About KWA Partners – Canada

KWA Partners is an organization owned and operated by Canadians and is one of this country's largest providers of career transition management and job-search support services. We are dedicated to individual service, local market expertise and national strength.

Our strategic commitment is described in our vision, mission and values statements:

Vision: To be Canada's most respected provider of career management services.

Mission: To inspire and support our clients to succeed in their careers.

Values: Respect, relationships, stewardship and leadership.

Working exclusively at the request of client organizations, we serve people at all levels, from senior executives, professional specialists and management to supervisory, administrative and hourly employees. Our expertise encompasses a full range of industries, including financial services, IT, telecom, health care, entertainment, retail, manufacturing, hospitality, utilities and non-profit.

The materials that form the core of this book have evolved from the work that we have done with individuals who are in career transition. What we offer here are the practical tools and proven methodologies that help people attain the work they want. With this book we are pleased to offer our expertise to a larger audience, and yet, we are convinced of the value of the personal consultation to facilitate the best possible career transition.

At KWA Partners, we believe that individual attention is the primary factor in helping people manage a career transition. Our staff is the key to our ability to continually deliver service consistent with our vision, mission and values. We understand the practical realities of the employment market and dedicate ourselves to guiding people toward their next employment opportunity—one that will be an excellent fit with their style, skills, interests and values.

To our corporate clients:

We appreciate the ongoing trust you have placed in us by choosing KWA Partners to serve your employees. Without your support we would not be able to accomplish our mission.

To our individual clients:

We wish you all the best in your career transition, and we commit our support to you.

Marge Watters

It's Your Move

A Personal and Practical Guide
to Career Transition and Job Search
for Canadian Managers, Professionals and Executives

Collins

HarperCollins Publishers Ltd
2 Bloor Street East, 20th Floor
Toronto, Ontario, Canada
M4W 1A8

www.harpercollins.ca

Library and Archives Canada Cataloguing in Publication

Watters, Marge
It's your move / Marge Watters. — 3rd ed.

ISBN 978-0-00-639153-1

1. Career changes. 2. Career development. 3. Job hunting.
I. Title.

HDF5384.W37 2007   650.14   C2007-901685-5

*This book is dedicated to the many people
I've had the privilege of helping with their career transitions.
They have inspired me by teaching me
the tremendous resilience of the human spirit.*

*This book is also dedicated to you,
as you begin your journey
toward the work you want.*

Contents

Part Two — Develop Your Strategy   35

Part Three — Gather Your Resources   101

Part Four — Move into Action 207

Part Five — Cross the Finish Line 253

List of Worksheets

What You Need to Know Before You Start

You can't control the wind, but you can adjust the sails.

Good career management skills are your ticket to continually having work that is challenging, rewarding and meaningful to you. Though an employer might assist you at times, the long-term responsibility for planning and directing your career is yours alone. From the time you first enter the workforce until you retire permanently, you need to be deliberate about moving from one opportunity to another, pursuing your interests, honouring your values, leveraging your knowledge and engaging the skills that you most enjoy using.

Finding the work you want can be a daunting challenge. Employment opportunities come and go with changing economic cycles, industry trends, technological innovations and demographic shifts. Every time you're planning a career move, it's a new game. The rules have changed, the playing field has been rearranged and the players are unpredictable. In order to succeed, you must refresh yesterday's strategies and embrace today's reality. Those who play smart will learn a lot about themselves and the dynamic environment of the workplace.

It's Your Move fully explains the steps you need to take to make a positive career change. It offers a logical process and practical tools designed to help you make choices that are right for you. It explores the challenging issues you will face at every stage of the career transition process, and provides proven methods for identifying and landing your next opportunity.

Have a look at the complete picture. The content of the book follows the sequence pictured on page 2. At every step, you will find practical advice accompanied by exercises, guidelines, worksheets, samples, tips and stories from real-life experiences. Resist the temptation to jump in at Step 3 or 4. The wise strategy is to take time for the first two steps before charging ahead.

Throughout the book, you will be invited to complete extensive and thought-provoking exercises. To do the exercises thoroughly you'll need more writing space than I have given you in the book. Set up a three-ring binder or open a new folder on your hard drive, dedicated to your career transition process. Carve out the time and prepare to do some challenging and enlightening work. As you go through the exercises, spend a third of your time recalling your past and describing yourself accurately, a third of your time writing and the balance reflecting on your answers. Look for patterns, themes and consistent factors. It's the reflective process that opens the door for creative thinking about your future.

1

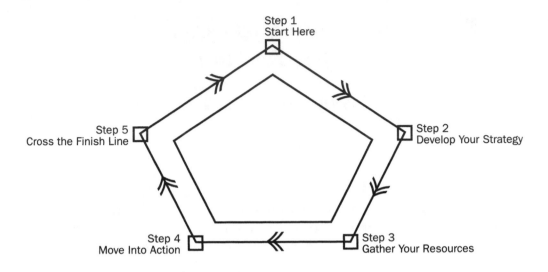

Before you begin, you'll need to understand what I mean by some of the terms and phrases that are used frequently. When I say "career change" I include looking for a job that is very similar to your most recent one, as well as making a dramatic shift into an entirely different occupation or industry. "Career change" can mean looking for a fresh opportunity within your organization, changing employers or going out on your own. Also, I use the terms "career change," "career management" and "career transition" interchangeably. I consistently use the title "career transition consultant" to describe professionals who assist individuals as they go through the career transition and job search process. "Career consultants," "career coaches," "career transition counsellors" and "outplacement counsellors or consultants" all provide the same type of services.

It's a whole new game. Playing well promises the rewards of flexibility, freedom and unlimited possibilities. But, unless you have the opportunity to work with a career consultant, it's also a lonely game, one in which you are your own strategist, marketer, administrator, advocate and friend. That's why I wrote this book. I hope that it will encourage and motivate you, show you where some of the hazards lie and give you the practical help you need to find the work you want.

Get Your Head in the Game

Winning relies as much on attitude as it does on hard work.

Objectives

Whether you have decided to move on, or the decision has been made for you, this first step involves ending your current employment situation with confidence and professionalism. By taking care of the details of transition and dealing with the emotions you experience, you can make a positive start. The chapters in Part One cover:
- Evaluating your readiness to move on.
- Handling the announcement of your departure effectively.
- Reasons for seeking legal advice.
- Financial planning for transition.
- Building a support network.
- Practical strategies for coping with your emotions.

Rules to Follow

- Be committed to moving on. Fence-sitting is not good for you or your career.
- Pay attention to your finances up front. Establish the maximum length of your transition period on the basis of your finances. Set a minimum remuneration requirement for your next opportunity.
- Separate the emotional issues from the legal issues.
- Choose your confidants wisely. Don't bare your soul to anyone and everyone.
- Plan carefully what you will say about why you are making a change.

Moves That Can Set You Back

- Being negative about any organization or person, thereby appearing unprofessional.
- Sharing your plans for moving on with anyone inside your organization before you are ready to act on them.
- Being dishonest with yourself about the feelings that change brings.

- Ignoring the effects that a career change will have on the significant others in your life, including children of any age.
- Jumping into the job market before taking the time to do a career assessment and create a strategy for finding the work you want.

Chapter 1

Start Here

*Nothing is more important
than your reputation with yourself.*

Getting your head in the game requires that a decision be made about managing your career. If your employment is terminated, the decision is made for you. You probably won't be consulted, and the news can be quite a shock. The quick hit can be devastating at first, but there are advantages; for example, you don't have to suffer the turmoil of indecision or the disappointment of slow rejection by your organization. The decision is made, and you're at the starting line.

"Working notice" is a common practice, and it isn't always easy to handle. In this situation, your current responsibilities end, often as the result of project completion or restructuring, and you are given the opportunity to conduct an internal job search. Organizations vary in the degree of clarity they provide regarding their processes and the level of assurance they give regarding job availability. Some offer excellent internal support; others, none at all. If you are given working notice, get your head in the game right away and start managing your career.

Early retirement can be good news or bad news. You're off to a great start if you've been waiting for the opportunity and you already have ideas about what you want to do next. However, if you'll be in bad shape financially, or you're unprepared emotionally and psychologically for this news, the phrase "early retirement" can seem like a euphemism for being fired. Regardless of your initial reaction, there are benefits. You will be able to position your leaving as an early retirement, and having some pension income, you probably won't have to replace all your income to stay even.

If the decision to make a career change is entirely yours, being decisive and making time to do it right will be the challenge. Deciding to leave on your own can be the most difficult starting point. It isn't easy to be proactive about making a move when you are spending all your energy keeping up with the demands of your day-to-day responsibilities. Not devoting the time needed to pay attention to your future, however, is one of the greatest errors in good career management. Doing so requires commitment, organization and discipline. Dedicating yourself to this task is something that only you can do.

In any of these circumstances, you can take control and be determined to make the moves that are right for you. Too many people make mistakes with the closing steps of leaving a job because it is such an emotionally loaded decision, regardless of who makes it. Be very careful about what you say and do.

How you handle your departure from a job will affect your reputation, your references and consequently your future.

Are You Ready to Move On?

If the choice is yours, there will be signs telling you when it's time for you to put yourself into the career management game. Sometimes, colleagues and family can see those signs more clearly than you. After a few years in the same job, some people simply find that they need a new challenge. Perhaps your enthusiasm has diminished because you've become too comfortable in your current role. If you are stale, restless or bored, it's time to consider a change.

Relationships can create or destroy satisfying work. Unproductive and unhappy relationships generate some of the most common reasons for making a change. A reconfigured team might generate too many conflicting opinions. It could be that you and the new boss or the new team can't find a way to work together well. If you've genuinely given it your best shot, consider moving. Chances are high that a move is being planned for you, and it may not be one you want.

When you gain significant practical experience or when you complete formal education adding relevant credentials to your résumé, you might be justified in seeking out a more senior role. Surprisingly, some organizations find it difficult to acknowledge the growing capabilities of their own people. You may have to move on to move up.

In bad economic times, downsizing is commonplace. In good times, mergers and acquisitions bring restructuring. In every economic climate, job loss can result from technological advances, process re-engineering, a change in strategic direction or the arrival of a new leader. Do you wait to see if the organizational change will affect your position, or do you become proactive before you are forced to find a new job? If you are still challenged and enthusiastic about your work, and if that work is likely to continue regardless of structural reorganization, stay put. In this era of non-stop change, you might dodge one upheaval only to land in another.

Regardless of your reasons for a career change, decide to get your head in the game. Don't wait for something magical to happen. You won't find out what else is out there until you go out and have a look. Terrific job offers seldom land in people's laps unsolicited. They're not like junk mail! Most people have to generate new opportunities through thoughtful and diligent effort.

Tip: If you feel so trapped or overwhelmed by your responsibilities or personal circumstances that you can't focus on managing your career, getting professional support is probably a smart idea. First, see your family doctor to make sure nothing is physically wrong. Then, find a qualified counsellor or a competent career transition consultant to help you.

As you work through the following guidelines, remember that you are simply making the decision to begin an active career management process. It doesn't necessarily mean that you will change employers. You might find the ideal opportunity within your current organization.

GUIDELINES FOR DECIDING TO MAKE A MOVE

- Fence-sitting is uncomfortable and unproductive. Find some way of making the decision. Make a list of the pros and cons of staying where you are. Evaluate your current job as if it were a new opportunity. Would you take it?
- Think about what it would take to initiate a career change. Can you dedicate the time and effort to doing it right? If not, can you make some lifestyle changes to make this dedication possible?
- Are you reacting to a temporary or recent situation? If you give this situation more time or effort, is there a chance that your discontentment will vanish?
- Do you like the organization overall? Would you be content with another job in your company if one was offered?
- Career transition consultants are skilled at helping people determine whether or not to look for a new job. Ask someone outside your organization to recommend one and make an appointment to see them.
- Be realistic about the benefits of staying where you are if you have long service with your organization. Consider that leaving might significantly reduce your pension and you might forfeit some types of deferred compensation.
- Once you've decided to look for a new opportunity, commit specific blocks of time to carrying out your intention. Become organized and disciplined.
- Do not discuss your thoughts about leaving with anyone in your organization. Deal with points of dissatisfaction about your job as if you fully intended to be part of the long-term solution.
- Do not make direct or veiled threats about leaving. If you are unhappy, deal with the specific issues directly and with the appropriate persons.
- Work through confidential channels. Be cautious with your network and find out which search firms are working for your company so that you do not contact them.
- Use private email and voice mail systems to avoid the possibility of having your search discovered.
- Consider getting legal advice before engaging in conversations with any of your employer's competitors.

A senior risk manager found herself increasingly dissatisfied with her work and decided to leave her corporate role to pursue a completely new career that would involve a significant salary reduction. Over the course of several discussions with her boss, she focused on aspects of her role where changes might convince her to stay. At the same time, she planned her exit but did not reveal this to anyone associated with her work. On the morning that she intended to resign, she received an emergency call from her husband. He told her that his employment had been terminated. As a result, she continued to work in the same position for three years before she could pursue her plan. It was a good thing that she had kept her plans to herself.

You've Decided to Resign

Once you know that you are leaving and where you are headed, give the amount of notice required by your employment contract or company policy. Do not announce your departure too far in advance. Deliver the news of your resignation or retirement respectfully. You never know when you might need to return, or when you might have to deal with your boss or co-workers in another setting.

If a counter-offer is presented by your organization, think about it very carefully. If a substantive change in your role or mandate is on the table, weigh it against your external opportunity. However, if the counter-offer is based solely on remuneration, moving on might be wise. Regardless of what is said, employers have a hard time seeing you as a committed team player after they have had to pay a ransom to keep you. Search firms and placement agencies also become significantly less interested in you after you have jilted them by accepting your company's counter-offer.

Think about what you will say to colleagues, senior management, clients and suppliers about your reasons for leaving. Say more about the new opportunity and less about what you're leaving behind. Be truthful in your explanation, but be respectful. Do not disparage your current employer or anyone who works there.

You've Received Working Notice

Your boss has told you that your current role will be ending, and you will have a specific period of time to look for work while your salary continues to be paid. If you are given the option of looking for another job internally, you can sometimes access internal job boards, career centres or telephone hotlines for help. Here are some questions to guide you.

GUIDELINES FOR DEALING WITH WORKING NOTICE

- Is it possible to receive pay in lieu of working notice and leave immediately? If so, would this be preferable to you?
- How much freedom will you have to look for work internally during the notice period? Will you be given the time to plan your next move, make contacts and attend interviews?
- How likely is it that you will find suitable work within the organization? Will your current boss recommend you for other positions?
- If you find a new job internally, will you feel the same way about the organization? Can you be happy staying if you feel you've previously been rejected?
- If you choose to forego the internal job search, how much time can you take to make contacts and look for work externally?
- Is the support of a career transition consultant available during the working notice period, and, if you haven't landed a job within that time, what quality, level and length of career transition support will be provided?
- If you do not land a new position internally, at what point will you be advised of the details of your severance package?
- If you land a new job outside the organization, can you be released before the working notice period is over? Would you receive any portion of the severance package?
- How would either of these early exits affect your benefits, pension and deferred compensation?

A marketing director received working notice when his department was restructured. He had 90 days to find a new job within the organization. He asked to use the services of a career transition consultant right away, and during the 90 days he split his time between doing his job and looking for the next opportunity. He quickly eliminated the internal options and used his network of contacts to pursue outside opportunities. He landed a job at a higher level with more pay, starting two weeks following the end of the 90-day period. He and his wife enjoyed a nice holiday and banked a substantial amount of his severance payment.

You've Been Offered Early Retirement

The opportunity to retire early can feel like a long-awaited blessing, or it can be an unwelcome and abrupt end to your years of service. Your reaction depends on both your financial situation and your interest in and energy for continuing to work. Increasingly, people are viewing early retirement as an opportunity to find work that is less demanding but more fulfilling. This usually means less pay, which is often feasible with supplemental income coming from a pension plan. To help you decide what to do, a thorough review of your financial situation is imperative.

If your finances allow you to stop earning an income, don't make hasty decisions about what retirement might be like for you. It's difficult to know how you will fill your time until you are out of the working world and at home with no obligations to an employer. You might be perfectly happy, or you might feel the need to get back to work in some capacity.

Explore what combination of work, leisure and volunteer activity is right for you by following the exercises in this book. They are designed to accommodate partial retirement and other part-time work arrangements.

You've Been Told That Your Services Are No Longer Required

Out of the blue, you've been called into a meeting and informed that your employment has been terminated. In the space of a few minutes, you find yourself out of a job and in the employment market. Even if you anticipated this or wanted it to happen, the emotional impact of the moment can be overwhelming. Here are some guidelines to get you through.

GUIDELINES FOR DEALING WITH A TERMINATION MEETING

- Just listen. You don't have to say anything. All of your comments and questions can come later.
- You should be told clearly what your last day of work is and what is expected of you in leaving the premises. If you are not told, ask!
- Don't expect to be able to absorb the contents of your severance letter during the termination meeting. If you are a long-service employee, a quick glance at the dollar amount can be helpful. Otherwise, wait until you are at home and read the letter in privacy.
- This is not the right time to confront your boss. Probing for explanations won't resolve or change the situation. Your goal is to make a dignified exit.
- Take the time to talk to a career transition consultant if one is there for you. This can give you some breathing room and some understanding of the level of support available to you.

- Cry if you feel the need. No one expects you to be a hero, but avoid creating a scene in front of your co-workers.
- If you have been asked to leave immediately, do not try to say goodbye to all your co-workers before you leave for home. Call them later, or arrange to meet them in a few days when the initial shock has worn off.
- Arrange to pick up your personal belongings later or ask to have them sent to you.
- Give all keys, passwords and company cards to your manager or career transition consultant.
- Do not touch your computer. If you have personal files or email, ask your manager to have them downloaded and sent to you.
- Take time to compose yourself before you leave. There is no rush to be out the door quickly.
- Think carefully about how you will get home. Arrange for a taxi or call someone to accompany you. This may not be the time to be behind the wheel of a car or alone on a long commute.
- Plan how you will break the news to your spouse or partner. Consider whether telling them immediately by telephone or later in person would be best.
- Walk out with dignity.

Informing Family and Others

Telling loved ones and close friends about your job loss, early retirement or working notice will help you come to grips with the reality of the situation. Unless you have very special circumstances, it's important to tell your spouse or partner immediately about what has happened. Withholding the information for any reason will add to the considerable stress of job loss. If you wait, you risk creating the impression that you do not trust your spouse's or partner's ability to cope. You also deny them the opportunity to be supportive.

Your children should also be told as soon as possible. From as early an age as three they will be able to grasp the basic facts, and they deserve to know what is happening. Everyone in the household will be affected by your transition. It's best if both parents agree on the wording and the tone of the message. Make it reassuring and age appropriate.

Inform other immediate family and friends that you are no longer with the organization. It's better for them to hear this directly from you rather than by trying to call you at work. Many people find that telling their parents is very difficult, as their reaction may be influenced by both the dynamics of the relationship and their potentially limited exposure to the realities of today's workplace. Do not let your reluctance keep you from telling them. They might surprise you with their acceptance and understanding.

Think about friends and neighbours. If you have a spouse or partner, it's wise to decide together what you will say. Your spouse should be ready with the same story that you are telling. When people offer to help and support, assure them that you will call on them when you know what you plan to do.

Keep the explanation of your leaving simple, honest and consistent. You don't need to tell every detail, but everything you say must be true and not misleading. Try to depersonalize the story with a very brief explanation of the context for the decision. What you say must be a reasonable match with what your former employer will say.

Finally, consider your contacts from work. As the news of your leaving spreads, you might receive phone calls offering support and assistance from co-workers, colleagues, suppliers, clients and other contacts. What you say to these people can either build bridges to future employment opportunities or sabotage your prospects. It is extremely important to put on your game face, remaining professional and discreet in what you say. Saying less is usually best.

GUIDELINES FOR HANDLING EARLY CONVERSATIONS WITH BUSINESS CONTACTS

- Decide who you want to contact personally. This might include clients or suppliers with whom you have current dealings. When you call them, be clear that you are making a personal call, not as a representative of your former employer.
- Do not let any anger or bitterness toward your former employer show. Address the facts and try to sound confident in the belief that you will be moving on to better things.
- Respond graciously to non-specific offers of help by assuring the caller that you will be in touch when you are ready.
- Temporarily postpone specific offers to arrange meetings or make introductions for you. You will need this kind of help when your search is in full swing, but meeting important contacts before you have had the time to think and prepare can do more harm than good.
- Keep a record of names and phone numbers from these early conversations. This list will be invaluable when you start your search.

If your employment has been terminated, you're at the starting line for career transition whether you like it or not! You're in the game, and *it's your move*. Taking care of yourself, your loved ones and the closing steps comes next.

Tip: Most terminations result from some change in the work environment. Once you have gained perspective on your loss, you will most likely be able to explain why your employment was terminated by citing that change rather than speaking from your emotions.

Chapter 2

Take Care of the Closing Steps

Good beginnings start with good endings.

If your employment is terminated, you need to understand your legal rights and financial situation before you agree to the terms of the severance package or sign a release. This kind of analysis requires clear thinking, at a time when you might be in an emotional fog. It is also entirely normal to have strong feelings of anger, fear and sadness. To help yourself through this difficult time, get good, objective advice from professionals. This chapter will help you decide what professional advice you need. Do not rely entirely on your family and friends for this important step.

Saying Goodbye

In the days immediately following the termination of employment most people feel confused and alone. Knowing what to do first is a challenge. These guidelines will help.

GUIDELINES FOR THE DAYS FOLLOWING TERMINATION OF EMPLOYMENT

- Until the news settles in and you're thinking more clearly, do not make any immediate, drastic changes or big decisions. Don't cancel holiday plans or call the real estate agent!
- Do not sign a release or the severance letter until you understand it completely. Check the date for returning the completed forms, and if you need more time, ask for an extension. You might want to have the severance letter reviewed by an employment lawyer, but it is not essential to do so.
- Do not make a round of emotionally loaded calls to your colleagues and business contacts. Diatribes and hasty explanations of future plans can severely diminish their willingness to stay connected. You will need their help once you have decided what you want to do next.
- Do not activate your employment search until you have achieved some equanimity. Do not call placement agencies and search firms, even if you have regularly received calls from them. Take the time to think about how you will position your leaving and your future plans.
- Allow yourself some time to recover from the news. Be patient with yourself as you work through the shock and emotional impact.
- If a seemingly perfect job opening presents itself in the early days following your job loss, do your best to respond by getting your résumé together quickly and preparing for interviews. Try

not to pin all your hopes on this single opportunity. Most employment searches take a lot of effort and a fair bit of time. There will be other options if this one doesn't work out.

- Remind yourself that losing a job is a common occurrence. It no longer carries a stigma, and you will find many capable people who have successfully navigated similar circumstances.

Tip: If you have been dismissed because you made a mistake or an error in judgment, choose at least one confidant and share the entire story. This could be your lawyer, your career transition consultant or a very close and discreet friend who has no connection to your working life. You will appreciate having a sounding board as you go through the career transition process.

Consider Getting Legal Advice

This section is not intended to give you legal advice. It is meant to make you aware of some of the basic legal issues and to encourage you to seek specific advice from an employment lawyer. Most companies, especially larger ones, ensure that they are in compliance with severance regulations. However, you need to feel that you have been treated fairly, especially if you are a long-service employee. One conversation with a competent and caring employment lawyer may be all that you need to resolve the situation directly.

Common misconceptions about severance packages include the notion that a severance payment is a reward for long service or a pay-off to assuage an organization's guilt over an employment termination. This is not the case. *Severance packages are usually required by law to satisfy an employer's obligation to provide an employee with reasonable notice of termination.* Severance will provide at least some financial assistance to an employee while they search for their next employment opportunity. Therefore, a number of subjective elements come into evaluating the fairness of a severance package.

There are two kinds of law that must be considered: statutory law and common law. Statutory law is written and can be found in the relevant federal or provincial act. If you know the jurisdiction of your former employer, you can find the applicable document on the Internet. However, statutory law is not the complete picture. Common law emerges as cases are heard and judges decide what constitutes fair treatment in specific circumstances. The decisions that are made by judges regarding severance payments take into consideration the economic situation in the area, and the individual's age, skills, length of service, income and level of responsibility. To fully understand your rights under common law, you will need to consult an employment lawyer.

An employment lawyer is the best choice because they specialize in dismissals and compensation, and are current on court decisions in their region. Labour lawyers usually specialize in unionized situations. If you were part of a union, your severance terms may have been pre-negotiated in the collective agreement, in which case your union representative can give you information.

An employment lawyer should help you separate legal issues from emotional ones, construct a list of negotiating points and suggest that you try the first round of negotiations yourself. By handling these discussions directly, you might get what you want without needing to take an adversarial position, incur significant expense or lengthen the time it takes to reach an agreement. Of course, if you are not willing or able to do this, your lawyer will take over and do it for you. Litigation is not the preferred route. However, if you do proceed, leave the case in the hands of your lawyer and try to get on with your life. Don't let unresolved severance issues and the pursuit of a claim hold you back from whole-hearted engagement in career planning and the employment search, or unduly affect your family.

Tip: As long as you are making progress, negotiate for yourself with your lawyer's advice guiding the process. Once you ask your lawyer to write a letter to your former organization, the negotiating will most likely be handled between your lawyer and theirs. This will likely increase the expense and the time required for settlement.

GUIDELINES FOR CHOOSING A LAWYER

- Ask for a referral to an employment lawyer from your own lawyer or a career transition consultant, or call your provincial Law Society.
- Ask for a preliminary meeting or consultation by phone or in person, and explain your situation briefly. Ask these questions of a lawyer before you make your choice:
  - Do you have a conflict in representing me against my former employer?
  - How many non-union termination situations have you handled in the past few months?
  - Do you represent both individuals and organizations?
  - What percentage of your cases are settled out of court?
  - Will you support me if I want to do the negotiating myself, or do you think it is important that you handle the negotiations?
  - How much do you charge? Is there a minimum fee?

If you have been offered the services of a career transition consultant, do not hesitate to use this service right away, even while you are negotiating your package. They should not reveal any information about you or your plans to anyone, and they should have only your best interests in mind. Working with them right away can be a significant benefit to you both professionally and personally. They will help you sort through your issues and avoid the common mistakes associated with job search.

Tip: The courts expect you to do everything you can to mitigate your damages by taking steps to find your next employment opportunity. Using a career transition consultant from the earliest moment will help your case. If you are worried about impartiality or confidentiality, talk with your consultant and ask for written assurance.

Often funding for financial counselling is included in the severance package. It might be provided through the career transition firm. If so, use it. Even the most capable managers of family finances usually learn something from a session with a financial professional.

Do a Financial Review

The benefits of undertaking a financial review at the time you leave your job include making the most of tax shelters, considering the life, disability and medical benefits that you and your family need, and developing a realistic budget for the transition period. Your primary goal in doing a financial review is to establish a comfortable timeline for finding your next employment opportunity, and to alleviate some of the anxiety that accompanies job loss. Think of your severance as your pay in advance for your career transition work. If you are re-employed before your severance pay runs out, you have earned yourself a bonus.

Start by completing a thorough list of your monthly expenses. You have fixed and discretionary expenses. It is often an eye-opener to see where the money has been going. With accurate information, you and your family can agree on areas for savings if needed. Compare your monthly expenses with your income from your severance package. How many months do you have until you need to be working again?

Next, take an inventory of your assets and liabilities. Have a plan ready to use in case your job search takes longer than your severance package will carry you. Analyze your assets and liabilities to get a picture of your liquidity. If you need them, which assets would you use first? Do you need to make any investment changes now to provide for the possibility of raising more cash in the future? Do you have any liabilities that represent unnecessary luxuries? At what point would you give up those luxuries?

A man who worked for 28 years in one organization made a rather unique financial decision when he lost his job. He and his wife, who still worked, owned a house in the city and a large cabin cruiser that they loved using on a system of lakes several hundred kilometres away. They were tired of the city, and their children were grown and gone. The couple kept the boat, sold the house and rented a small apartment close to the wife's office. He landed a series of contracts and that income, combined with their investment income and his wife's salary, allowed them to afford a new lifestyle, tailored entirely to their liking.

Consider your life, disability and health benefits. Make sure that you understand exactly which benefits continue with your former employer and for how long. This will vary depending on the organization's policy. If you have a short time remaining in your group benefits plan, use it to the full. Make appointments with the dentist and doctor for everyone in the family while you still have coverage. Get your prescriptions filled.

Tip: During your transition period make sure that decisions regarding insurance reflect the appropriate risk factors. Life and disability insurance cover catastrophic, long-term needs. Medical and dental insurance assist with short-term cash flow. Where is the greatest risk for you and your dependants?

Check immediately with your spouse or partner to see if you can be covered by their employer's plan. There is usually a time limit involved. Your former organization's life, disability, health and dental insurance might be convertible to an individual plan without requiring evidence of insurability. This is expensive, but it eliminates insurability concerns. If you need to buy your own coverage, there are many good options available for health, dental and life insurance. Fewer options exist for disability insurance, but there are plans available that can be combined with your severance package to protect your ability to earn an income. Independent coverage is more expensive than group insurance, but being unprotected might be too risky. Call an insurance agent or broker for advice.

Use the worksheets that follow to assist in your financial review.

Tip: By completing a budget you may find that you have more time for transition than you thought. Some people discover that they can double the number of months available by careful planning and frugal spending.

WORKSHEET 2.1
Calculate Your Monthly Living Expenses

Rent	_____	Allowances	_____
Mortgage	_____	Pet care	_____
Taxes	_____	Computer equipment	_____
Property insurance	_____	Computer & Internet	
Hydro	_____	services	_____
Gas	_____	Public transportation	_____
Water	_____	Haircuts & care	_____
Telephone	_____	Club memberships	_____
Cable	_____	Hobbies	_____
Household purchases	_____	Cosmetics, toiletries	_____
Repairs & maintenance	_____	Prescriptions	_____
House cleaning	_____	Dental care	_____
Lawn care & snow removal	_____	Eye care, glasses, contacts	_____
Auto –loan or lease	_____	Tobacco, alcohol	_____
–insurance	_____	Babysitting	_____
–plates	_____	Lessons	_____
–license	_____	Dry cleaning	_____
–gas	_____	Entertainment	_____
–parking	_____	Magazines, newspapers	_____
–repairs	_____	Donations	_____
Groceries	_____	Other expenses	_____
Lunch money	_____	Other loan payments	_____
Eating out	_____	Credit card payments	_____
Childcare	_____	Income tax installments	_____
Activities & lessons –you	_____		
–spouse	_____	**Annual Expenses**	
–children	_____	Gifts	_____
Tuition	_____	Holidays	_____
Clothing & shoes –you	_____	Family celebrations	_____
–spouse	_____	RRSPs/savings	_____
–children	_____		
Insurance (life, disability)	_____	Total and	_____ ÷12
Insurance (medical, dental)	_____	monthly equivalent	_____

**TOTAL MONTHLY
LIVING EXPENSES** _____

WORKSHEET 2.2
Your Assets and Liabilities

Non-Registered Assets	Owner You/Spouse	Financial Institution	Amount or Market Value	Maturity Date	Monthly Income
Bank accounts					
CSBs & money market funds					
GICs/term deposits/bonds					
Employer savings plans					
Mutual funds					
Stocks					
Cottage					
Residence					
Rental or investment properties					
Life insurance CSV					
Other					
Total					

Registered Assets	Owner You/Spouse/Child	Financial Institution	Amount or Market Value	Maturity Date
RRSPs				
RESPs and trusts				
Total				

Liabilities	Lender	Outstanding Balance	Renewal Date	Rate	Monthly Payment
Mortgage					
Car loan					
Line of credit					
Credit cards					
RRSP loan					
Other debts					
Total					

WORSHEET 2.3
Your Financial Picture for Transition

Other Sources of Income

Part-time work	_____
Fees & honorariums	_____
Maintenance payments	_____
Investment income	_____
Rental income	_____
Disability benefits	_____
Government benefits	_____
Pension income	_____
Other	_____
Total other income monthly	_____

Upcoming, Non-Recurring or Contingency Expenses

Medical	_____
Dental	_____
Personal	_____
Travel	_____
Education	_____
Home repairs	_____
Car repairs or purchase	_____
Other	_____
Total	_____
Estimated monthly payments	_____

Transition Budget

Regular monthly expenses	_____
(Minus) Realistic cost-cutting estimate	– _____
(Plus) Monthly payments re: non-recurring expenses	+ _____
Total monthly expenses for the transition period	_____
(Minus) Monthly income from other sources	– _____
Total monthly amount that must be drawn from the severance package or savings	_____
Number of months the severance package could last:	_____ **Months**

Important: File your claim for Employment Insurance (EI) within four weeks of your last day of work regardless of your receiving a severance payment. Delaying in filing your claim may cause loss of benefits. File online at www.hrsdc.gc.ca or in person at your nearest Service Canada Centre.

Tip: An honest look at how you spend money and a discussion with your spouse or partner early in your transition period can reduce anxiety and prevent problems down the road. Drafting a comprehensive plan now can give you the freedom to take the time you need for a good transition.

Using a professional financial adviser to help you maximize tax shelters and use your severance package to its fullest advantage is a very good idea. Fee-only Certified Financial Planners (CFP) or Registered Financial Planners (RFP) are planners with nationally recognized designations who have completed education and examination requirements, and are required to meet standards for annual continuing education. Other qualified professionals include Fellows of the Canadian Securities Institute (FCSI), Chartered Accountants (CA), Certified Management Accountants (CMA), Certified General Accountants (CGA), Chartered Financial Analysts (CFA) and Certified Public Accountants (CPA). Be sure that the professional you choose operates on a fee-only basis.

Many investment representatives, financial product salespersons and brokers are paid a commission or fee for the products they sell. You may wish to seek advice from them after you have decided how you will allocate your severance monies; however, they may not be an unbiased source of information for you at this point.

GUIDELINES FOR CHOOSING A FINANCIAL PLANNER

- Ask your bank manager or your career transition consultant for a referral to a qualified, fee-only financial planner. You can also be referred through Advocis, The Financial Advisors Association of Canada, either by calling (416-444-5251 or 1-800-563-5822) or visiting their web site (www.advocis.ca), which allows you to search for financial planners by province and type of service.
- Call and explain your situation briefly. Ask these questions before making your choice:
  - What credentials do you have?
  - Do you operate on a fee-only basis? If so, what is your fee?
  - How many meetings do you think we will need? Can we do follow-up by phone?
  - How many clients with severance packages have you advised recently?
  - What should I bring to the meeting?
- Rapport is important. If you don't feel comfortable with the preliminary call, try someone else.

The meeting itself should take between one and two hours. Encourage your spouse or partner to attend the meeting. Hearing the planner's advice first-hand and having an opportunity to ask questions can contribute to their peace of mind. To make the best use of the time with your financial adviser, do some preparation. Complete the worksheets in this book or those provided by your adviser and bring the following to the meeting:

- a detailed list of your assets, including RRSPs, investments and savings
- an itemized list of any outstanding debts, including mortgages and credit-card balances
- your personal monthly household budget with estimates in all categories

- your last income-tax assessment
- a recent pay slip
- your last statement of account for your pension plan and employee savings plan
- a copy of your severance letter
- your current insurance portfolio, including life, disability, medical and dental

Decide on your objectives before the meeting. Are you most concerned about debt reduction, benefit replacement, pension issues, sheltering the severance through RRSPs (tax minimization) or personal budgeting? Any thoughts on what you'll do next provide helpful information to your financial planner. Are you considering early retirement, financing a new business, moving your residence, looking for a similar job, taking some time off or changing direction completely? The more prepared you are going into the meeting, the more focused the information your planner provides will be.

Build a Support Network

An empathetic and supportive network of family, friends and professionals can help you tremendously during transition. Sometimes a support network evolves naturally as people offer to be a resource. The phrase "Let me know if there's anything I can do" is usually genuinely meant, but it is seldom backed by specific ideas of what might be done. At the appropriate time, you will have to tell people.

Choose your support network wisely. A person who has been through career transition successfully can provide a wealth of first-hand experience. Former co-workers and bosses can give you insightful feedback on your career plans once you've done a thorough assessment. Any colleague with whom you feel comfortable can become an on-going source of encouragement and advice. Be judicious about how you use the support of family and friends; some are more capable than others of helping you carry the burden. Set clear guidelines from the outset by asking them directly how much they want to know. Keep the lines of communication open, but be careful not to lean too heavily on those who are struggling to cope with their own reactions to your career change.

The formation of your own board of advisers is a more strategic and intentional approach to creating a support network. Your board could include four to six people from varied backgrounds who are willing to offer you advice, feedback and encouragement on a regular basis. You might call on your advisers individually or gather them together in an informal session to do some brainstorming on your behalf. The best combination of people will include those who have different perspectives. They will be people who have your best interests at heart. You will need to feel comfortable receiving feedback and constructive suggestions from them. It also helps to include people who have well-developed networks.

A human resources director, whose employment was terminated when her company was acquired, asked six colleagues from different walks of life to act as her board of advisers. She included a recruiter, a lawyer, a colleague from her MBA class of many years past, a politician and two friends from her volunteer work. She sought advice individually for the most part, but she also chose a convenient pub as a venue for the group to meet on the occasional Friday evening. It turned into a welcome opportunity to network, wind down and help a friend with her search.

Tip: Begin to think about who might provide references for you to a prospective employer. Record the names of those who offer this support. Consider whether this is an appropriate time to broach the topic with everyone. Some of your references will be an integral part of your support network. For others, you will need their contribution only when an offer of employment is imminent.

Remember that as part of your support network, a career transition consultant can be a tremendous help. If your employment has been terminated and your organization has not provided transition service, ask for it and negotiate the length and quality of service. If this move is your own decision, consider engaging a consultant. Many people think that they don't need this sort of help, but a capable consultant in a firm with a reputation for individualized service can aid your transition process significantly.

GUIDELINES FOR CHOOSING A CAREER TRANSITION CONSULTANT

- Don't let the titles confuse you. Career counsellors, outplacement counsellors, career transition consultants and career coaches all do substantially the same work.
- The industry is not regulated, and there are no specific designations or credentials to ensure competence. The best consultant for you will have a background that you respect. A good consultant should offer a listening ear, challenge you to stretch your thinking, and provide practical advice that is appropriate for you and your industry.
- If your organization has engaged a particular firm for you, stick with it unless you know exactly where you'd rather go or you have a strong dislike for the consultant, the program or the environment. Shopping around for a new firm can open a new round of negotiations with your organization and can significantly delay your engagement in the transition process.
- If you are on your own, ask a human resources professional, your employment lawyer, a financial adviser, or others who have been through the process, who they would recommend. Call the Human Resources Professionals Association in your province and ask for a list of firms.
- Evaluate the service according to the level of expertise it offers and its reputation. Spending three months with a high-quality firm focused on individualized service will probably do more for you than twice that time with a firm that emphasizes group sessions or self-directed tools.
- Call and describe your background and circumstances briefly. Ask these questions before you make a choice:
  - May I come in and meet you and see your facilities?
  - Who will work with me? What is their background? Please give me a general profile of some of the clients this consultant has advised. How senior were they? What industries were they in?
  - May I have an outline of the programs? What parts of my program would be delivered through workshops or delegated to a junior staff member? (Individualized service supplemented by optional workshops is best.)
  - How often will I meet with my consultant, and what access will I have to consulting support between scheduled appointments?

- What efforts will my consultant make to contact me and remain proactively involved with my job search?
- What access will I have to office space? May I see the facilities that I will be using? Are there times when I will not have access because the facilities are full?
- Are organized networking opportunities part of my program? How often? What are typical backgrounds of the people who attend?
- What level and length of service has the most appropriate content for me and my situation?
- What are your fees?

Give Yourself a Time Frame

If you are employed and you've decided it's time to make a move, give yourself a deadline for finding a new opportunity. Be intentional about allocating time to your search so that your busyness does not cause months to pass without effort being directed toward it. Each step in the process is likely to take longer for you because you cannot dedicate your full attention to it. Looking for work can be a full-time job in itself.

If you are not working, the financial review has helped you establish the maximum number of months you have to make this transition. Even if you have the luxury of ample time, it's wise to make an initial estimation of how long it might take you to find work. It will help you determine how urgent it is for you to get going. Be realistic so that you don't get caught short of time.

Taking a temporary break can be an excellent strategic move, especially if you have been working for years without one, or if your last role was particularly stressful. Regardless of what you choose to do during your time off, be clear about how long you intend to delay your search activities. Let your support network and references know when you intend to begin, and be sure to live up to that commitment. Make your time out a purposeful step in the process.

It's very difficult to predict how long your career transition and employment search will take. Talk with your support network and anyone you know who has successfully gone through the process in order to understand the parameters. Most people underestimate the time needed to prepare for entering the marketplace and few realize how time-consuming an active search can be. The factors that will affect your time frame include how radical a career change you plan to make, your degree of flexibility regarding terms of employment, the buoyancy of the market for your skills and how effectively and diligently you work at your search. Last but not least, being in the right place at the right time never hurts.

To get an overview of where you're headed, look at the charts in the appendices. Reference will be made to them many times as you move through the steps in the process. Appendix A offers a strategic view of the career transition and employment search process. Appendix B is a table that sets out your search activities as a project plan with a timeline. Start using the template in Appendix B now by inserting the date by which you would like to begin working in your next role.

Tip: If you choose to take some time off, it is often very helpful to meet with your career transition consultant before doing so. They will help you through the closing steps and introduce you to the transition process. Their input can help you enjoy the time you need with more peace of mind.

Achieve Closure and Move On

Settling the legal and financial aspects of your severance and building a support network will move you toward closure. Saying your goodbyes and offering to help the transfer of your work to someone else will be beneficial but may be emotionally difficult. A huge part of ending well is how you handle your feelings about leaving your job and facing the future. The next step deals with your emotional well-being.

Chapter 3

Make It Through the Emotional Maze

*What happens to you is less important
than what happens inside you as a result.*

Every change marks the end of something. Endings involve loss. When you lose something important, you have an emotional reaction to the loss and there's nothing wrong with that. Leaving a job, whether by choice or not, carries with it a loss and the accompanying feelings.

What you do to earn a living gives you purpose in many ways. It provides challenges and opportunities to solve problems. It offers the chance to keep you learning. It lets you interact with others, individually and in teams. It offers recognition and status, as well as the means by which you pay the bills and plan for the future. Your job forms part of your identity. Making changes to something this important requires special care. Dealing with your emotions is an important step regardless of who initiated the change.

Reactions to Change and Loss

The nature and intensity of your reaction to loss depends on several factors. Without question, your degree of control over the situation is a major factor. If you made the decision to change jobs, you might feel some sadness about leaving behind colleagues and a familiar environment, but excitement about the opportunity ahead probably outweighs the sadness. Moreover, you will have had time to prepare for your goodbyes.

A young woman who decided to leave a high-powered job in advertising knew that she would greatly miss her colleagues and her team's cohesiveness. In the weeks before she announced her departure, she carried a piece of paper with her. On it were two columns. One was labelled, "Things I'll miss about this place," and the other, "Things I won't miss." To her surprise, when she actually said her goodbyes, a significant amount of her sadness had dissipated through keeping this inventory.

If your employment was terminated suddenly, both the shock and the lack of control will affect the intensity of your reaction. If you were a long-service employee or your organization was your first and only employer, your attachment to it could be very strong. You may have made a number of personal sacrifices in the line of duty to your employer. It could be that over the years you passed up excellent offers to work elsewhere for the sake of loyalty. People who have a long history with an organization usually have deep feelings about losing their job.

Another very significant influence on your ability to deal with career change is the other changes that are occurring in your life. Changes in health, family circumstances, finances, personal goals or lifestyle can make change easier to manage or much more difficult. It is noteworthy that people who meet with career transition consultants seldom have only one change to consider. There are usually other personal circumstances that need attention.

It is impossible to predict how an individual will feel about any change, including job loss. There is no right or wrong reaction. Our feelings are just what they are. There's no point in trying to change, ignore or banish them. Good management of your emotions is essential to healthy change management.

Good management starts with understanding. The range of emotions that we experience is enormous. However, most human emotions can be categorized using one of these four words: sad, mad, glad or afraid. Think about it. You might describe your mood as blue, discouraged, gloomy or devastated. These are words meaning "sad." Frustrated, annoyed, disappointed, angry and #!*@#$ are ways of saying "mad." Relief and gratitude are expressions of gladness. Worry denotes fear. Simplifying the range of emotions to a few broad categories might help you achieve clarity regarding your feelings.

Tip: Learning to name your feelings is an important part of good emotional health. Admitting that you're angry puts you in touch with the feeling, gives you clarity and puts you in a position to choose how you will express it.

Feelings often overlap. It's entirely possible to feel sad and afraid at the same time. People who say that they feel depressed are probably sad and angry. With depression, the anger is usually turned inward. Any combination of feelings can be experienced at the same time.

Use the following worksheet to put some of your feelings down on paper. This exercise might seem unnecessary, but it allows you to identify and air feelings that might otherwise stay bottled up inside. The objective is recognition and good management of your emotions.

WORKSHEET 3.1
Identify Changes and Feelings

Think about the changes that are occurring for you in each of these areas of life. List each situation and all of the accompanying losses. For example, termination of employment could mean the loss of financial security, camaraderie, status, hopes for advancement, business travel, etc.

Name your feelings. Stretch your imagination and list the beginnings that this change might bring.

	What has changed?	What was lost?	How do you feel about each loss?	Possible new beginnings
Work				
Relationships				
Health and Age				
Community/ Society				

The type and intensity of feelings that you experience will fluctuate. Initially, you might feel paralyzed by anger and fear. These feelings may give way to sadness or even relief, and then return. People recovering from a significant loss often describe their experience as being similar to riding a roller coaster. At first the ups and downs are enormous in their contrast. Eventually, the ride evens out, and a sense of control and stability begins to return.

Physical reactions to loss are not unusual. When you are dealing with intense emotions, your body is vulnerable to illness, aches, sleeplessness, excessive fatigue, changes in appetite, confusion and even diminished memory. People often worry about these physical symptoms, thinking that grave illness has accompanied their loss. Usually, your physiological reactions to your emotional state will be temporary.

One senior executive had trouble concentrating in the weeks following his job loss. He would be halfway through a sentence and completely forget what he was saying. This was embarrassing and disconcerting for one so reliant on his thought processes. He decided to treat his problem with honesty and a bit of humour. Simply admitting what was happening helped solve the problem.

When you are coping with loss, take special care of yourself. Rest, exercise and follow a well-balanced diet. Watch your use of addictive substances, including caffeine, alcohol, tobacco and over-the-counter medications. Consult your doctor. Any of the symptoms described above could require medical attention. It would be a mistake to ignore them, assuming that they will go away once you are over your loss.

Important: If you are feeling so low that you think there is no reason to carry on, or that others would be better off without you, STOP! Call your doctor, a clergy person, a counsellor or a crisis line. There are people who care about you and want to help you make it through this difficult time. Reach out for help right away.

A less well-known reaction to loss is the tendency to remember and grieve past losses in the midst of coping with a current situation. People often find themselves shedding tears over an event that happened years ago. If this happens to you, don't worry. It's not unusual to take an emotional inventory of past losses as you work through your feelings about a current one. It's okay to remember and appropriately express your feelings regarding your divorce, the death of a loved one, an unwanted move, hopes unfulfilled or any other change from your past.

Be aware that there is a future-oriented aspect to change and loss. Every ending creates a new beginning. You might not be ready to feel optimistic, but it can help you to think about the possibilities that might open up for you.

Why Worry about Feelings?

Nothing sabotages the career transition process more than unresolved feelings of anger, sadness and fear. Anger is the worst culprit. Sadness that spirals downward into a state of gloomy inactivity scores a close second. Fear is usually manageable through focused activity directed at creating a positive outcome. Gladness is a welcome feeling.

If you have lost your job, you are probably angry. This is not a bad thing in itself. What can be destructive is the way in which you choose to express your anger. Spreading your version of the story, complete with blame and bitterness, will only hurt you. There may be a lot of truth in what you say, but saying it indiscriminately is not helpful to your future prospects. Find safe confidants with whom you can vent your anger in privacy.

A manager had the unhappy task of telling a long-service, well-liked subordinate that his employment was terminated because the organization wanted to build a new culture in the division. The employee was devastated. However, only his wife, his closest friends and his career transition consultant heard the full extent of his reaction. Everyone spoke highly of the professional and dignified way in which he handled his departure. His former boss and colleagues made every effort to support his transition.

Email can be a very dangerous thing in the hands of an angry person. There is something about the immediacy and informality of this medium that tempts people to write regrettable things. Unfortunately, sending a venomous email is worse than saying something in anger, because, while the spoken word is sometimes forgotten, the email lives on in print. If you are angry, don't touch your email!

Anger not only burns bridges between you and the past, it can destroy your best path forward. Your professional community is small. The more senior your position, the smaller the community. If word gets around that you are openly expressing your bitterness, your contacts will not want to have more than one final conversation with you. If you go into interviews without having your emotions under control, a skilled interviewer will hook you every time. You will not be offered future opportunities if you are perceived as being unable to cope with the past. The fact that you have lost your job is less important to others than how you are perceived to be dealing with it.

Tip: Before talking with your business colleagues and contacts, write down your explanation of your job loss. Practise saying it to a confidant, and be sure that it is completely free of anger and bitterness.

Do not misunderstand this point. It *is* okay to feel angry, sad and afraid. It is *not* okay to express those feelings to anyone and everyone you meet or in ways that are harmful to you or others. To cope well with change, you must find appropriate ways to acknowledge and express your feelings.

Unresolved feelings not only harm your relationships, they drain your energy and rob you of your creativity. To engage in a positive, forward-focused career management process, you must find your way through the maze by dealing with your emotional reactions to loss. You might need several weeks before you start to find your way, and it could take a long time to exit this maze entirely, but you need to be making progress. There is no way over, under or around these feelings. You must move through them to get past them.

It's a Personal Journey

The strategies that work for you in making your way through the narrow passages, hidden intersections and unmarked turns of this emotional maze will be unique to you. No one can predict what will help you and what will set you back. Your support network can offer suggestions and cheer for you, but you are the one who will discover what works for you. The key is to keep trying different tactics until you begin to make progress.

When your feelings are intense, talk is the most reliable healing agent. Even the most introverted individuals find relief in getting their concerns off their chest. This is why so many people make the mistake of saying too much and talking to the wrong audience. You need to talk to a good listener. This will be an objective person who is removed from the situation. It will be someone who won't judge or give simplistic or trivial advice. In fact, while you are hurting, no advice is often the best advice. A good listener just listens. They don't turn the conversation to address their own needs, and they won't breathe a word about your talk to anyone else.

When you find such a person, tell them the unabridged story with as much colour commentary as you wish. This is your chance to let it go! Talking through everything allows you to acknowledge the extent of the situation you are handling. Recognize the feelings that accompany each change. Name your feelings. Shout them out, or cry them out if that's helpful. A good listener won't mind. Talking should help you achieve clarity.

Tip: Express your feelings in a safe way. Cry, yell, punch a pillow, go for a long run, play a hard game of tennis, sing at the top of your lungs or clean the house to within an inch of its life. Do whatever works for you without hurting yourself or anyone else.

There are many additional strategies that you can try as you search for ways to progress through the emotional maze. The list that follows offers suggestions. Some of these activities will work for you, and others won't. Try as many as you wish.

GUIDELINES FOR COPING WITH THE EMOTIONS ACCOMPANYING CHANGE AND LOSS

- Do something symbolic to mark what has ended. Go to a goodbye lunch or party if your co-workers want to do this for you. Burn your business cards. Shred a copy of your company's annual report. Pop the champagne. Create your own way of saying goodbye to familiar places and routines.
- Write about your experiences. Sit down at the computer, or buy a spiral notebook and put everything that happened in writing. Consider starting a journal. Tracking your feelings through the career transition process can be enlightening and helpful. Not too long from now, you will be able to see how far you've come.
- Arrange for a temporary time out, preferably at a place that you love. Spend some time on your own to rest, and be reconciled with what has happened. Solitude is often a great healer.

- Pay attention to your health. Eat a balanced diet. Get lots of sleep. Exercise. If you do get sick, be patient and take the time to recover fully without being anxious.
- Lounge in a hot tub, go for a massage, do deep breathing exercises or attend yoga classes. You hold emotions in your body more than you may think possible. Relax your muscles and let your feelings go.
- Do something creative. Work with your hands. Renovate a room, plant a garden, build a deck, paint, knit, cook, do woodcarving, repair things, sculpt or sew. As long as you find it relaxing and fulfilling, do it!
- Rely on your spirituality. Meditate or pray. If you belong to a community of faith, turn to the people who share your beliefs for support.
- Read the biography of someone you admire. There are countless stories of individuals who have coped with overwhelming difficulties, and left a legacy of courage and inspiration.
- Take stock of how you have handled changes in the past. Were you able to get through them without a lot of difficulty? If so, can you use the same strategies this time?
- Take every opportunity to limit the number of changes happening in your life.
- If you are very frightened, sit down and think about the worst possible outcome this situation could bring. Then practise inverse paranoia. Think about the best possible scenario, and visualize it happening. Write down what you would need to do to make it happen. Try to set at least one attainable goal.
- Be serious about having fun. Doing what you truly enjoy is often one of the first things to go when you're faced with difficult times. It may seem frivolous to schedule time for play, but you need to kick back now more than ever.
- Find reasons to laugh. Look for humour everywhere. Watch a funny movie. Invite your most easygoing friends to dinner. Ask people to tell you the best joke they've heard lately.

Help Your Loved Ones Deal with Your Career Change

When you lose your job, you are not the only one who experiences loss. The people who love you and depend on you can feel the loss of everything from financial security to the company convention in Bermuda and the daily chats with your assistant. Compounding this is their inability to control the situation. For them it's like hitting a patch of black ice when they're not behind the wheel.

Loved ones will experience emotions that can be completely different from yours. Your spouse might feel very angry because you have been hurt, while you are filled with fear and sadness. This can cause tension between you unless you understand that those close to you need the freedom to have their own reactions and cope in their own ways. Communication, understanding and support are vitally important for you and everyone who is close to you.

The turmoil of uncertainty plus the varied emotional reactions of loved ones often puts extraordinary stress on relationships. Even if you have been strong for one another initially, the long journey can be a challenge. These basic principles might help:

- First, take good care of yourself and manage your own emotions well.
- Give your loved ones the freedom to have their own reactions and cope in their own ways.

- Establish a plan for communication with each person who needs to be informed of your progress. Agree on a regular time to talk and put some structure around the conversation. This way, you can avoid unwanted, poorly timed interactions that seem like criticism or nagging.

After days of anxiety and conflict, a husband and wife decided to limit the discussion of the job search to once a week. They set aside Thursday evening, and developed a format for their conversation. They each answered these questions in turn without interruption: "What was this week like for you?" "What was encouraging?" "What was discouraging?" "Is there anything I can do to help you?" "What can we do this weekend that's fun?" Suggestions, judgments and advice were not permitted unless specifically requested. No solutions were expected. This process considerably eased the tension between them.

If you have children living at home, don't be surprised if they begin to act out. Fighting with siblings, letting grades slip and defying household rules are some of the ways that children of various ages express their anxiety. If you ask them what's upsetting them, don't expect them to be able to connect their behaviour to your current circumstances. The best response is to acknowledge their feelings and do something special or different to help them handle their specific problem. Children differ in their resilience and reactions. Some behave in surprisingly supportive ways at first, but a prolonged period of stress in the household will present challenges for them.

Very young children will feel the stress regardless of your words. They will be frightened if they witness their parents' tears and tirades. Continue to show your love for them and manage your intense feelings in a healthy way, out of their sight. Children need assurance that they are not the cause of the tension in the house. They will take their emotional cues from you, so keep your messages as upbeat and positive as possible.

Young children are interested in their own routines. They want to know if they will be able to continue their favourite activities like hockey or swimming lessons. Once you tell them what will be different for them while you are looking for work, and assure them that everything will be okay, they are usually very accepting as long as *you* seem okay. Help them with what they will say to their friends and how they will respond to any questions about your circumstances.

Eight- to twelve-year-olds will take most of their reactive cues from you, but they are also forming their own ability to make sense of things. Some preteens will ask very direct questions, and they deserve honest answers. Tell them a bit about how you are feeling, and at the same time assure them that you are in control of the situation. For example, you might say, "I'm a bit scared, but I'm talking to a lot of people to find work. It will all work out for us." Others at this age might brood or imagine catastrophes. Spend time with them and keep talking to them. If you keep the lines of communication open, you will be better able to address their concerns. The influence of peers can be significant for preteens. Immature and ill-informed ideas might bombard them. It's critical that your children receive your input and frequent reassurance.

Teenagers can be more realistic about the implications of job loss. They can separate the circumstances from their role in it, and they will have their own emotional reaction. They will look to you as a role model. Tell them the facts and ask for their support in whatever way makes sense for your family. Don't allow the classic teenage hyperbole to throw you. The solutions aren't as simple as they might think, and it can be challenging to be patient with their input. On the other hand, some teenagers will respond in remarkably mature ways and offer to make practical contributions. Accept this help with gratitude, but don't let them take on unrealistic responsibilities. Again, communication is the key. Teens will learn a lot from how you handle this situation.

When you are coping well with the emotions accompanying your career transition, it will have a calming effect on your children and everyone close to you. Offer frequent reassurance that everyone in the family is going to get through this tough time. Tell them that you love them. Hug them often.

The Return of Hope

Making it through the emotional maze will take time. There will be ups and downs, progress and setbacks. Give yourself credit for every step forward. Your goal is to remain aware of the dynamics of your emotions and use good coping strategies. Hope will return.

Gradually you will feel like you're back to what's normal for you. You'll find that you can concentrate again and take more interest in what's happening around you. Flashes of creative thinking and short bursts of energy will herald your discovery of the way out of the maze. Keep heading in the right direction and keep noticing how you feel.

The early moves in this game of career transition have been about ending well. With the decision made, the details settled and your journey through the emotional maze under control, it's time to move on.

Develop Your Strategy

What a person does tells you who a person is.

Objectives

This step invites and challenges you to think in-depth about what you've done and what you want to do next. It will help you identify all that you have to offer the marketplace. You will do a thorough analysis of your situation that concludes with a strategic targeting exercise. The chapters in Part Two cover:

- Career review and personal assessment.
- Identifying your strategic advantage.
- Evaluating the balance between work and the rest of life.
- Options to a traditional job.
- Looking ahead to retirement.
- Identifying the ideal employment opportunity for you.
- Initial assessment of the market.
- Setting targets where you think your potential to contribute coincides with market needs.

Rules to Follow

- The reflective work you will do is pivotal. Allow yourself the time and freedom to fully explore the questions presented in the following chapters.
- If you get stuck at any point, don't try to force the answers. Let the questions remain with you to answer later or to serve as areas for future exploration.
- Once you've completed a section, reread and reflect on what you have written to assess the patterns and themes.
- Use your own style to record your thoughts. Work at your computer, draw diagrams or pictures, use charts, graphs or mind-maps, dictate an audio recording or write longhand.
- Use career assessment tests only after you have done your own reflective work.
- This is personal and private information. You do not need to share this with anyone unless you would find it helpful.

Moves That Can Set You Back

- Dismissing this section as a waste of time.
- Thinking that you'll get back to doing this later and skipping to the résumé section so that you can get into the marketplace quickly.
- Giving only superficial answers.
- Thinking about the questions without recording your thoughts.
- Overlooking jobs that were unsuccessful or unenjoyable for you. There can be tremendous learning in adversity.
- Neglecting to get input from your support network and advisers that can offer you a reality check.
- Allowing the expectations of others to dominate your thinking. This is an opportunity to be yourself.
- Setting targets that lack clarity or are too broad.
- Spending an excessive amount of time on this reflective process, resulting in procrastination.

Refer to Appendix A: Strategic View of Targeted Employment Search Process. In Part Two you will work on your situational analysis and strategic targeting.

Chapter 4

Take Time Out
for Reflection

All that is past is prologue.

It takes careful self-assessment and good planning to move forward on the career path that is right for you. In the past, you might have followed your organization's prescribed progression through the ranks or responded to a headhunter's call, taking new opportunities as they presented themselves. In that old style of career management, there was often more emphasis on traditional advancement than on doing the work that you wanted and liked to do. In contrast, you are now expected to understand who you are and where you best fit in the workplace.

You are not the same person you were when you started your career. You're not even the same person you were ten years or even five years ago. This is a rare opportunity to evaluate where you've been and where you are today in order to generate options for where you want to go. Take the time to complete the following exercises in detail. Record your thoughts using a method that is comfortable for you. Relax and enjoy the process; it can be very affirming and do wonders to restore a damaged sense of self-worth. You have tremendous value to offer, and all of your experiences count for something.

....

Tip: If you are considering a major career change, take yourself on a retreat to do this reflective work. Organizations usually send their people to an off-site, facilitated session when long-term strategic thinking is needed. Plan your own off-site! Get away to a place where you feel totally relaxed, and enjoy solitude while you go through this process.

....

Create Your Timeline

Take a long look into your past by creating a timeline. Start with your earliest memories and work forward chronologically, recording the people and events that have affected your opportunities and shaped your decisions, especially as they relate to your career direction. Divide your history into blocks of time or chapters that have been significant for you. Be sure to include your experiences from outside the workplace. Look at the timeline provided and create your own, using the worksheet. Then follow the guidelines to help you recall how your career direction evolved.

GUIDELINES FOR TIMELINE ANALYSIS

Answer the following questions for each chapter of your personal history:
- What was your ambition and career direction at that time?
- What significant events or experiences influenced your expectations and outlook?
- Who were your role models?
- Who provided examples of undesirable behaviours and attitudes?
- What were the roads taken and not taken?
- What opportunities did you wish to have and why weren't they available to you?
- What caused you to close this chapter and move to the next?
- What did retirement mean to you at this time?
- If you could re-write parts of your personal history, what would the revised edition say?
- What elements of your lifelong dreams remain unfulfilled?

An Entrepreneur's Timeline

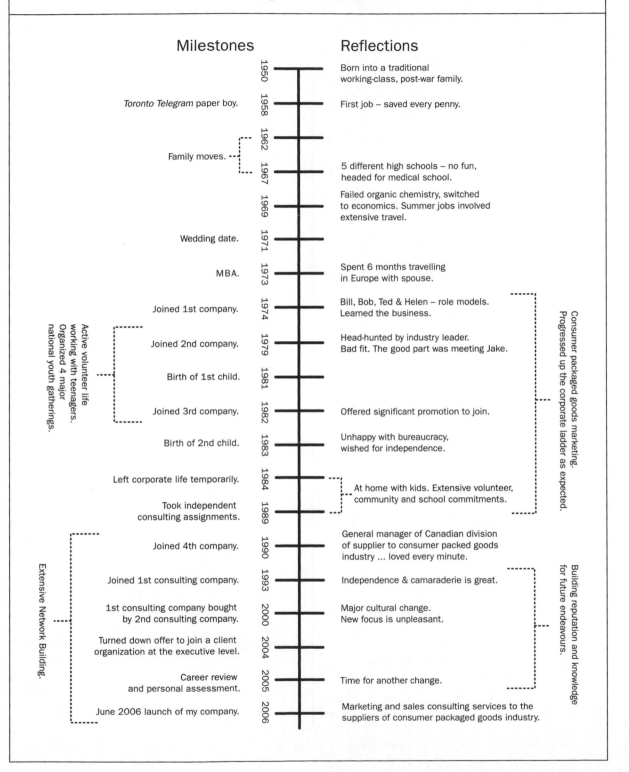

Milestones

Toronto Telegram paper boy.

Family moves.

Wedding date.

MBA.

Joined 1st company.

Joined 2nd company.

Birth of 1st child.

Joined 3rd company.

Birth of 2nd child.

Left corporate life temporarily.

Took independent consulting assignments.

Joined 4th company.

Joined 1st consulting company.

1st consulting company bought by 2nd consulting company.

Turned down offer to join a client organization at the executive level.

Career review and personal assessment.

June 2006 launch of my company.

Active volunteer life working with teenagers. Organized 4 major national youth gatherings.

Extensive Network Building.

Reflections

Born into a traditional working-class, post-war family.

First job – saved every penny.

5 different high schools – no fun, headed for medical school.

Failed organic chemistry, switched to economics. Summer jobs involved extensive travel.

Spent 6 months travelling in Europe with spouse.

Bill, Bob, Ted & Helen – role models. Learned the business.

Head-hunted by industry leader. Bad fit. The good part was meeting Jake.

Offered significant promotion to join.

Unhappy with bureaucracy, wished for independence.

At home with kids. Extensive volunteer, community and school commitments.

General manager of Canadian division of supplier to consumer packed goods industry ... loved every minute.

Independence & camaraderie is great.

Major cultural change. New focus is unpleasant.

Time for another change.

Marketing and sales consulting services to the suppliers of consumer packaged goods industry.

Consumer packaged goods marketing. Progressed up the corporate ladder as expected.

Building reputation and knowledge for future endeavours.

Timeline years
1950, 1958, 1962, 1967, 1969, 1971, 1973, 1974, 1979, 1981, 1982, 1983, 1984, 1989, 1990, 1993, 2000, 2004, 2005, 2006

WORKSHEET 4.1
Your Personal Timeline

Milestones   Reflections

Identify Your Accomplishments

Think back over your career and volunteer history, and recall the times when you had a sense of pride or satisfaction in something you did. The important stories are the ones in which your accomplishments were significant and satisfying to *you*. They might or might not have been part of your job. They could have attracted recognition and reward, or perhaps you were the only one who noticed. They could have taken years to unfold or only a moment's time. Think about this for a while. You are recalling times when you might have said or thought, "It's great to be me, doing what I'm doing." These stories are often called "accomplishment stories" or "peak stories."

Experiences from your personal life, volunteer commitments and community involvement are important for this exercise, but they cannot totally substitute for accomplishments on the job. Keep thinking until you have at least five work-related stories. Stop at ten stories as a maximum to avoid belabouring this exercise. Embedded in these stories are your key skills and core values. Use these guidelines and the following worksheet to record your accomplishments in detail and reflect on them.

Tip: At this point, don't worry about what you are going to do next. Plumb the depths and harvest the riches of your experiences—they contain the clues to your future!

GUIDELINES FOR RECORDING AND ANALYZING YOUR ACCOMPLISHMENTS

- First, relax and simply let the stories from your past surface. Collect as many as you like. Don't edit any out.
- Choose approximately ten stories that mean the most to you. For each of these, record the circumstances, the places and the people who were involved. Note the approximate dates.
- Analyze each story using this formula: Situation—Action—Result:
  - **Situation:** What was happening? What was the challenge, problem or opportunity at hand? What were the obstacles you faced? What could have been at risk if you hadn't got involved? Why did this matter to you? What motivated you to act?
  - **Action:** What did you do?
  - **Result:** What resulted from your efforts or activities?
- What common elements are present in your stories? Is it being in charge, advancing your career, making a profit, building a team, solving a problem, helping someone, improving a process, creating something new or shattering the status quo?
- What skills did you use in achieving these accomplishments?
- What themes are emerging?

A human resources manager in a large decentralized company was transferred to the region with the largest employee population. Her mandate was to transform the human resources function so that it would both contribute to the business strategy and establish standardized policies and procedures. She began by surveying the needs and expectations of the line managers. Within 18 months, she initiated recruiting and orientation programs that reduced turnover from 25% to 15%; tied the results of customer satisfaction surveys to group rewards, resulting in a 30% improvement in overall ratings; and restructured the ratio of professional staff to customer service staff, generating savings of 16% in salaries. Her model was subsequently used across the company.

You might struggle with identifying your accomplishments if your emotions are still heightened or if you have been working in an unsatisfying role for too long. If so, try identifying "rut" experiences— times when you were really frustrated, discouraged or burnt out. These stories will probably illuminate situations in which the skills you enjoy using were not engaged and your most important values were ignored or contravened.

The purpose of this exercise is to put you back in touch with what's important to you and what gives you a sense of being valued. Whether you have come at this renewed awareness by recalling good times or bad, you now have top-of-mind several key stories that demonstrate the best of what you have to contribute.

Tip: Accomplishment stories told using the Situation—Action—Result formula will become the backbone of your communications as you go through the search process. It is a powerful way to make your skills and strengths known to others.

WORKSHEET 4.2
Record Your Accomplishments

List at least five work-related accomplishments plus several from your volunteer commitments, community involvement and personal life.

Sample:
Situation: Lack of appropriate and effective family support for Alzheimer's patients in chronic care due to inadequate family education.
Action: Led a committee of physicians, nurses and others to create training and support programs.
Result: Delivered 36 sessions over an 18-month period resulting in greater understanding and involvement by families, and less pressure on nursing staff to deliver sporadic information.

1. **Situation:**
   Action:
   Result:

2. **Situation:**
   Action:
   Result:

3. **Situation:**
   Action:
   Result:

4. **Situation:**
   Action:
   Result:

5. **Situation:**
   Action:
   Result:

The People in Your Past

Your co-workers and colleagues on the job can make any assignment or situation more enjoyable or more difficult. To do a thorough career review, it's important to reflect on the personalities, styles and skills of the people who were part of your past work experiences. By doing this, you will improve the likelihood of choosing a positive work environment for your next employment opportunity.

Think about past bosses, other superiors, peers, subordinates, clients, suppliers and others from your past. Using Worksheet 4.3 as a guide, list the names of as many individuals as you can recall in each category. Then use the prompting questions to reflect on the characteristics of each person who had a notable influence on your success, development and enjoyment, either positive or negative. Reflecting on bad experiences is often more enlightening than reflecting on good ones.

The final prompt in each section of the worksheet invites you to develop a general profile of the sort of people that would create an inviting and energizing work environment for you at this point in your career.

The information that you collect here will be used later as you develop your vision statement describing the ideal employment opportunity for you.

A semi-retired businessman in his seventies works with a consulting firm and intentionally seeks assignments with start-up organizations focused on software development. These organizations tend to be populated with people in their twenties. The exposure to fresh ideas and different expectations keeps this man feeling young and energetic. His clients receive the benefit of wise counsel and access to an extensive network of contacts across many industries. It's a win-win situation!

Tip: There are many books on management and leadership style that could serve as additional guides for your reflection.

	WORKSHEET 4.3 **Reflect on People in the Workplace**
Names to Consider	**Personal Characteristics, Style and Skills**
Bosses and other supervisors	For those who brought out the best in you, was their delegating style specific and complete or general and more directive? How did they communicate, confront, make decisions and represent you to others in the organization? How did they give recognition and rewards? What were they particularly good at doing? Was it team building, developing subordinates, planning strategy, implementing, organizing, selling or communicating? Answer the same questions for those who brought out the worst in you. How have your needs for leadership changed over time? Develop a composite profile of the ideal boss and other superiors for you at this point in your career.

Names to Consider	Personal Characteristics, Style and Skills
Peers and colleagues	How would you describe the colleagues and peers with whom you accomplished the most?
	Answer the same question for those with whom you accomplished the least.
	How would you describe the colleagues and peers whom you enjoyed the most and the least?
	What were the usual causes of friction between you and your co-workers?
	How has your need for interaction with co-workers changed over time?
	How would you describe the ideal group of colleagues and peers for you today?

Names to Consider	Personal Characteristics, Style and Skills
Subordinates	As a supervisor or manager, what have been your most rewarding experiences?
	Who were the subordinates you recall as outstanding? Who were the most challenging? Why?
	What were your greatest challenges as a manager?
	How do you think your most outstanding and most challenging subordinates would describe your management style?
	If you could build a team from the ground up, what characteristics, styles and skills would you seek in your team members?
	Do you like managing people?

Names to Consider	Personal Characteristics, Style and Skills
Clients and others outside the organization	How would you describe the clients and other external contacts with whom you built excellent relationships? What personality and style issues caused conflict between you and people outside the organization ? How do you think your key contacts would describe your personal characteristics and style? What sorts of people would comprise an ideal group of clients and contacts for you today?

Organizational Culture

Organizations have unique personalities and characteristics that profoundly affect the way work is done and determine what type of persons will feel comfortable working there. If you are not compatible with the true personality of your workplace, it can be a major struggle for you.

An organization's culture is revealed in what gets done, what is said and how its people think. Culture affects the way employees interpret their experiences. It makes some behaviours praiseworthy and others taboo. It governs the way individuals relate to one another and to customers, suppliers and competitors. The true core values of an organization are exhibited in its culture.

Most organizations have a published values statement, but few can claim these stated values are genuinely and consistently reflected in the daily experiences of their employees. To analyze an organization's culture, take a critical look at its behaviours. Listen to stories about its achievements. Ask people about its successes and failures. Be careful to identify any possible differences between the expressed cultural norms and values versus those actually practised. There is often a large gap.

> *The charismatic CEO of a small, entrepreneurial financial services company developed a values statement that put customer service at the top of the priority list. He worked hard to ensure that his staff and external contacts heard this message. However, day in and day out, the questions that he would ask his people were, "What deals are you working on?" or "How's the XYZ deal going?" Everyone knew what was truly valued!*

Analyzing your fit with the organizational cultures you have experienced is an important step in deciding what you would like to do next. Each organization, separate department or specific team you have been involved with in the past will have had a unique culture and you will have responded differently in every case. If your career has taken you into numerous situations, narrow these down to the few that seem most significant.

Use a separate copy of Worksheet 4.4 to analyze each experience. Recall what was good and bad about that culture for you. Determine how various aspects of culture affected your job satisfaction. Make note of the characteristics you will look for in your next employment opportunity.

Tip: If you are interested in moving from one sector to another, consider the differences in their cultures. Business, social services, the government and not-for-profit organizations, to name a few sectors, have notably dissimilar characteristics. Do thorough research and a careful analysis of your fit with the prospective environment. This will help you avoid culture shock, which could limit your potential for success in a new sector.

	WORKSHEET 4.4 **Analyze the Organizational Cultures You Have Experienced**		

Cultural Characteristics	Questions to Consider
Values	• Was there a written statement of values? • Was there a gap between the expressed values and those actually practised? • Were the core values integrated into recruitment practices, orientation, performance management and reward systems? • What was the track record regarding diversity and equity?
Resilience	• How has the organization adapted to its changing environment? • Did it grow or diminish as a result of setbacks? • Was there an open exchange of ideas without reprisal? Were internal disagreements resolved or did they result in divisiveness?
Leadership	• How did the leaders get people to follow them? Was it through command and control, through incentives or by influence and inspiration? • Describe the characteristics of those who got ahead. • Was the culture one of entitlement or was it a meritocracy? • Were senior individuals in the organization visible to the rank and file? • How did leaders show appreciation to employees for good performance?
Creativity	• Were new ideas encouraged by the leaders and your co-workers? • Were new initiatives supported without reprisal or ridicule in the case of failure? • Was there an atmosphere that encouraged playfulness and the use of humour?
Communication	• Was communication honest? • Were important messages conveyed thoroughly and promptly to the appropriate people? • What was the style of communication? Formal or informal? Were important decisions delivered in writing or in person? • What did outsiders say about the organization?
Decision-Making	• How were decisions made? Did you have access to the decision-makers? • Was decision-making delegated to the lowest appropriate level?
Legends and Rituals	• What sense of the organization's history and future possibilities did employees have? • What stories were told and retold? Who and what were admired or denigrated in the stories? • What was celebrated and how? • What were the characteristics of ordinary occurrences such as meetings, performance reviews, lunches and coffee breaks?

Pursuits Beyond the Workplace

Education and Professional Development

Is this period of career transition an opportunity for you to return to the classroom? What would you study and how would it add to your strategic advantage? If you are lacking credentials that are expected at the next level in your profession, consider taking the time to get them. Having fresh knowledge of the most current theories and practices is a tremendous benefit in any area. In some fields, training in the leading-edge technologies and processes is essential for making a good move.

If you have any interest in advancing your education, be sure that you have thought through your long-term plans. Mid-career education is very costly. The time commitment and sacrificed earnings will be significant. Choose the institution and the courses wisely. Be certain that you know exactly what will be required of you and how this study can advance your career.

Through your contacts, determine how prospective employers will value the education you intend to pursue. Make an appointment to see the dean or the program director and ask where recent graduates are employed. Interview a few of them, and ask what other institutions they considered, or why they made the choices they made. Ask if they would do anything differently now.

Community Involvement and Volunteer Experience

In creating the timeline and identifying your accomplishments, you were encouraged to include experiences from your non-working life. At this point, think about the people that you have gotten to know through these other commitments, experiences and interests. Choose appropriate questions using the worksheets as a guide to reflect on your relationships outside the workplace. The people with whom you have enjoyed working on volunteer and community commitments and other non-work experiences can serve as models for the ideal group of future colleagues.

Look at the organizations where you allocate your time and energy. Are you active in your industry or professional association? Do you help with fundraising or other work for a charity? Are you active in politics? Do you help out at your children's schools? Are you a member of a religious or service organization? Are you on the board of a member-owned sports club? What role do you typically assume in these organizations, and are you happy with what you are doing? Are there other groups or organizations you have considered joining? If yes, why haven't you done so? What roles would you like to fill?

A time of career transition will offer the opportunity to make changes in your volunteer life. Examine what you value and make careful choices as you move forward. Plan to back away from commitments that drain your energies without providing sufficient personal rewards.

Hobbies and Interests

When your time is truly your own, what do you enjoy doing? Even if you haven't had time recently for your hobbies and personal interests, bring them back to mind. While you are moving through the transition process, engaging in your favourite pastimes can help keep your spirits up.

Some people consider turning their hobby into a livelihood. This often depends upon having a pension or some other source of income. It is more often the case that hobbies and interests provide balance in life rather than significant income opportunities. Carving out time for these things is a worthwhile goal as you choose your next employment opportunity.

Two friends who enjoyed going on bike tours together decided to open a tour operations company to organize and lead excursions through Europe. They delighted in planning the routes, choosing quaint hotels and creating lists of recommended restaurants. Their inaugural summer was successful because a number of friends and acquaintances came along, but the second summer things did not get off the ground. The marketing, administration and management of overseas suppliers was more than the friends could handle. They reverted to planning and enjoying trips for two.

Wrap Up Your Reflections

Ideally, this broad look at your past has generated some fresh ideas for your future. At least it should have helped you remember what you disliked in the past and prefer not to repeat. As a conclusion, answer these questions: If you had to choose a specific period of your past working life and relive it, which would you choose? Why?

The next step in the reflective process will provide you with a snapshot of who you are today.

Tip: You may still feel bogged down or overwhelmed by negative feelings about your last job. Perhaps all you need is more time to move through your feelings; however, the problem could be more complex. Be kind to yourself and get the help you need from a professional counsellor or your doctor.

Chapter 5

Identify Your Strategic Advantage

Compete where you have an advantage.

Play to your strengths. Your point of greatest marketability and highest degree of job satisfaction is found where your style, skills, knowledge, interests and values intersect. It's the unique combination that makes it very difficult for anyone to imitate your approach and contribution. This is your strategic advantage. Don't try to find work where none of these attributes are needed or valued. Take the time to define your strategic advantage precisely and you will have the means to find an employment opportunity that integrates *what you do* with *who you are*.

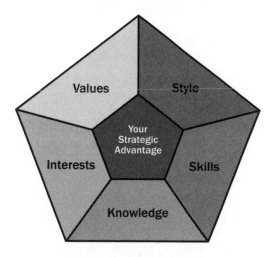

Whether you are considering only a slight shift in focus or a radically new direction, you must take stock of your skills, knowledge and personal style. These are the traditional components of job specifications, and the core attributes on which you can build your future. If you are also able to incorporate your interests and values in your next employment opportunity, you will have made the most of this transition.

Tip: Don't look for a career assessment test that will circumvent this work. No test can tell you who you are and exactly what you should do. Complete your own reflective process first. You know yourself well. It might take time for the picture of your ideal career to come into focus, but it's on your radar screen somewhere.

As you work through the following sections, take notes. You will use your notes to develop a description of yourself that is specific, factual and businesslike. It will become invaluable to you as you move through the career transition process.

Your Personal Style

Your personal style is the summation of your distinguishing qualities. It describes the characteristics and attributes that you bring to your work and your interaction with others. It governs how you work. When you understand your personal style, you have the option to choose tasks and relationships that will engage your strengths. You can avoid unsuitable situations and adjust your style to accommodate circumstances where your strengths will not be helpful.

You are likely to be aware of your dominant characteristics. You know yourself, and you have been praised for your strengths and criticized for your weaknesses. The more subtle aspects of your style will be somewhat hidden from you. Look for clues in past performance reviews and informal feedback. Ask trusted colleagues to help you with this exercise.

A young woman described herself to a career transition consultant by talking about what she enjoyed doing in high school, in university and in summer jobs. It was obvious that she was creative, quiet, intellectual, unconventional and spontaneous. No wonder she was very unhappy as the manager of a large operations department in the back offices of a huge bureaucratic organization.

If you are considering a major career change, your personal style stays with you even if you leave everything else behind. In fact, it is often a person's most striking personal characteristics that lead the way into new territory. For example, an altruistic, pragmatic manager with a persuasive communication style might use his skills to run a charitable foundation.

To develop a description of your style, use the following worksheet and choose words that are appropriate for you in each category. A list of descriptive words is included to prompt your thinking.

WORKSHEET 5.1
Describe Your Personal Style

Choose a few words, or write a very short phrase, to describe yourself in each of the following areas. Do not limit your choices to the examples given; use the inventory of adjectives on the next page for ideas.

Thinking style   This is the way that you approach a problem or opportunity. Descriptors might include realistic, visionary, strategic, analytical, logical, perceptive, concrete, etc. There are many others.

Communication style   This might elicit words such as enthusiastic, cautious, comprehensive, persuasive, inspiring, reserved, straightforward, etc.

Management style   Here you might describe yourself as fair-minded, authoritative, caring, democratic or non-directive. You might write, "I delegate tasks and give minimal specific direction."

Subordinate style   How do you like to be managed? Are you self-reliant, consultative, a conscientious task implementer, a questioner or a loyal follower?

Team style   What role or task usually falls to you? Are you the innovator, the detail monitor, the implementer, the communicator, the relationship caretaker, the organizer or the leader?

Work style   Are you highly organized, spontaneous, meticulous, flexible, process-oriented, a team player, a loner, results-focused, decisive or a perfectionist?

Resilience   How are you hard-wired? Are you a worrier or are you relaxed? Do you take things too personally? Are you critical or accepting, optimistic or pessimistic, driven to achieve or non-competitive?

Think of a story from your past to exemplify each of the words that you used to describe yourself. Is the picture accurate and complete? What else should be added?

Inventory of Adjectives

accepting	consultative	forward-thinking	open-minded	self-reliant
accommodating	cooperative	friendly	opportunistic	sensible
accurate	creative	future-oriented	optimistic	sensitive
achieving	credible	generous	organized	serious
adaptable	customer-focused	hands-off	outgoing	shrewd
affirming	deadline-driven	hands-on	participative	sincere
aggressive	decisive	hard-working	patient	skillful
agreeable	dedicated	helpful	people-oriented	sophisticated
altruistic	deliberate	high-impact	perceptive	spontaneous
ambitious	demanding	high-potential	perfectionist	straightforward
analytical	democratic	honest	persevering	strategic
articulate	dependable	humorous	persistent	strong
artistic	detail-oriented	imaginative	personable	subtle
aspiring	determined	impressive	persuasive	successful
assertive	diligent	incisive	philosophical	succinct
assured	diplomatic	independent	poised	supportive
astute	direct	individualistic	positive	sympathetic
authoritative	discerning	industrious	powerful	tactful
aware	disciplined	ingenious	practical	tasteful
believable	discreet	initiating	pragmatic	team builder
calm	dynamic	innovative	process-oriented	team leader
candid	easygoing	insightful	productive	team player
capable	effective	inspiring	professional	technical
careful	efficient	integrative	proficient	tenacious
caring	eloquent	intelligent	project-oriented	thorough
cautious	empathetic	intense	punctual	thoughtful
charismatic	empowering	intuitive	quality-driven	tolerant
cheerful	energetic	investigative	quick	top performer
clever	engaging	judicious	quiet	top producer
collaborative	enterprising	kind	realistic	to the point
committed	enthusiastic	knowledgeable	reasonable	tough-minded
communicative	entrepreneurial	logical	refined	troubleshooter
competent	ethical	market-driven	reflective	trustworthy
competitive	experienced	methodical	reliable	truthful
compliant	expressive	meticulous	reserved	unconventional
comprehensive	facilitating	motivated	resilient	understanding
composed	fair-minded	multi-talented	resourceful	unrelenting
conceptual	far-sighted	non-competitive	respected	upbeat
concerned	firm	non-conforming	responsible	versatile
concrete	flexible	non-directive	results-focused	visionary
confident	focused	objective	results-oriented	well-balanced
conscientious	formal	observant	risk taker	well-spoken
consistent	forthright	open	savvy	willing

Your Key Skills

This part of your strategic advantage comprises the professional credentials and technical skills you have acquired through formal education and training plus the functional skills that have grown out of your practical experience. Skills constitute what you do.

To create a complete inventory, start by recording all of your credentials and core skills. Include any processes, methodologies, systems or programs in which you are qualified or where you have substantial experience. Add your functional skills, which are most easily identified by considering the areas of responsibility where you have gained expertise. Include the skills you have acquired in your volunteer and community work as well. Use the samples below as a guide.

Tip: Many skill sets cross boundaries and provide the credibility to move from one industry to another. Focusing on your skills gives you an independent identity based on your capabilities. You no longer need to describe yourself simply as a former employee of an organization.

Samples of Professional Credentials

CHRP	Certified Human Resource Professional
RN	Registered Nurse
CFRE	Certified Fund Raising Executive
P Eng	Professional Engineer
CMC	Certified Management Consultant
CFA	Chartered Financial Analyst
CMA	Certified Management Accountant
CFP	Certified Financial Planner
FLMI	Fellow of the Life Management Institute

Samples of Technical Skills

Human Resources Information Systems
ISO quality registration
Six Sigma
ERP Implementation
Project Management
Alternate Dispute Resolution
Systems Applications
Programming Languages
Databases

Samples of Functional Skills by Occupation

CEO	vision, strategy, marketing, operations, finance, corporate governance, selection and communication
CFO	strategy, corporate governance, budget control, reporting, risk management, finance, taxation, raising capital and communication
CHRO	strategy, organizational development, change management, leadership development and communication
CIO	strategy, business process improvement, systems architecture, data integrity and security, infrastructure management, business alignment and technology solutions and communication
Account Manager	sales forecasting, territory management, client relations and business development
Controller	financial planning, budgeting, treasury, cash management, auditing, and financial reporting and analysis

General Manager	team leadership, strategic planning, managing processes and systems, business development and customer relations
Health Care Director	management of staffing, volunteers, patient care and facilities, admissions and discharge planning, budgeting and proposals
Human Resources Manager	recruiting and selection, compensation and benefits, training and development, performance management and labour relations
Journalist	writing, editing, interviewing, research, layout and design
Lending Officer	business development, credit analysis, asset recovery and portfolio management
Marketing	product development, pricing, distribution and promotion
Plant Operations	team leadership, project management, logistics, resource allocation, quality control and continuous process improvement
Property Management	building systems, tenant relations, maintenance and upgrading, leasing and staffing
Retail Operations	merchandising, promotions, inventory and cost control, staff training and development

---

WORKSHEET 5.2
Your Skills Inventory

Professional credentials:

Technical skills:

Functional skills:

When your list is complete, think about which skills you enjoy using and which ones you'd rather leave behind. Being good at doing something does not automatically mean that you like doing it. Many people enter the workforce without a clear idea of where their interests lie. They develop expertise in an area that is not a good fit and stay in a role because the cost of change is too high.

Tip: If you are serious about walking away from your current set of technical and functional skills, be prepared for a longer search, the possible need to re-train, a significant orientation period and a cut in pay. To do this, plan your finances, get your support network in place, muster your courage and go for it! You are making a courageous decision.

Your Knowledge Base

Your knowledge can be separate and distinct from your formal education and your professional skills. It consists of everything you have learned about everything! It includes your understanding of various industries, companies, products, market segments, regions, regulations, cultures, special interest groups, etc. It is the combination of information, exposure, experience, savvy and acumen about people, places, things, activities and ideas.

You have gained knowledge about many things that can be useful to other people and organizations. In some instances, a confidentiality or non-compete agreement will restrict you from sharing what you know. This is clear evidence of the value of this knowledge. Your integrity depends on respecting these agreements, but you will also have a large amount of unrestricted knowledge that you will be able to contribute to your next employment opportunity.

Use the worksheet to bring to the surface some of your most significant points of knowledge. Think expansively. Do not be restricted by the categories listed.

Tip: Every industry segments its market in some way. Organizations adjust their product and service offerings to better serve targeted groups. Your knowledge of specific market segments will be a valuable transferable asset.

A nurse who had moved into an administrative role lost her job when her hospital amalgamated with another. While she was in transition, her 82-year-old mother had a stroke and became in need of a chronic-care facility. As the nurse went through the time-consuming and difficult process of arranging for her mother's care, she realized how daunting it could be for people who knew very little about the health care system to find and gain entry to a facility that would meet the needs of both the family and their loved one. She parlayed her interest into full-time work by offering her knowledge and skills on a consulting basis to families in similar situations.

WORKSHEET 5.3
Your Knowledge Inventory

List the industries you know well. Which ones do you know marginally?
E.g., advertising, health care, telecommunications, retail

In addition to your previous employer, which companies or organizations do you know well?
E.g., competitor A, supplier B

What products or services do you understand in depth?
E.g., derivatives, home appliances, small engines, wine, waste management

In which types of transactions or strategic initiatives do you have experience?
E.g., acquisitions, outsourcing, re-engineering, turnarounds, collective bargaining

List the market segments you know well.
E.g., institutions, retail, high income, business travellers, women

List the regional markets or geographical areas where you have expertise.
E.g., South America, Atlantic Canada, China

List the languages you speak fluently or conversationally.
E.g., French, Spanish, Mandarin

Include other knowledge that you have accumulated that will make a contribution to a future employer.
E.g., chaired capital campaign for local hospice

Your Interests

Your interests can be a significant component of your strategic advantage. If your work allows you to be involved with something that genuinely fascinates you, you are fortunate. People who are curious and passionate about their product, service or market have a natural enthusiasm that is unmistakable. If you can, expand your work to include your interests. For people considering a career change, your interests can be a guide to ideal employment opportunities.

Some people have no trouble identifying their interests, while others find it surprisingly difficult. If you have been working too hard or you are under too much stress for any reason, your interests might have been pushed so far into the background that you can't think of what they really are. On the other hand, if you are one who is curious by nature, you might have so many interests that it's impossible for you to identify the ones that could be incorporated into your working life.

What are your interests? Think beyond your hobbies and athletic pursuits. Interests include ideas or issues and philosophies that fascinate and attract you. Some may be lifelong interests; others may be emerging and evolving. Your interests are a large part of what makes you unique. If the answers are obvious to you, jot them down. If not, the worksheet and the inventory of interests are designed to help you.

Tip: Many people who have the option to retire early focus on their interests when choosing their next endeavour.

A professional engineer who was the CEO of a small consumer packaged-goods company spent his spare time designing and managing residential renovations with his wife, who was an interior decorator. Together they transformed several run-down houses into showcases. When his position was eliminated as a result of international restructuring, he landed a role as the CEO of a software development company that creates products for the interior design industry. He was fortunate to be able to integrate an avid interest with his paid employment.

WORKSHEET 5.4
Assess Your Interests

What social, environmental, cultural, health-related, religious, judicial, political or business issues do you find the most compelling?

On the job, when you choose a course or read an article in a trade or professional journal, what topics attract your attention because you are truly curious?

In the workplace, what departments, roles, projects and activities seem appealing?

What magazines, books, TV shows, movies or Internet sites interest you?

Who are your role models and heroes?

How do you like to spend your time outside the workplace?

At social events, what topics of conversation do you welcome?

If you were to return to school, what would you study even if it had no obvious practical application?

If money were not an issue, how would you spend your time?

If you need more input, look at the following list to prompt your thinking.

Inventory of Interests

accounting	decorating	human rights	process re-engineering
acting	designing	information	product development
adolescent issues	digital photography	technology	psychology
alternative	disaster recovery	interior decorating	public relations
medicine	e-commerce	international	quality control
amateur theatre	education	development	research
antiques	environmental issues	investments	recruiting
archeology	ethics	journalism	real estate
art	event coordinating	judicial system	religious studies
astronomy	executive coaching	keynote speaking	retail business
auto mechanics	exercise	labour relations	risk management
biotechnology	falconing	landscaping	sales
birding	fashion	languages	security
boards of directors	film	law	seniors' issues
boating	financial planning	leadership	small business adviser
branding	fishing	development	snowmobiling
carpentry	fitness	lecturing	special interest groups
catering	flying	literacy	spirituality
charitable foundations	forensics	literature	sports
chemistry	franchises	marketing	strategic planning
child development	fundraising	market research	stock market
child poverty	gardening	martial arts	succession planning
children's causes	genealogy	massage therapy	teaching
coaching	gerontology	media	tennis
collecting	geriatric care	mentoring	theatre
community issues	global issues	merchandising	translation
communications	golf	music	travel
competitive	gourmet cooking	organizational	university courses
intelligence	governance	behaviour	volunteering
computer	graphic design	organizational design	web site design
programming	health issues	painting	wilderness
condominium laws	history	philosophy	adventuring
conservation	homelessness	photography	women's issues
counselling	home restoration	physics	woodworking
creative writing	horticulture	poetry	writing
criminology	hospitality industry	political issues	yoga
debating	human resources	politics	

Your Values and Motivators

Values are your personal guideposts. They go hand-in-hand with the motivators that drive you. Ideally, these principles exert enormous influence over your choices regarding work. They are informed by your upbringing, role models, expectations and experiences, and comprise your unique inner rationale. Following them generates a sense of fulfillment. If you are in a situation that continually requires you to act against your principles, you will become unhappy, unduly stressed or burnt out.

Thinking about values and motivators is very important to the career transition process. They can be a powerful part of your strategic advantage. The highest degree of job satisfaction is found where your principles align closely with the requirements of your role and the expectations of your organization. Success on the job usually follows. "Know thyself" is a proverb that is often quoted because it's so important.

Tip: Values and motivators are not necessarily lofty ideals. For example, being an expert in your field is a value held by many. The desire to earn a lot of money can be a powerful motivator. Be honest with yourself, and be clear about your priorities at this time in your career and life.

It may be difficult to maintain a grasp on your values and motivators for two reasons. First, they change and evolve as you move along your career path and through different stages of life. Second, they are often conflicted within you, and with those of people who are important to you. Some people spend a lot of time contemplating these aspects of their lives, while others are less concerned.

To gain some clarity, consider your preferences and needs in the workplace separately from the responsibilities and values in your personal life. For the purposes of identifying your strategic advantage, first consider only what is important to you in the work that you do. Think of your present needs and expectations as they pertain to your work. You will be invited to bring the rest of your life into the picture in the next chapter.

WORKSHEET 5.5
Prioritize What's Important in the Workplace

Prioritize the following list by identifying each statement as A (primary importance), B (secondary importance) or C (little or no importance). Feel free to add anything else of importance in regard to your work and include these in your ranking. Next, review your A list and identify no more than three non-negotiable needs that will drive any decision regarding your next employment opportunity. Then develop a secondary list of things you would like to have.

_____   Performing work that contributes to the good of society

_____   Helping or caring for individuals and adding value to their lives

_____   Having bottom-line accountability and being responsible for results

_____   Working in a competitive environment, having a chance to win at something

_____   Having stability and security at work through a structured environment

_____   Having an opportunity to bring change to an organization

_____   Having an opportunity to preserve tradition and protect proven processes

_____   Being free of bureaucracy and entrenched policies, a more entrepreneurial approach

_____   Defining your own work schedule, having flexibility

_____   Mentoring or training other individuals either formally or informally

_____   Managing a group of people, building an effective team, being the leader

_____   Having freedom from management responsibilities

_____   Being acknowledged as an expert in a technique, field or specialty

_____   Developing a strong industry profile and gaining the recognition of peers

_____   Working for an organization that is recognized as best-in-class

_____   Having opportunities to travel or work outside the office

_____   Having direct contact with people outside the organization such as customers and suppliers

_____   Using and developing presentation skills by speaking to small and large groups

_____   Having lots of contact with people during the day

_____   Having plenty of time alone to think, write or work on a task

_____   Working with intelligent colleagues who are experts in their field

_____   Being part of a closely knit team where challenges, opportunities and credit are shared

_____   Being part of a cross-functional team that touches every part of the organization

_____   Being able to work independently, deciding on your own how to achieve objectives

_____   Working with a group of people who enjoy social activities and have fun together

_____   Having clear, step-by-step direction and supervision

_____   Solving new and complex problems that challenge your thinking and use your skills

_____   Being responsible for implementation of ideas created by others

_____   Exercising your creativity to develop new ideas, solutions and products

_____   Enjoying variety and regular change in the mandate or job content

_____   Having a stable, predictable routine month after month

_____   Enjoying access to the latest technology

_____   Being offered opportunities for further training and development

_____   Being offered potential for career advancement, a ladder to climb

_____   Working in a fast-paced environment with a rush of urgency and a demanding schedule

_____   Having opportunities to work with people who are ahead of you in job title and status

_____   Having a job title and status

_____   Being recognized for work well done, receiving awards, verbal praise, commendations

_____   Building a sense of personal and professional growth

_____   Having an opportunity to make a lot of money through bonuses, commissions or stock options

_____   _____

_____   _____

_____   _____

Do not confuse this exercise by adding things like time for the family, location or a minimum level of remuneration. Stay with what you need from the work itself.

What work have you done that truly reflected your values?

What work have you done that was contrary to your values?

List your non-negotiable criteria for being satisfied and motivated in your work.

List the values and motivators that are desirable but could be traded off.

Career Assessment Testing

Now that you have done a thorough self-assessment, consider taking advantage of the many career assessment tests that are available. These tests can affirm your thinking and bring to the surface things that you have not considered. They cannot tell you exactly what to do with your career. They categorize the interests, abilities and attributes that you report, and provide lists of the careers in which people with similar profiles report success and satisfaction. The more sophisticated tests explain the reasons why specific careers match your profile. Don't expect miraculous revelations. Expect a helpful analysis that complements your own work.

It's best to work with a professional, such as a career transition consultant, psychologist, executive coach or therapist who is qualified to administer the testing. They will help you understand the results and integrate them with your self-assessment work. However, you can do this on your own, using tests that are available in books or on the Internet. The following guidelines should help you through the process.

GUIDELINES FOR CHOOSING CAREER ASSESSMENT TESTS

- Tests alone cannot tell you what to do with your career. Consider the results of career assessment testing as another step in the process.
- Determine if testing is for you. If you are comfortable with your self-assessment and know exactly what you want to do, or if you have been through the testing process numerous times with the same results, it may not be worth your while.
- There is no one test that is more conclusive or gives better results than another. Each one has a unique approach, so it's best to use several.
- Much-used and well-respected tests that look at career choice include the Myers Briggs Type Indicator, the Strong Interest Inventories, the Campbell Interest & Skill Survey and the 16PF. Each of these has a cost associated and should be administered by a qualified professional. Look at samples of different reports to see if the type of data generated is what you need.
- If you are working with a career transition consultant, counsellor or coach, ask if the feedback session can be audiotaped for you. This is very helpful for your subsequent review.
- Don't expect a definitive answer. Sometimes there are discrepancies between test results. You might also get results that don't seem to fit your self-image. Remember to put the testing in context. Talk this over with your career transition consultant or your support network. Your own analysis and feedback from people who know you should take precedence.

Get Input from Others

At this point, go back to your support network, board of advisers or references for input. You might be overlooking some of your most significant strengths because you don't think of these qualities and abilities as anything extraordinary. Your colleagues from the workplace and anyone from your volunteer and community endeavours will most likely have valuable insights. Gather a group together or approach each person individually, provide them with a summary of your notes, and ask for their views using the following guidelines.

GUIDELINES FOR REQUESTING AND RECEIVING INPUT

- Choose your input providers wisely. Relatives and close friends might be good choices, but they probably haven't seen you in the workplace. Include some people from your work environment.
- Choose people who will be honest in their responses but sensitive to your situation. This might not be the best time for you to hear too much negative feedback.
- Decide how you will record their responses. Usually allocating time for taking notes following the conversation will be sufficient. If you're getting a group together, appoint a recorder. If what's said is not written down, you might forget it.
- Ask questions such as:
  - What are my most natural talents, skills and abilities?
  - How would you describe my style for each category on Worksheet 5.1, "Describe Your Personal Style"?
  - In what areas do you recognize me as particularly knowledgeable?
  - In your opinion, what are my three greatest strengths?
  - Do you think that I overuse any of my strengths? In what way?
  - What skills do I need to develop?
  - From your perspective, what do I appear to value highly?
  - What are the kinds of jobs or roles that you think I would do well in and like doing?
- Try to receive this input without defensiveness. Just listen. Asking for clarification and examples is a good way to increase your understanding of what is being said.
- Remember to thank these people with a written note.

Tip: The most significant input is often that which you don't expect.

Put It All Together for Presentation

With all of the data that you've collected in thinking about your strategic advantage, it might be a challenge to narrow it down and explain it clearly, but it's worth the effort. Presenting yourself in terms of your skills, knowledge, style, interests and values is a powerful way to communicate to the marketplace. A verbal synopsis of your strategic advantage breaks away from the use of titles and names of previous employers, expanding the possibilities for your future. It positions you as an individual with a unique and independent set of talents and attributes, seeking opportunities to add value.

In Part Three: Gather Your Resources, you will develop a script that describes you using a few key points from each component of your strategic advantage. It will be your capsule profile. The following example can be used as a template for putting your capsule profile together. It packs a lot of information into very few words.

I'm a retail operations executive with extensive experience in managing a nationwide chain of over 100 franchise stores selling specialty kitchen items. My particular strengths include inventory and cost control, merchandising and the provision of training and development support for store managers. I understand the challenges facing small retail franchise owners in Canada. I am at my best when handed a mandate and given the flexibility to do it my way. I am a manager, not an innovator. My creativity emerges in finding solutions to very practical problems.

Your strategic advantage, expressed in a capsule profile, brings together who you are with what you do, what you know and what you care about. Once it is clearly identified, this powerful combination can give you the leverage to find an employment opportunity that meets your needs.

Tip: Don't confuse your strategic advantage with passion. If you view your work only as a means of making a living, don't think there's anything wrong with that! What you care about and enjoy most may never have anything to do with your work. Have confidence in being who you are!

Chapter 6

What Really Matters to You?

Life is all about choices.

What you value in your work and the things that motivate you on the job rightfully have a powerful influence on your career choices. However, you have responsibilities to your family, friends, community and volunteer commitments. You also have personal needs and dreams. All of these compete for your time, energy and talents. Their importance to you must be considered as you plan your next career move.

There's more to think about regarding employment. The analysis of work-related values and motivators that you did in Chapter 5 covers only a part of the picture. The work environment, your terms of employment and market factors beyond your control can significantly affect your ability to achieve the balance that's right for you. This chapter invites you to examine these things as both a reality check and an opportunity to re-set your priorities.

Goals to Achieve

Everyone is motivated to do or have different things that make life and work personally satisfying. Your career goals can be as ordinary as providing for your family's needs or as grand as finding the cure for cancer. Perhaps your most compelling goals have nothing to do with your career. If this is the case, you need to adjust your career to make room for achieving goals that truly motivate you.

Most people are motivated by several things at once, and motives change over time. It can be difficult to acknowledge and describe your true motives, but they are there. One way to identify what really matters to you at this moment is to think about what you hope people will say about you in the future.

Imagine that you are turning 90. Your friends and family are planning a big party to which guests from every phase and sphere of your life have been invited. A toast will be offered to you, and you have the privilege of writing it. What would you like it to say? Use the worksheet on the next page to create it.

WORKSHEET 6.1
A Toast to You

Here's to [*You*] _____ .

Your friends and family appreciate you for

_____

_____

_____

Professionally, you are known for _____, and made significant
contributions to _____

You are dedicated to (a cause, organization, group, activity, hobby, spiritual practice)
_____ that has inspired or influenced you to

_____

Everyone here admires and respects you for _____

_____

Please join us on this very special occasion in a toast to [*You*] _____ .

Tip: There is no better time than the present to make the things that truly matter to you your priority!

Personal Well-Being

Are you satisfied with the vitality of your body, mind, emotions and spirit? Feeling completely balanced with regard to your own well-being is elusive. Multiple responsibilities and challenges cause most people to either neglect self-care or become obsessed with one facet of it to the detriment of others. A temporary period of unemployment offers the opportunity to review your priorities and reclaim healthy practices and good habits that you have allowed to lapse. It also allows you the time to form new habits.

Use the following worksheet to reflect on your personal needs. Make some realistic commitments to yourself.

Tip: Life is a gift. Good health is an extra blessing. Are you living with an appropriate sense of gratitude?

WORSHEET 6.2	
WORKSHEET 6.2 **Evaluate Your Priorities Regarding Yourself**	
Physical health *Your body is the only permanent home you have!*	Are you comfortable with your physical condition and appearance? Is this affecting your career in any way? Can you make a realistic commitment to change without creating impossible hurdles? Are you putting inordinate importance on this aspect of your well-being?
Intellectual stimulation *If you don't use it, you'll lose it!*	What do you do to keep your mind active? Are you dependent on your job for intellectual challenge? If you have been either bored or out of your depth at work, how does this inform your career choice? What level of additional formal education or professional development would you be willing to pursue to assist you in achieving your career goals? Is more education an accessible, affordable and attractive prospect for you?
Emotional balance *Are you competent in managing yourself and handling relationships?*	Self-awareness, self-control, self-esteem and emotional stability are very important for success on the job. Have you experienced difficulties in these areas that have affected your job performance? What are you prepared to do about making changes?
Spiritual well-being *Religion is cultural. Spirituality is universal.*	What spiritual practice helps you cope with challenges and appreciate good fortune? For example: • Enjoying nature, art or music • Solitude • Meditation or prayer • Yoga or tai chi • Following the practices of a religious denomination • Reading inspirational works If you would like to devote more time to your spiritual well-being, what are you prepared to give up?

Commitment to Your Family, Friends and Community

Where do you draw the line between the time and energy you put into your own well-being, your work and time devoted to loved ones? If you have responsibility for small children, adolescents or aging parents you are probably performing a difficult balancing act. You could always work more at the expense of the family, or do more caregiving at the expense of the job. Volunteer commitments and community activities could soak up every spare moment if you were to allow it. Finding a compromise is challenging.

On the following worksheet, use the sections that are relevant to you as a guide for your reflections on your commitments to others.

WORKSHEET 6.3 **Evaluate Your Responsibilities and Priorities Regarding Family, Friends and Community**	
Spouse or partner	Is your spouse or partner financially dependent on you? Does your spouse or partner have special needs? Do you have responsibilities associated with his or her work? How does his or her career influence your career choices? How supportive of your career plans is he or she likely to be?
Children	At their ages, what do they need from you? Do any of them have special needs? How much support do you get from their other parent, extended family members or paid child care? What lifestyle do you want for them?
Parents	Are they dependent on you in any way? Do they live close by or far away and does this influence your career choice?
Friends and neighbours	Do you have obligations or interests involving friends and neighbours that are important to you and require your time and attention? How much of a priority is this?
Volunteer commitments **Community responsibilities** **Service or religious affiliations**	How much time do you devote to these types of activities? Are you satisfied with your choice of activities and level of involvement? How will your career choice affect your involvement?

A woman in her late forties lost her management job with a large retailer when it was acquired by a competitor. She had never liked working in a business environment, but because she carried responsibility for her large extended family, she had persevered. Her love was working with children. Having none of her own, she volunteered at camps on her holidays, taught church school and worked occasionally at a local daycare centre. When her employment was terminated, she decided to use her severance to return to school and obtain a certificate in Early Childhood Education. Upon graduation, she landed a job and now manages programs for several centres while enjoying working with children.

Work Environment and Terms of Employment

In Chapter 5 you analyzed what is important to you in the workplace, looking at the content of the work, relationships, autonomy, responsibility and advancement potential. There is much more to consider. Many people willingly trade some aspects of job satisfaction for a more favourable work environment or more suitable terms of employment, such as a shorter commute or flexible hours. Use the worksheet to focus your thinking on these issues. Your responses will begin to clarify the strategic targets you will define in Chapter 8.

WORKSHEET 6.4 **Evaluate Your Priorities Regarding Work Environment and Terms of Employment**	
Remuneration	What is the minimum income that you must earn to maintain the lifestyle you want and to take care of your dependants? How much of it needs to be base salary, and how much can come from variable pay such as bonuses, profit sharing, stock options or commissions? What is your long-term plan regarding the accumulation of sufficient financial resources for permanent retirement?
Mobility	Are you willing and able to relocate? Would your spouse and children be willing and able to relocate? If so, what would be your preferred location?
Commuting	How much time and expense will you tolerate? What mode of transportation is available and acceptable? Will you commute by car, bus, subway or train? Would you like to work from a home office? How much time would you be willing to spend there?

Benefits	Do you need full insurance and health benefits from an employer or can you purchase what you need independently?
Physical environment	How important is the style and quality of your physical surroundings?
	Do you need to work in a private office or is a cubicle acceptable?
	Do you need any special accommodations?
Travel	What amount of job-related travel is possible for you?
	Do you like to travel for your work?
	What destinations are acceptable and desirable?
Vacation	Are you accustomed to long, uninterrupted vacation periods?
	Are you willing to take fewer vacation days?
Schedule	Do you work in the evenings and on the weekends?
	Does your industry or profession have peak periods in the year?
	Are you willing to be accessible 24/7?
	Would you like flexible work hours or job sharing?
	How many days are you willing to work every week or month?
	Is part-time or seasonal work an option for you?
Your future	What would you like to achieve professionally in the next 3, 5 or 10 years?
	How many more years will you be working?
	What are the steps to retirement for you?
	Can you make short-term sacrifices for long-term gains?
	What would that mean for you?

Other Factors That Influence Career Choice

Freedom to make career choices is often limited not only by personal priorities and circumstances, but also by market factors beyond your control. Markets evolve, governments bring in decisions, political influences shift and economic conditions change. Many roles require specific professional credentials. Graduate-level education is a prerequisite for advancement to senior roles in some organizations. Age and gender can be unofficial but real barriers. Let's face it, the law protects you, but you can't become a ballerina or make the NHL at age 56.

It is crucial to be realistic about these factors. Direct your energy toward choices that have no barriers for you. Resist becoming overly pessimistic during tough economic times or unduly optimistic when market conditions are good. Many cycles are temporary and simply require you to wait it out. Some trends are permanent and recognizing them as such is wise. Accepting ongoing change is part of good career management.

Tip: There is opportunity in every situation. It takes resilience, creativity and often perseverance to find it.

WORKSHEET 6.5 **Consider the Realities That Affect Career Choice**	
Economic and regional determinants	What economic conditions and regional factors will influence your search for employment?
Industries in transition	What are the current and future prospects of your industry? What industries are advancing? Which ones are contracting?
Government initiatives	Is your work dependent on government funding, protective tariffs or specific government-driven initiatives?
Educational requirements	What professional credentials or level of education is required for further advancement in your field or entry into a new field?
Age	How will your age affect your employment prospects?

In the late 1990s, when the federal government balanced the budget for the first time in years, there were devastating implications for individuals who worked in the fixed-income securities market. Because there were no more new issues of government bonds, a number of traders and salespeople lost their jobs. One young trader decided to take a step down in remuneration in order to make the switch to an analyst's role. A seasoned salesman moved into selling retail investment products and joined a franchise operation that was establishing offices in Canada. A woman with young children took the opportunity to stay at home with her family for a while. She also recognized that her true interest lay in working with physically disabled children. She enrolled in a Master's program part-time to pursue her ultimate career goal.

A Realistic Look at Values

How do personal priorities and other circumstances affect your career choices? For many people, very significant and limiting factors exist, making a major career shift unthinkable. If this is true for you, make your goal the revitalization of your career through a change of venue or focus. By transferring current skills and knowledge to a similar role in another organization or by identifying a role that requires a variation on well-known themes, many achieve a renewed sense of interest and energy in their work.

Your challenge is to incorporate as much of what you value into a realistic career plan.

Tip: Most people are free to make choices as long as they are willing to make sacrifices. You can't have it all, but you can aim to have what's most important to you.

Chapter 7

Consider Alternatives to a Traditional Job

Look for work versus a job.

Do you want another full-time, permanent job, or will you consider alternatives? Have you thought about striking out on your own and working independently? Could you start or buy a business? Is retirement on the horizon and would you like to ease into it gradually? What work arrangement would best suit your current lifestyle, and what do you think the future holds?

The current employment market is characterized by non-traditional work arrangements. Organizations see the benefit of just-in-time workers, and there is an increasing willingness to hire outside expertise and assistance for specific non-core tasks and projects. This has created a large market for occasional, variable and part-time employment. Interim executives, contract workers and consultants are frequently engaged. Think about the options this provides for you, each with its benefits and drawbacks.

There are many valid reasons to focus on finding work in whatever form it may come, rather than limiting your options to a permanent job. If the market for your skills at your level is slow, you're in for a wait regardless of how capable you are. Through contract employment, you might find very interesting work that strengthens one part of your background or immerses you in a new area. Or perhaps you are at the stage of your career where your knowledge is your most valuable asset. If so, contributing as a consultant could be the appropriate role for you.

The ex-COO of a multinational manufacturing firm discovered that prospective employers were more interested in his experience establishing manufacturing operations in China than in his other considerable skills. After initially putting a damper on conversations regarding consulting assignments, he finally agreed to help a former colleague by taking a look at his business plan for building a facility in China. His advice proved to be of exceptional value. Subsequently, he took consulting assignments from others, and eventually landed several board appointments as a result. This unanticipated form of employment turned out to be exactly right for him.

In a traditional job, you trade your skills and knowledge for remuneration, title and status, development opportunities and a modicum of job security. In non-traditional employment relationships, you negotiate flexible, time-limited terms under which you exchange your skills and knowledge for remuneration.

With a business, you deliver products and services to the marketplace under your own banner and employ others to assist you. This diagram illustrates a range of options:

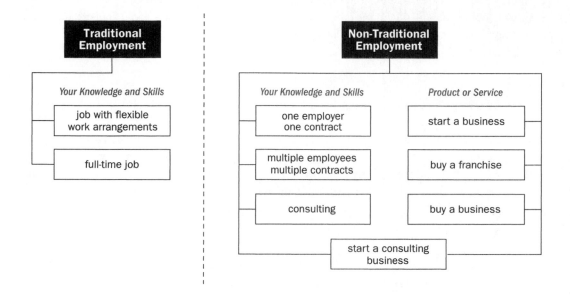

Traditional Employment—Flexible Work Arrangements

Flexible hours and telecommuting have created the opportunity for many employees to have some of the advantages of working independently while staying in a traditional job. It is increasingly common for executives, professionals and managers to regularly work from home, or organize their hours in the office according to their personal priorities. Job sharing is a possibility, but only where the work lends itself, the participants are suitable and the organization's culture accepts the arrangement. Part-time opportunities at the executive level are few and far between, but they can be the answer for people who want to improve the balance between work and personal interests. Seasonal work is a possibility for some professionals such as accountants.

While employers have created flexibility that works extremely well for some, the trade-off can include lower earnings, no benefits, limited professional development opportunities, difficulty maintaining a sense of belonging and less chance of upward mobility within an organization.

Contract Work

Contract work usually involves joining the ranks of an organization for a short time. The contract assignment might be related to a specific project or a peak in the organization's business. Alternatively, the contract worker fills the shoes of a permanent employee who is on temporary leave. The length of contracts can extend from a few weeks to months and even to years. The work might be full- or part-time. You could be paid as an employee, or submit invoices as an independent supplier.

Tip: To be able to claim self-employment status, you must exercise control over the way your work is done, the schedule and the location. You must bring your own tools and materials to the job, provide a service that is not an integral part of the organization's core business and bear some financial risk in the contract. Check www.cra.gc.ca for details. Consult your accountant for tax advice and your lawyer for help with contracts.

There are several ways that contract work can fit into your plans. One is as a stop-gap. This involves taking contract opportunities that come along while you are looking for a full-time position. Doing this keeps your skills sharp, broadens your experience, adds new contacts to your network and generates income in the process. Many organizations use contract assignments as a way of evaluating a candidate's skills and fit before making a permanent hiring decision. The downside of taking a full-time contract is that you will be much less active in the job market, leaving you with little or no time to market yourself.

Tip: Expressing interest in non-traditional employment can provide the quickest route to re-employment. It can also open a door that eventually leads to permanent employment.

Contract work can also be a career choice. Either as an independent or working for an organization that supplies contract workers to its many clients, you have the benefit of constant change in your work environment. This option usually involves some business development responsibility. If you strike out on your own, the challenge of finding the next assignment will always be with you.

Some people use contract work as a step toward retirement. It's not unusual for employers, suppliers or competitors to ask a recently retired individual to accept a contract position. These people often find that being valued in a completely new culture is one of the most affirming things that has happened in years. You might be surprised to find that you become busier than ever, pushing the notion of retirement far into the future.

A senior manager who accepted an early retirement package from a major financial institution decided to continue deploying his skills and interest in internal auditing by seeking contract work. He had been on the leading edge in using business intelligence and data-mining technology to eliminate the hit-and-miss sampling technique common to audit procedures. His ability to apply software built for market research to other business solutions quickly caught the attention of several financial institutions, and his venture into the arena of contract work soon took precedence over his plans for having more leisure time.

Consulting

Consulting refers to the process of offering information and recommendations at a strategic level to the managers of an organization or to an individual. Implementation is usually left to the client. Consultants are typically engaged when something is going wrong, when existing processes and systems are inadequate or when changes are needed or being anticipated. They are expected to bring to their clients the best practices in their areas of expertise. An expert consultant will review the situation, identify the issues and make suggestions for interventions and change, with practical advice for implementation.

To become established as a consultant, you usually need to have recognized expertise in your field, good contacts and strong marketing, negotiating and facilitation skills. It also helps to have the appropriate professional designations and formal education at the graduate level. Consultants can choose to work independently, in association or partnership with other professionals or with a consulting firm. To be successful, independent consultants must have the ability to originate business.

Tip: When you work independently, you need to pay attention to your record-keeping, tax status and insurance needs. Purchase and use a software package for bookkeeping. Hire a Chartered Accountant to get you set up, and to do your annual statements and tax filing. Insurance and medical and dental benefits may be available through your professional association or the Association of Independent Consultants. Check their web site at www.aiconsult.ca.

Independent contractors and consultants are free from the infrastructure of an organization. They are usually able to work from the location of their choice and perhaps employ sub-contractors and administrative staff. Often they handle more than one assignment at a time, providing variety, breadth of exposure and an ever-increasing knowledge base built on experience. Independence can be exhilarating.

The allure of self-employment also includes the perception of having freedom to work when you want, for whom you want and at what you want. It seldom turns out to be utopia. To replace an employer's demands, your clients will have ill-timed crises and unrealistic deadlines. In the absence of workplace politics, you will have the challenge of balancing your clients' expectations with your actual ability to perform miracles. However, with hard work, these options to a traditional job can be made to fit your interests and needs.

After managing three acquisition integrations, a senior human resources professional decided to establish herself as an independent consultant. To augment her MBA, she became a Certified Management Consultant and contacted her broad network of business colleagues to solicit assignments. After two years of building her practice, she works long hours and weekends to meet the needs of her ever-growing list of demanding clients. Her expertise in managing people through times of significant organizational change has generated great success and a frenetic lifestyle.

Business Ownership

The thought of owning and operating a small business has appeal for those who want to be in charge of an enterprise. The impetus is usually the recognition of a niche market. This could be a new product or service, or the need for improvement on what is currently available. Whatever the inspiration, you can look at building a business from scratch or buying an existing business or franchise.

Before investing too much time and money in the start-up phase, use the guidelines at the end of this section to test your readiness. Then write a thorough business plan. Financial institutions provide excellent templates, and many are available on the Internet. Your plan must include a full description of your product or service, including its features and competitive advantages. Establish pricing and calculate the cost of sales. Do a thorough market analysis.

A couple decided to start a small business providing computer software training programs. To begin the venture, they needed to lease office space with training facilities, purchase furniture and equipment, and hire administrative staff. They constructed a plan that calculated the precise point where they would have to abandon the venture without leaving their family's finances in irreparable ruins. They each knew how they would orchestrate a quick return to paid employment. Once the plan was in place, they took an optimistic and tenacious approach to building the business without second-guessing their strategy.

Decide how much you can afford to invest without a financial partner. Don't expect financial institutions to provide funding for your business without collateral or your personal guarantee backed by solid assets such as your house. Get financial and legal advice before you start.

Tip: Choosing the appropriate form of business is critical. Incorporating, establishing a partnership or operating as a registered or unregistered sole proprietor are your choices. Each carries advantages, risks and costs. Ask your professional advisers which is best for you.

To build or buy a small business, you can go it alone, team up with one or more colleagues or get the backing of an existing organization that has interests matching yours. On the surface it might seem that going it alone is the most risky option, but that's not always true. Partners with an investment and interest in your business should add ideas, effort and support. It could turn out that their priorities and abilities are not as advertised.

A would-be entrepreneur decided that his skills in internal communications and employee relations would work well in the field of diversity training. He was introduced to a potential partner who was working as an executive coach and had a similar interest. The pair incorporated, entered into a complex shareholders' agreement, leased an office and developed a model for their service before either one focused on their target market and how they would actually bring business in the door. As time passed, one partner kept himself so busy with his coaching practice that he was unable to generate leads

for the joint effort. The other lacked contacts and the confidence to develop them. After much expense,
their venture had to be wound down.

Another route to business ownership is buying rather than building. The simplest and safest approach is buying a franchise. Reputable franchise vendors have done most of the groundwork for you. They know the product or service and the market very well. There should be an established formula for operating the business as well as training and support to get you started. Your ongoing fees pay for marketing and advertising, and there may be preferential supplier arrangements negotiated for you. The downside includes the potentially staggering cost of purchase and the reality that you will probably have to work morning, noon and night for limited potential earnings. It's crucial that you like the sort of work that you'll be doing, and thrive in structured situations. Buying a franchise is not a good idea for people with high needs for independence and variety.

Tip: Before buying a franchise, do your research and planning as if you were going to build the business from scratch. Your bank manager and the Canadian Franchise Association are reliable sources of advice and caution.

Buying an existing business is another story altogether. The best advice here is "buyer beware." Make sure that you know and have confidence in the current owners' reason for selling, and do not proceed unless you get a clear and thorough answer to every question you ask. As with building a business, you need to understand the product or service well and have a grasp of the market. Look at the financial situation with a critical eye, and most importantly, look at the people who work in the business. You need to be confident that the team will rally around you and do their best to take things forward.

Tip: If you are considering buying an existing business, surround yourself with a team of qualified professionals. Even if the entity is very small and you think you know it well, hire help! You will need a lawyer, an accountant and, ideally, a business broker, venture capitalist or co-investor to look over your shoulder. Do not try to do this alone.

An experienced general manager learned that a small office furniture manufacturing company was for sale. He asked a neighbour who owned his own small manufacturing business to accompany him on a fact-finding visit to the target company. After two hours of looking at the financials, touring the plant and interviewing the owner, the two men left to ponder their findings. The asking price was $750,000. On the way home, the small business owner said, "For that much money, I'd just as soon start up fresh. I can make a lot of mistakes for $750,000." The decision was made, and the purchase was not!

- Identify the skill, service, product or type of advice you will offer your potential clients or customers. Define it clearly and specifically.
- Identify the benefits of your service or product. What's different about it? Why is it necessary for or advantageous to the buyer? Why would your clients or customers choose your offering over the competition's?
- Assess the market. Who will pay for your advice or buy your product or service?
- Do you have access to the market? Meet with several potential clients or buyers to discuss the potential of your endeavour. You will be successful only if qualified decision-makers will meet with you.
- Plan how you will manage a fluctuating income stream.
- If your endeavour requires an upfront investment of capital, how much money are you willing to put at risk?
- Identify the variety of skills you will need to be successful. These could include skills related to business development, administration, project management, written communications and more. Do you have the necessary skills or will you need to engage someone who has them?
- Think about what working in this new, non-traditional employment arrangement will mean for your family. Building a business is nearly always an all-consuming task. Contract or consulting work could give you more time at home, but lower earnings. In every case, the stress on relationships can be great. Make sure that you have your family's support.
- Talk with people who have gone in a direction similar to the one you are considering. Learn from their experiences, both good and bad.

Non-Traditional Employment Options Are Transforming Retirement

The growing acceptance of non-traditional employment arrangements has had a profound effect on retirement issues. Instead of abruptly moving from full-time work to permanent retirement, many people are progressing toward it via flexible work arrangements, contract work or consulting. The process of gradual or semi-retirement can be a welcome alternative for both employers and employees.

Demographers have been warning of a serious shortage of workers should all baby boomers retire permanently in their early sixties. Smart employers recognize that older employees can offer valuable advice based on experience and can often act as mentors for younger workers. Employees in their late fifties and beyond are known to have lower rates of absenteeism, fewer accidents, higher levels of job satisfaction and possess a stronger work ethic than their juniors. Why wouldn't organizations create employment arrangements that are attractive to this group?

Semi-retirement is an increasingly popular and productive career phase. It is usually characterized by the need for less pay, as a result of having at least a partial pension or investment income. This phase might be initiated by an early retirement package from your long-standing employer or simply by your desire to gear down. Even individuals who have received a package often return to their former employer on a contract basis to do a special project or to fill a temporary vacancy. Many build second careers in related fields. Former executives become executive coaches; an accountant may teach CMA courses or keep the books for a charitable organization; an executive from the hospitality industry might buy a small inn.

Whether you choose semi-retirement or find that the employment market has thrust you into it, remaining actively engaged in the workforce in some capacity may offer you some of the best experiences of your career. Many people of traditional retirement age enjoy the independence and flexibility of non-traditional employment arrangements because it gives them better work/life balance. Moreover, they can often choose what sort of work they will do, and with whom they will be associated.

The choices are yours. Decide what's most important to you and make this transition a good one.

Chapter 8

Set Your Targets

*Where does your ability to contribute
coincide with market needs?*

You've reviewed your career history, gathered your accomplishment stories, identified your strategic advantage and reflected on your values. Now it's time to pull all of this together into a vision statement of the ideal employment opportunity for you. Next, have a preliminary look at the marketplace and consider industries and sectors where you could make a contribution. Combine this with your preferred terms of employment, and your strategic targets are set. These targets are working hypotheses that will give your search focus and direction. This diagram illustrates the targeting process.

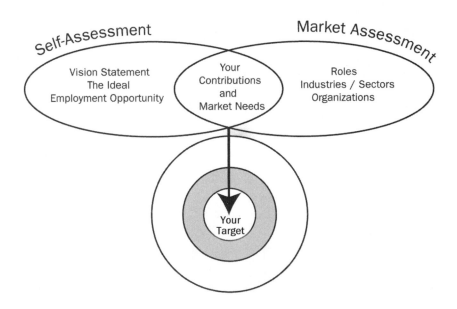

Self-Assessment—The Ideal Employment Opportunity for You

To summarize the self-assessment work you have done using Chapters 4–7, create a vision statement of the ideal work for you. It will describe the activities or functions to which you are best suited and the types of cultures or environments you prefer. It will not name specific job titles or organizations. This vision statement will be forward-looking, yet grounded in the realities of your talents and experience. As you progress through your search for work, use it as a touchstone to keep you on the right track.

Use worksheet 8.1 on page 88 to create your vision statement. Share it with your support network. Ask if they think it's an accurate description of you. Have you missed anything that is key?

A top-performing salesman had spent the most recent two years of his career working on the implementation of new sales support technology. This detail-driven, internal role left him feeling burnt-out and out of touch with his key skills. As he recalled accomplishment stories from earlier years and identified his strategic advantage, he described himself as charismatic and competitive. He claimed to understand the emotional dynamics of successful sales. Sales management held little interest for him, but achieving higher monetary rewards was important. He wanted variety and travel opportunities in his next role. After he shared his vision statement with his support network, they suggested that he become a motivational speaker. After taking a few courses, he succeeded in getting on the speakers' circuit, and now makes his living addressing sales conferences and conventions for a variety of organizations.

WORKSHEET 8.1

Self-Assessment—Your Vision of the Ideal Employment Opportunity for You

What are you motivated to achieve in your career (Chapter 6)?

List the elements of your strategic advantage (Chapter 5) that you will take to your next role.

- Skills

- Style

- Knowledge

- Interests

- Values

Describe the type of people with whom you most want to associate in your work (Chapter 4).

Identify the culture and type of organization that most appeals to you (Chapter 4).

What other personal values, obligations and priorities will affect your career decisions (Chapter 6)?

What are your remuneration requirements?

What is your preferred geographical location?

On what terms will you accept a non-traditional employment arrangement (Chapter 7)?

How will your next career step move you toward your long-term goals?

Identify the Possibilities

Where can you find an opportunity that meets the criteria you've listed? Now that you have a working description of the qualities and components of the work you want, think about the various roles that would suit your needs and wishes. Then think about the markets, including industries, sectors and organizations, that have a need for people in such roles. Note the names of people who could provide information and help. Do not think strictly in terms of job availability.

Note: The term "market" as used here refers to industries, sectors and organizations. The words "industry" and "sector" are often used interchangeably. For example, the financial services industry is often called the financial services sector. The government is more often considered a sector, as is the world of not-for-profit.

This is the time for you to do some brainstorming and let your imagination range as broadly as possible. If you are comfortable with asking others for input, enlist your support network or a few key people to help you with this exercise. It's important to move past the potential limitations of your own thinking. Distribute copies of your ideal employment opportunity vision statement to the people who have agreed to help you brainstorm and enjoy the process.

Then use the following worksheet to record the roles and markets you've identified that align with your ideal employment opportunity. The example given in the first part of the this worksheet is drawn from the previous story about the top-performing salesman.

WORKSHEET 8.2
Identify Roles and Markets that Align with Your Ideal Employment Opportunity
Example

Roles	Industries and Sectors	Organizations	People
• corporate trainer • sales trainer • selling anything • politician • religious leader • motivational speaker • TV broadcaster • talk-show host • sports announcer	• corporate training suppliers • retailers selling luxury items • office products suppliers • radio/TV industry	• MICA • IKON Office Solutions • The Liberal party • The Anglican Church of Canada • Speakers' Forum • CBC • KDKA - FM	• Mary Mills • Joe Jones • Etc.

Your Data

Roles	Industries and Sectors	Organizations	People

Market Assessment

Begin the process of assessing industries, sectors and organizations where you might find one of the roles you've listed. Use worksheet 8.3 on page 92 and record the information that you know or can find easily. Be realistic about the remuneration and the level of seniority you could achieve in a new sector. Consider staying in the sector where you have experience and moving to an organization of significantly different size.

The industry or sector in which you have worked most recently is a good place to start because you know it well. For markets that are less familiar to you, do some very preliminary research. Check a few web sites and talk only with your close contacts. Later in the search process you will do in-depth research that will include reaching out to knowledgeable people who are not in your immediate support network. Research and networking will provide answers to the questions that are forming now. At this point in the exercise you are making assumptions to help clarify your thoughts and organize your search. You will likely return to this market assessment exercise many times.

Make several copies of worksheet 8.3 and use a separate copy to record your existing knowledge of each industry or sector and organization that you listed on Worksheet 8.2.

The National Sales Manager of a multinational documents company was interested in transferring her skills to an area in which she had more of a personal interest. Two markets were attractive to her. The first was the retail industry, with a particular focus on home decorating stores. The second was not-for-profit organizations dedicated to helping women in times of personal transition. She completed an assessment of each market, which made her aware of how much she needed to learn. Doing this exercise also allowed her to form excellent questions, which she subsequently used in her networking activities.

Refer to Appendix A: Strategic View of Targeted Employment Search Process and review the diagram to see where you are. Once you have completed the market assessments, your situational analysis is done and you are ready to set your targets.

WORKSHEET 8.3
Market Assessment

Industry or sector:

Organization(s)

Name	Size/Number of Employees	Location

Key People — List people who work in this market or who might know about it.

What are the current trends in this market or organization? What issues or challenges does it face? What does the future seem to hold? What skills are in demand?

How large is the market? How much time will it take you to explore employment opportunities in it? Is it large enough to sustain a full-time search? Which organizations are hiring?

Are there a number of organizations of varied size and scope in this market? How will their different strategic issues affect opportunities for you?

Which organizations are best-in-class or the most successful? On what basis do you make this judgment? Are acquisitions or mergers expected? Will there be new entrants to the market?

What roles exist in this market? At what level of seniority would you fit in?

What background and educational or professional credentials are required? Do they typically hire from outside the industry?

How do they recruit? Which search firms or placement agencies work in this market?

What level of remuneration is typical in this market?

To what extent are alternate employment arrangements available?

How do you think your ability to contribute coincides with the needs of this market?

Strategic Targeting

You now have the data you need to identify targets for your employment search. This step creates a strategy for your search and establishes the agenda for your research and networking. Set several targets, making them distinct from one another. Include only one role and one market in each target. Eventually your targets will overlap and elements of each one will apply to several others, but for clarity at the outset, keep it simple.

Choose one market that you have assessed in the previous exercise and develop a scenario in which you play a specific role within that market. Be as specific as possible when assessing a market that is well-known to you. Name an organization or a division or a team if you know of one that particularly interests you. You might even name a person with whom you are certain you would like to work.

For markets that seem less familiar to you, set targets that are quite broad. It is not unusual to lack specific information about markets that interest you at the outset of your search. Remember, your targets are going to act as working hypotheses that you will test later. Look at these examples of strategic targets:

Example: *"I am interested in working with John Smith as a member of his project team, testing new sales strategies in Asian markets. I see myself as the project leader for the China group."*

Example: *"I would like to explore the possibility of taking my sales management skills into the retail industry. I am particularly interested in do-it-yourself landscaping and gardening."*

It's that simple. A clear statement describing each of your targets will give your search focus.

The next step is to fully develop your rationale for setting each target. Use the following worksheet to organize your thoughts. Thorough work on this part of the exercise will enable you to speak of each target as a logical next chapter in your career. Your plans and ambitions need to be framed as a consistent progression from what you've done in the past to who you are in the present as you move toward your desired future. With the full explanation, your story will feel and sound natural and credible. Networking contacts will be able to assist you in concrete and helpful ways once they understand your targets and the logic supporting them.

WORKSHEET 8.4
Your Strategic Targets

Describe the target:

What elements of your skills, style and knowledge do you expect to engage in this scenario?

How do you think your ability to contribute coincides with the needs of the market in this scenario?

What value would you add in this scenario?

How will you differentiate yourself from others competing in this market?

Why are you interested in this target?

What is most compelling about this target for you?

What are your expectations regarding remuneration, level of seniority and employment arrangements?

What key questions will help you determine the practicality of this target?

Reality Check

Each of your strategic targets should involve only one market and one role. The possibilities are: stay in your current market or move to a new one; fill a role that is the same or similar to your most recent one or shift to a new role. Each of the four possible combinations carries a different expectation for the length of time your search will take and level of remuneration and seniority you could achieve.

Place each of your targets into the appropriate quadrant.

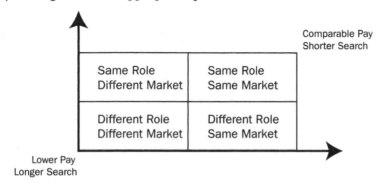

If remaining in the same market and role is an attractive and viable option for you, you will likely succeed more quickly and with better remuneration than with any of the other three options. While the top right quadrant of the model represents what is often the optimum route to quick re-employment, this is not always the case. Markets change with economic cycles, innovation and new trends. Familiar roles can be significantly altered or vanish completely. If staying in the same role and market has become unachievable or undesirable for you, your goal must be to seek opportunities in different roles and/or different markets. You may land successfully in the bottom left quadrant of the model, the one representing the most challenging career transition. It takes the most time and often requires a step down in remuneration, but it can be the beginning of a refreshing new chapter of your work experience.

Tip: An alternative employment arrangement could be the solution that allows you to land in the quadrant of your choice. If a traditional job in your desired market is unavailable, you might find contract work or consulting assignments that are on target.

An Example of an IT Professional's Strategic Targeting Process

To see how this targeting process flows from the self-assessment and market assessments, walk through the following examples of one person's work. Read the story below and look at the summaries of this individual's assessments. Notice that her seemingly diverse targets are logical and easily understood once given a full explanation.

A Senior Vice President (SVP) from the technology division of a large bank set three targets at the outset of her career transition experience. She felt confident that she could land a role as Chief Information

Officer (CIO) of a smaller financial services company. She was also interested in organizations doing research in the health care field because of her dedication to helping her niece, who had cystic fibrosis. She surmised that consulting roles would be more accessible to her in this new sector. Finally, she wanted to explore the possibility of moving into the not-for-profit sector, where she could contribute more directly to helping children with chronic health issues. To use her leadership capabilities and business acumen, she thought she should aim for an Executive Director's role in a foundation or association.

Prior to setting these targets, the SVP-IT had done a thorough self-assessment. The key points in her "Vision of the Ideal Employment Opportunity" are shown below.

SELF-ASSESSMENT
VISION OF THE IDEAL EMPLOYMENT OPPORTUNITY

Achievement motivation:

> In IT - to be the senior resource for an organization, aligning the IT strategy to the business strategy.
> Personally - to contribute more to helping children with chronic health issues.

Strategic Advantage:

Style — Strategic, innovative, logical, persuasive, reliable, a consultative leader

Skills — Strategic planning, team leadership, ERP implementation, vendor management

Knowledge — Financial services institutions, large-scale IT systems

Interests — Health care industry, cystic fibrosis research, gerontology, travel, skiing

Values — Doing work that contributes to the good of society
Variety and complexity in the work

Personal values, obligations and priorities affecting career decisions:

> No dependents. 10 years to retirement.

Remuneration requirements:

> Financial security is already established.
> Willing to earn significantly less to achieve other goals.
> $100,000 minimum if working at a not-for-profit.
> Market compensation is expected for senior IT roles.

Interest in non-traditional employment arrangements:

> Full-time, permanent job preferred.
> Would consider consulting to achieve other goals.

How will your next career step move you toward your long-term goals?

> Have enjoyed success in long-tenure at the bank.
> Looking for a venue where I can make a significant impact...not just another job.

The relevant points from the SVP-IT's three market assessments are shown below.

Market Assessment #1

Industry: Financial Services

Organizations:
ABC Credit Union,
European Ads Bank,
Big Life Insurance Co.

Key People:
Former co-workers from the Bank,
Suppliers,
Colleagues from industry association

Trends: Outsourcing, Off-shoring, ERP systems implementation, vendor management

Size: There are less than 5 credit unions of sufficient size and scope; there may be more foreign-owned banks; there are many small insurance companies

Best in Class: ABC Credit Union, Better Health & Life Co.

Possible Roles: CIO or consulting assignments

Remuneration: comparable

Possible Contribution: Current knowledge of trends, systems, vendors, compliance requirements, ERP experience should be highly marketable.

Market Assessment #2

Sector: Health care

Organizations:
Ministry of Health,
teaching hospitals,
research foundatons

Key People:
The Deputy Minister,
Hospital board members,
none known personally

Trends:
Rapid change
Need for efficient information management is critical.

Size: Market is huge and growing, both in the public and private sectors. Large and small organizations exist.

Best in Class: unknown

Possible Roles: Consulting assignments

Remuneration: unknown

Possible Contribution: Experience with large scale systems and complex organizations should be transferable.

Market Assessment #3

Sector: Not-for-Profit

Organizations: Foundations and associations for chronic health in children

Key People: unknown, but accessible through sister's contacts

Trends: Assume that business practises are increasingly needed.

Size: Numerous small organizations and a few large ones focused on my interests

Best in Class: Canadian Cystic Fibrosis Association

Possible Roles: Executor Director

Remuneration: Lower earnings would be expected and acceptable

Possible Contribution: Make an impact through using leadership principles. Use persuasive abilities to raise awareness and funds.

With her three markets identified, the SVP-IT set the targets described in her story and illustrated on the next page. Notice how different elements from her self-assessment provide the rationale for her diverse targets. The strategic targeting process gave her search a distinct focus and clear direction. When she explained her thoughts to others, her strategy made sense. As it turned out, several of her market assumptions were incorrect, but nevertheless, she landed successfully.

With her strategic targets in place, the SVP-IT set out to do her research and networking. She soon learned that the not-for-profit sector was more sophisticated than she thought in its use of business practices. Moreover, with no previous volunteer experience, she was not viewed as an acceptable candidate for an executive director's role. In the health care sector she discovered that innovative insurance companies were focusing on consumer-driven health plans. Her expertise, interests and values all helped her land a CIO role with a cutting-edge insurance company that provided consumers with information regarding their health care options.

Once you have set at least three strategic targets and done a thorough analysis of each one, you have completed the second phase illustrated in Appendix A. You are ready to move on to the next step, which is gathering your resources. Your targets will influence the content of your marketing resources. As you write your résumé and prepare your verbal pitch for interviewing and networking, keep a specific target in mind. You will return to these targets when you are fully prepared to move into action.

Wrap-Up

There has been much to consider during this time out for reflection. Congratulations for staying with the process. You're headed in the right direction if you're building on what's best from your past and unique about you today, then moving toward what's right for your future. Regardless of which employment opportunity you take next, the assessment and planning that you have just completed ought to help guide your decisions for years to come.

Now you need to acquire or refresh your marketing and search skills in order to move into action.

An SVP-IT's Strategic Targets
Where the Ability to Contribute Meets the Market Need

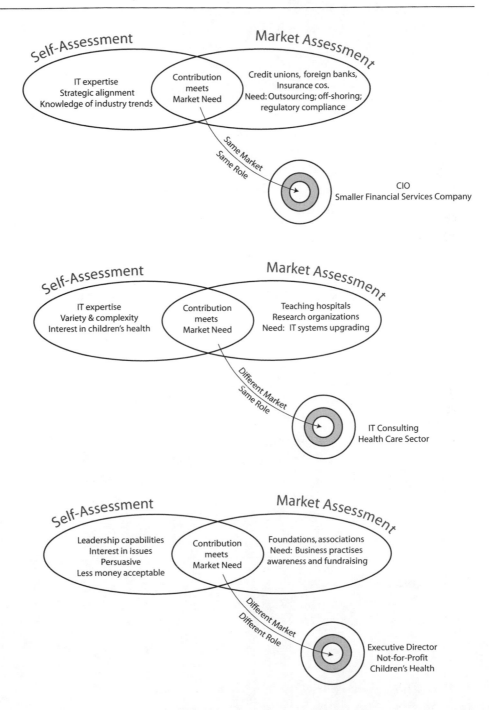

Gather Your Resources

The brilliance is in the details.

Objectives

This section helps you create the materials and develop the skills you'll need to conduct an active search. It offers detailed explanations and numerous samples to guide you. This is the most painstaking, detailed work you'll do. The chapters in Part Three cover:
- Why research is an essential part of your job search.
- Researching industries, trends and companies.
- Establishing a good record-keeping system.
- Writing a résumé that markets your skills and supports your intended direction.
- Developing additional materials, biographies and brochures.
- Creating five sound bites as a foundation for excellent interviews.
- Preparing for interviews.
- Understanding the various interview formats.
- Writing effective correspondence.

Rules to Follow

- Use a variety of research mediums, including print, the Internet and your network of contacts.
- Make sure that your résumé supports your intended career direction.
- Write an accomplishment-focused résumé, not a reiteration of your job description.
- Include quantified results in the accomplishment statements on your résumé wherever possible.
- Rehearse your answers to the most difficult interview questions.
- Tailor every piece of correspondence to the specific circumstances and the recipient.

Moves That Can Set You Back

- Rushing through the résumé-writing process in an effort to get into the market quickly.
- Going into interviews without thorough preparation.
- Being less than straightforward about your reasons for leaving your last job.

- Approaching companies before you have sufficient background information on them.
- Conducting superficial research without digging into the real issues.
- Neglecting to write thank-you letters.
- Spending an excessive amount of time developing marketing materials you don't really need.

Chapter 9

Research

Information is power.

Most people who embark on a career change begin with a limited amount of information about the options that might be available to them. Not knowing what's happening beyond the walls of your organization or the boundaries of your industry is a common deterrent to exploring new opportunities, and yet, access to a vast amount of information is readily available. Almost everything you need to know to find the work you want can be learned through purposeful research.

Tip: It may have been a long time since you've done the kind of in-depth research necessary for a job search. Most positions don't require it, and people in more senior roles usually delegate research tasks. Don't let lack of familiarity hold you back. You'll probably enjoy doing research once you get started.

The Value of Research for the Job Search

Research is a primary tool for implementing and advancing your search plan. You will narrow, broaden, revise or eliminate your targets by finding out as much as possible about the roles, organizations, industries and trends that interest you. Every piece of information you set out to find should be focused on pursuing your targets. When you think of research as one of the most important means to your goal, your job search activities will broaden significantly, going well beyond looking for ads and job postings that sound as if they might match your interests and skills.

A financial services executive set one target that involved finding work that would enable him to use his expertise in fraud prevention and risk management. His research focused on finding organizations with a record of increasing fraud losses and insurance claims. After identifying 40 organizations representing four industries, he found out who had responsibility for these areas. This generated a list of over 95 names for his networking initiatives. Through this research he expanded his search horizons and gathered reading material to help him form meaningful questions for discussion in networking meetings. He had no difficulty landing opportunities for contract work.

Your research will also improve your ability to compose pertinent and persuasive written materials. As you dig for information, you will become more familiar with the issues that are relevant to the people you will be contacting. You will also learn how different organizations and industries use and interpret various words and phrases. This will help you choose keywords for your résumé and use current industry jargon in your letters, making you sound knowledgeable and drawing the attention you want.

Research is also crucial to interview preparation. You need to learn everything you can about an organization before presenting yourself as a candidate for employment. Knowledge of the market, the industry and the people who are influential in the organization and the industry sector is important. You should read all the relevant publicly available information and talk with your advisers and networking contacts about the company before going to the interview.

Networking involves research in two important ways. First, research prepares you for networking calls and meetings, and second, research is the subject of networking. More is said about this in later chapters, but note that seeking information is the credible reason for contacting and meeting with people who can advance your search. Furthermore, information that you have obtained can often be of interest or assistance to the individuals you meet in the networking process.

Tip: By doing thorough research and sharing what you've discovered, you will be perceived as exceptionally knowledgeable and up-to-date. Prospective employers will want you working for them, not the competition.

Perhaps the greatest value of research is that it keeps you active in the market, learning more and meeting more people. While you are seeking to follow trends, understand industries, evaluate organizations and discover the names of decision-makers, you will come across new ideas that will expand your search and keep you thinking creatively. You will also meet people who can give you valuable insights and possibly open doors that you never knew existed.

Research Is a Four-Step Process

Like any other skill or ability, the value of research increases dramatically if it is executed well and used wisely. Give yourself credit for having done a good job once you've completed these four steps:

1. Collect the information:
- Be focused. Clearly define what you want to know, form your key questions and stay on topic.
- Be open to finding information where you don't expect it.
- Use a wide variety of resources.
- Consider people to be a primary research resource.
- Be creative in tracking down information. Think like a private investigator.

2. Organize it:

- At the outset, establish a meticulous filing and record-keeping system using electronic or hard-copy files.
- Create a system of cross-references for efficient retrieval of information.
- Record the date, page number and name of the publication on every clipping or print-out.
- Keep Internet bookmarks organized efficiently.

3. Assimilate it:

- An active thought process is the most important element in making research useful.
- Look for patterns and trends. Make connections and note contradictions. Let additional questions arise.
- As one idea leads to another, record off-topic ideas for future research.
- Form hypotheses. Draw conclusions.
- Make notes as your thoughts evolve.

4. Use it:

- Share your research with your board of advisers, support group and networking contacts.
- Become an information distributor, armed with reprints of articles, web addresses and tips on sources of information, including the names of knowledgeable people.
- Discuss what you've gleaned from your research with everyone possible, asking for their opinions and related ideas.
- Use research as an essential preparation tool for networking and interviewing.
- Look for opportunities to mention points from your research in networking meetings and interviews.
- Let research play a key role in evaluating employment opportunities.

Tip: A complete job search record-keeping system requires a calendar or diary, a database for contact information, correspondence files organized by name and cross-referenced to organizations, and separate files for information and articles on people, organizations, industries and trends. Detailed records allow efficient retrieval of information and prevent embarrassing duplications.

People Are the Best Research Resources

People are the best providers and interpreters of information. Most people enjoy being asked for their opinions, advice and help, especially when your questions are specific and thoughtful. You can ask the same questions of a large number of people, even when you are certain that you have uncovered every possible fact and opinion on a topic. People are flattered to have been asked, and you never know when your questions will elicit a new idea.

The variety of ideas and viewpoints that you gather from your networking contacts gives you an invaluable word-on-the-street perspective that no amount of formal research can match. You usually obtain the truly interesting and useful information only from individuals who are willing to speak candidly and off-the-record. If you want to know what it's really like to work at Your Target Co., ask around; don't rely exclusively on press releases or what the analysts and business reporters say. There could be some critical points of view that you will only discover by talking to other people.

Arranging an opportunity to job shadow is an excellent way to get first-hand information, especially if you are considering a significant change of occupation. Of course, the nature of the work, type of organization and seniority of the role must be conducive to an observer's presence.

A commercial banker was considering changing careers after over 26 years working for the same organization. He was interested in teaching business courses, and had done his research regarding the additional education that he would need at both the high school and community college level. To help him with his decision, he asked a neighbour who taught at the local high school if he would consider allowing him to tag along for a week. The arrangements were made and the commercial banker got a very realistic job preview. He decided to teach part-time at a community college as an interim step.

Tip: Your research questions give you reasons to contact the people in your network. A quick phone call or email with a specific question keeps you in touch and brings your networking contacts up-to-date with your search. For example, writing: "I'm trying to find out which companies are planning to build bitumen-upgrading facilities in Alberta," gives your contacts an opportunity to help you. It also lets them know what topic you're exploring. It's much better than simply saying, "I'm still looking."

How to Focus Your Research

The best way to focus your research is by forming targeted questions. Throughout the job search, there are four topics that will require your research skills: trends, industries, organizations and people. Use the following questions as guides.

Questions for Researching a Trend
- What is meant by the terms commonly used to describe the trend (e.g., "risk management")?
- What industries are being affected by the trend? How?
- Is there a social, cultural, political, demographic, geographic, technological or ethical factor involved?
- What books, articles, studies or government inquiries have been published?
- Is legislative change involved?
- Who stands to gain from this trend and who stands to lose? In what ways?
- What is the range of opinion on this trend? Who is saying what?
- What occupations are becoming obsolete and what new opportunities are opening up as a result of the trend?
- What sort of education or training is becoming valuable in response to this trend?
- How do you think it will affect your career change?

Questions for Researching an Industry

- What factors have affected the development of the industry?
- What are some of the current trends?
- Are there any factors limiting growth?
- Has any recent legislation affected the industry? Is there any pending?
- What environmental factors are affecting the industry?
- What new products or services are influencing the way business is being done?
- How has the use of technology impacted on the industry?
- Are there any specific lobbies or consumer groups that are influencing the industry?
- Are there any global factors that may affect the health of the industry?
- Who are the respected industry analysts? What are they saying?
- What skills are in demand? What skills or occupations are in decline?
- What organizations lead the industry?
- Who are the industry gurus?

Tip: Even if you are at the executive level, pursuing your research as if you were a student entering the field will yield keywords, names of organizations, industry associations and current information that will advance and expand your search.

Questions for Researching an Organization

- Is it owned publicly or privately? What can you find out about the owners?
- Has there been a recent change of ownership or is a change pending or predicted?
- How is it structured? Does it have subsidiaries, divisions, branches, decentralized offices, etc.?
- How many employees does it have? In what locations?
- Who are the principals? Who is on the board of directors?
- What is the history of the organization? Has it grown or contracted by acquisition, divestiture or internal initiative?
- What is its financial situation?
- What are its products and services? (If they are available in the retail market, try them.)
- Who are the customers and why do they choose to do business with this organization?
- Who are the main competitors and what differentiates this organization from them?
- How does it market its products or services?
- Have there been any recent press releases or articles about the company?
- What new ventures is the company planning?
- How do people describe the culture of the organization?
- What is its reputation for how it treats employees, customers and suppliers?
- What charities does the organization support?
- What attracts you to this organization? Would you be interested in joining it?
- What would be the negatives about working there?

Information to Gather about People

- Contact information, including proper spelling of the name, current title, address, phone number, etc.
- Do some research on their organization and industry.
- What is their background, including previous jobs, achievements and education?
- Have they been published? What press coverage have they had?
- What are their interests, concerns, personal goals?
- Who referred you to them? Why were you referred?
- What information do you expect them to have?

In this age of information, there is an enormous variety and quantity of research resources available. A few good starting points are listed in the section that follows. For resources that are not accessible on the Internet, go to a reference or business library and ask the librarian for help. Most of them will be pleased to direct you to the appropriate resources. As you gather information in your area of interest many more doors will open, and you will find excellent resources—far more than can be listed here.

Tip: If you are a novice at doing research on the Internet, these two web sites provide excellent introductions: Bare Bones at www.sc.edu/beaufort/library/pages/bones.shtml and WebTeacher at www.webteacher.org. The latter gives clear explanations of search engines and search techniques.

Research Resources

Business Information and Industry Profiles

- www.hoovers.com — This site is a valuable first stop for any research involving a business in Canada, the U.S. or around the world. Owned by Dun & Bradstreet, it provides a substantial amount of free information. The least expensive subscription package is worth considering if you do not have access to a business or reference library and therefore have limited access to other databases.
- www.strategis.ic.gc.ca — Industry Canada's business information web site. It provides current information on specific industry sectors, export opportunities, company capabilities, international intelligence and business contacts, new technologies and processes, management experts, market services, government economic research and statistics, micro-economics and more. It's a researcher's gold mine.

General Business / Trade Directories

- Canadian Key Business Directory—This classic resource is not published on the Internet and is expensive in print or on CD. You will find the hard copy at most libraries. The web site www.hoovers.com provides much of the same information.

Specific Sector Directories

- www.fin.gc.ca/links/bankse.html is an example of a sector directory. Use a search engine to find a directory for a specific sector on the Internet, or ask the librarian at a reference or business library. Sector directories are invaluable for networking leads.

Associations Directories

- www.canadiancareers.com/sector.html has an extensive list of links to associations in Canada.

Organizations' Web Sites

Information about an organization's history, structure, principals, financial data, products and services can often be found on its web site. This information has been written by the organization and is intended to promote it. Be sure to check the "Investors' Relations" section of the site to discover what is written to comply with public disclosure requirements. To locate web addresses use directories or search engines.

Annual Reports

- TSX Group (www.tsx.com)
- U.S. Securities & Exchange Commission (www.sec.gov)

News Wire Services

- Canada NewsWire Ltd. (www.newswire.ca)
- Reuters Online (www.reuters.com and www.reuters.ca)

Tip: Full-text newspaper and magazine information databases with efficient search capabilities can often be accessed through your public library at no cost to you. CBCA (Canadian Business and Current Affairs) is the best. It cross-references newspapers and business publications from across Canada. You may search by company name, a person's name or by subject or keyword. Factiva is its U.S. equivalent.

Chapter 10

Write an Effective Résumé

*The quality of the result is proportionate
to the quality of the effort.*

Having a well-thought-out and carefully prepared résumé is essential for responding to interesting opportunities. A good résumé presents your experience and qualifications clearly and concisely to a potential employer, and helps to persuade them that you have unique value. The amount of planning, energy and strategic thinking you invest in developing your résumé is important to your ultimate success.

Before you begin your résumé, list and describe the skills you would like to use in your next employment opportunity, the kinds of roles you would find interesting and where you believe your talents could be well used. This might seem overwhelming if you skipped to this chapter without working on your career review or identifying your strategic advantage. Investing some time in those topics now would be wise if you have not already done so. However, if you know your key skills and where you're headed, carry on with writing your résumé.

Rule number one is to write it yourself! There are any number of services that will take this task off your hands, but crafting your résumé enables you to become totally comfortable with the points you want to discuss in your interviews and the ways in which you want to express them. Find someone to offer suggestions and reliable feedback, but make the content your own. You know yourself best and you will do the best job of reflecting and emphasizing the most important aspects of your background, achievements and employment interests.

Tip: One of the primary benefits of having a résumé is what you learn in the process of writing it. Spending time reviewing your career and developing your accomplishment statements are the best ways to put your experience at the top of your mind so that you can readily talk about your achievements, skills and strengths in an interview or networking situation.

There are many pitfalls in writing a résumé. Use the following guidelines to direct your approach to the process.

GUIDELINES FOR WRITING YOUR RÉSUMÉ

- Don't expect to be able to dash off your résumé in an hour or two. Putting together a good résumé takes time, often days. You want the quality of your résumé to be top-notch.
- If you have an old résumé, it is often a good idea to get a fresh start by beginning again. You can use your previous résumé as a reference.
- Create a résumé that truly reflects your expertise and strengths. The original version of your résumé may be sufficient to address a number of your targets (see Chapter 8) when accompanied by a well-written cover letter that focuses on specific market characteristics or position requirements.
- You may need to write different versions of your résumé, aimed at different targets. However, it is wise to minimize the number of résumés you have.
- More than roles and responsibilities, your résumé must talk about your accomplishments. Write about problems and issues you have addressed, actions you have taken and outcomes you have achieved.
- Quantify the results of your accomplishments wherever possible. A compelling case is created with data such as "achieved savings of $2 million annually" or "decreased staff turnover from 20% to 12%."
- Every statement that you make on your résumé must be factual and true. Your résumé forms part of the basis for a legal agreement and a good-faith relationship with your employer. If false representations are made, the consequences could be very embarrassing and costly to your career.
- Employers might be looking through hundreds of résumés for each of their advertised or posted positions. Yours must spark interest quickly. Your key skills, experience and style must come through in a clear and concise way.
- Limit the length of your résumé to two pages, three at the most. In a few employment sectors such as IT, science, medicine or university teaching, longer and more detailed résumés are expected. If you have written articles, had works published, completed significant transactions or made professional presentations, list these on a separate page.
- Appearance is important. Pay attention to the format and layout along with spelling and grammar. Use high-quality paper and a laser-quality printer.
- Don't be fooled into thinking that good appearance will make up for poor content.
- Proofread your résumé carefully and ask at least two other people to proofread it for you.
- Remember that your résumé is not your most important marketing tool—you are! Your résumé will help you get an interview and provide documentation to support what you say in the interview, but hiring decisions are based on personal interactions and the chemistry established between you and the people you meet.

As you begin to write, there are several formatting decisions that need to be made. The first involves the arrangement of your data, and the second, font and spacing. The best advice is to keep it simple.

Format the Résumé

Chronological Format

The chronological résumé is the accepted standard for organizing your information. This format describes your work experience in reverse chronological order, with the most recent job listed first. It emphasizes the names of employers, dates, job titles and primary responsibilities along with your key accomplishments. It displays your employment history sequentially and, where you have a record of increasing responsibilities and promotions with no major employment gaps, this is clearly an advantage.

Executive search and human resources professionals have a strong preference for chronological résumés. They are used to reading them, and they can find what they're looking for fairly quickly.

Functional/Chronological Format

An alternative to the chronological format is a combination functional/chronological résumé, which is organized according to the key areas of your work experience (also called "functional activities"). The chronological section of this combination format either precedes or follows the functional section and outlines the traditional information, including names of employers, dates, titles and additional information. It should be no more than one page. Résumé Sample #3 at the end of this chapter illustrates this format.

The functional/chronological résumé enables you to bring out the underlying themes running through your various positions and experiences, which can be particularly advantageous when some of your key accomplishments occurred several years in the past. By using this format you can also establish the transferability of your skills and accomplishments, which can be a real asset when you're planning to change career paths. Due to the nonlinear format of the functional/chronological résumé, gaps in your experience may not be as apparent. This is one reason this approach is less favoured by human resources professionals.

Tip: An exclusively functional format is not recommended. This type may include the names of employers but gives no dates. It merely outlines experience by functional area. A functional résumé that contains no chronological data gives the impression that you have something to hide.

Other details to consider include font, spacing and layout. Simplicity in these areas is more conducive to scanning and emailing. An 11- or 12-point type using either the Times New Roman or Arial font is recommended. Margins should be no less than 3/4 of an inch at the left and right, and no less than 1 inch at the top and bottom. The choice of layout is somewhat restricted by the need to put a lot of information in a small space. The creative use of columns and bullet points can make information stand out but reduces the amount of space you have for content. Leave as much white space as possible and take care to be consistent. This includes text fonts, heading fonts, underlining, bolding, spacing between lines, paragraphs and sections. Use white or off-white paper.

The samples in this chapter illustrate various formatting options.

An Outline of the Résumé

The Heading

Use one of the samples as a template for formatting the heading, and begin with your name, address and contact information. Use the familiar form of your name, and drop the middle initial unless you use it regularly. Include relevant degrees or professional designations after your name, but don't overdo it. You want to be perceived as qualified and competent, not a braggart.

Make sure that your email is current and confidential. If it is likely to be intercepted by your administrative assistant at work or your teenager at home, you might decide to get another email address and use it exclusively for your job search.

The profile statement follows the heading. However, since it summarizes the information contained in the résumé, it's best to write it last. Directions for writing the profile statement are given later in this chapter.

Career History and Accomplishments

The body of your résumé contains a review of your employment history. The primary objective of this section is to convey substantive evidence of your abilities and talents. A second objective is to demonstrate your level of expertise and achievement in the various functional areas that are relevant to your profession.

Tip: Information that dates back more than about 10–12 years won't capture much attention. If you have significant accomplishments that you want to highlight from earlier years, consider using the combination functional/chronological format.

There are many options for the title of this section. They include professional experience, business background, career highlights, background and achievements, selected accomplishments, etc. The choice is yours. Create an outline by listing all past employers, position titles and dates in reverse chronological order. Use copies of previous job descriptions and performance appraisals for reference.

Return to your career review and consider the accomplishments that you identified there. Sit back and reflect on each period of your career and identify what gave you the greatest sense of pride. Be sure to think about the challenging times when you learned a lot or were stretched to do more than you thought you could. Try to come up with at least 12 to 15 career accomplishments or highlights, and five that are recent.

In the body of the résumé, include these career highlights in the form of accomplishment statements, which are concise descriptions of a specific situation or challenge. They describe your actions and results, and are far more interesting to read than simple descriptions of duties and responsibilities. Accomplishment statements make your skills and interests come alive for the reader by creating a verbal picture of you doing the work that you are good at doing.

It's tempting to transfer phrases from a job description to your résumé, but try to resist doing this. The contrast between accomplishment statements and standard job description jargon is striking. For example:

- Responsible for business development and customer service in the Lower Mainland.
  becomes:
- Recognized the need for a more focused approach to attracting new business through a revised customer referral program. Worked with a team of five retail managers and developed the *Convenience Plus Program* to promote a full range of products and services. Achieved a 15% increase in sales in the Lower Mainland territory within the first six months.

This second version tells the reader much more about what you can do than the first statement.

To write accomplishment statements use the Situation—Action—Result formula (see Chapter 4):

- Describe the **Situation** or context of the work including the obstacles, problems or challenges you faced.
- Detail the **Actions** you took or directed others to take.
- Highlight and quantify the **Results** of your actions.

Begin each accomplishment statement with an appropriate verb (consult the Inventory of Verbs on page 116 to generate ideas). Tell your story in a few short, declarative sentences. Use the past tense and a newspaper reporting style of writing. Do not use the word "I." Add depth and detail to each accomplishment statement by quantifying wherever possible. Note size, volumes, percentages, dollar values and timelines. This allows your reader to gain an understanding of the level of responsibility you've achieved. When unsure of an exact number, use qualifying words such as:

approaching	less than
approximately	over
in excess of	ranging from ___ to ___

You do not need to claim all the glory in your accomplishment statements. Where appropriate, use phrases such as:

assisted with	participated in
contributed to	shared in the success of
in support of	worked with ___ to

Prospective employers want to know that you can produce results. The implication is that if you have done it once, you can do it again. Describe and quantify the results of your efforts by including statements such as:

achieved sales targets
avoided a potential problem
avoided potential losses
boosted staff morale
contributed to team effectiveness
created client awareness
created positive public relations
decreased staff costs
delivered on time
delivered under budget
developed new markets
eliminated capital costs
formed a strategic alliance
generated new business
generated savings of $__
identified new market opportunities
improved a reporting process
improved accuracy
improved client relations
improved customer service
improved product knowledge
improved product performance
improved profit margins by __%
improved recovery rate
improved retention
improved service delivery

increased customer satisfaction
increased/improved efficiency
increased market share
increased sales by __%
increased shareholder value
leveraged existing resources
met an urgent/demanding deadline
met company goals
organized better procedures
preserved a competitive edge
provided a tax advantage
provided more accurate information
reduced costs
reduced customer complaints
reduced downtime
reduced errors
reduced inventories
reduced processing time
reduced turnaround time
reduced turnover
resolved problems
secured government support
streamlined administration
streamlined operations
turned around a difficult situation
won an award for

Once you have written your accomplishment statements, decide which ones best support your intended career direction. Within the relevant position, put them first. Include accomplishment statements to cover every functional area in which you were involved and the full range of responsibilities you carried. Review your analysis of your strategic advantage (Chapter 5) and be sure that your accomplishment statements exemplify it.

There is no other element of a person's résumé that will have as high an impact on job search success as the *identification of key accomplishments*. It is crucial for you to put a great deal of thought and effort into this component of your résumé.

Tip: Do not overcrowd your résumé. Cramming too much on two pages, or expanding the résumé to four or five pages, will not necessarily impress the reader. Dense and lengthy résumés will not be read in detail.

An Inventory of Verbs

Achieving results
accelerated
accomplished
achieved
acquired
advanced
authorized
boosted
built
captured
delivered
drove
established
exceeded
expanded
improved
increased
introduced
launched
met
outperformed
overcame
pioneered
procured
produced
reduced
re-engineered
repositioned
resolved
restored
restructured
safeguarded
secured
solidified
solved
streamlined
sustained
systematized
surpassed
transformed
unified
united
won

Managing
analyzed
assigned
attained
capitalized
chaired
coached
consolidated
contracted
coordinated
delegated
developed
directed
enlisted
evaluated
executed
generated
guided
improved
inspired
led
managed
mentored
mobilized
motivated
normalized
officiated
orchestrated
organized
oriented
outsourced
oversaw
planned
prioritized
produced
recommended
recruited
rejuvenated
reviewed
scheduled
selected
set goals
solved
strengthened
supervised
trained

Selling
booked
campaigned
closed
cold-called
convinced
cross-sold
developed
explained
gained
generated
increased
influenced
launched
marketed
merchandized
met targets
negotiated
persuaded
proposed
positioned
sold
targeted
up-sold

Creating
changed
created
customized
designed
developed
directed
energized
envisioned
established
fashioned
founded
generated
illustrated
initiated
instituted
integrated
introduced
invented
originated
personalized
rebuilt
redesigned
reorganized
replaced
revamped
revitalized
shaped
structured

Communicating
addressed
advised
advocated
arbitrated
authored
briefed
clarified
collaborated
communicated
confirmed
corresponded
critiqued
crystalized

defused
developed
directed
drafted
edited
educated
formulated
influenced
informed
interpreted
interviewed
investigated
judged
lectured
listened
mediated
moderated
negotiated
oriented
persuaded
presented
promoted
proved
publicized
qualified
questioned
realized
recognized
recommended
reconciled
reinforced
related
relayed
represented
responded
resolved
spoke
transcribed
translated

verbalized
wrote

Performing tasks
adapted
administered
allocated
analyzed
applied
appraised
arranged
audited
balanced
budgeted
calculated
catalogued
charted
classified
collected
compiled
computed
developed
dispatched
documented
executed
finalized
forecast
generated
implemented
inspected
maintained
manufactured
modified
monitored
operated
organized
perfected
performed
planned

prepared
processed
produced
programmed
projected
reconciled
recorded
regulated
retrieved
reviewed
scheduled
screened
served
specified
structured
validated
verified
worked with

Teaching
adapted
advised
clarified
coached
communicated
developed
educated
enabled
encouraged
evaluated
explained
facilitated
guided
informed
instructed
led
stimulated
taught
trained

Serving customers
followed up
handled
listened
merchandized
met
processed
promoted
resolved
responded
satisfied
serviced

Researching
collected
investigated
located
mapped out
master-minded
networked
observed
piloted
pinpointed
predicted
rated
recorded
retrieved
reviewed
simplified
summarized
surveyed
systematized
tabulated
tested
translated
understood
verified

Tip: Be ruthless in your editing. Clear, concise copy is not easy to write. Eliminate repetitious words and phrases and look for ideas that can be combined.

Additional Information

At the end of your résumé, list other relevant information. This includes the following categories:

Education:

List the degrees or diplomas you hold and the name of each institution. Dates are optional; their inclusion is a matter of choice, depending upon your willingness to disclose your age. If you have not yet completed a course, use the term "in progress" or "currently enrolled."

Languages:

Use "fluent in," "conversational" or "written and spoken" to describe your level of expertise in other languages.

Professional Development:

Indicate the name of the course provider, title of the course and date completed. Include any in-house courses provided by former employers that are relevant to your future direction. Don't go overboard and list every training session you have ever attended.

Professional Affiliations/Memberships:

Use the full name of the organization to which you belong; then note its abbreviated form if appropriate. Indicate any offices you have held. If you have taken a key role in events or conventions hosted by your organization, note them as well.

Community Involvement:

Include any volunteer work or fund-raising activities in which you have participated in the last few years. Make special note of positions you have held.

Computer Skills:

List only the programs and languages that are integral to your professional work. Unless there is a specific reason for doing so, you need not list standard software packages like Word or Excel.

Awards:

Awards show that you have been recognized for excellence. They are an important addition to your résumé. Include both professional and volunteer awards, and the reasons they were given.

Publications:

Publications include any articles, columns or books you have authored or co-authored, or to which you have contributed.

Interests:

Including interests is optional, especially at more senior levels. If you include them, list hobbies, physical activities, outdoor activities, intellectual pursuits, unique interests and pastimes. These will identify you as a well-rounded person who manages stress and leads a balanced, active life. Interviewers may also refer to your interests at the beginning of your meeting as a way of breaking the ice and putting you both at ease.

Profile Statement

The last piece of your résumé to be created, and perhaps the most important, is the profile statement. As an advertising and positioning statement, your profile should immediately grab the reader's attention by summarizing the skill sets and themes found in the body of your résumé. Ideally, it should define what differentiates you and state your strategic advantage. It is as unique as your thumbprint and should be an accurate overview of your abilities, experience and personal style. Give it some marketing sizzle to make it compelling.

The terms "profile statement" and "objective statement" are sometimes used synonymously. However, an objective statement usually describes the job title or role being sought. In years past it was common practice to have an objective statement at the beginning of the résumé. For most people, an objective statement would be either so vague as to be meaningless or so specific that it would limit the range of possible employment options.

Tip: In addition to profiles, career or job objectives are customary for IT and technical positions. A statement describing your objective can also be helpful if you are targeting a major career change.

Since your profile statement is a summary, writing it will likely be more challenging than writing your accomplishment statements. Take your time and get it right. Employers tend to read this section first, and a well-written profile statement can make a strong impression. Despite the time and effort required, many people find that completing this section of the résumé crystallizes their thinking, raises their confidence and convinces them of their marketability.

Tip: Your profile statement makes claims about you and what you can contribute to an organization. Your accomplishment statements provide the proof.

Your profile statement lets the reader know the professional category in which you place yourself. Are you a human resources professional or a labour relations specialist? Are you a project manager or a business developer? This choice is very important because it either limits or expands the number of different roles for which you might be considered.

The profile statement should also give the reader a clear picture of:

- the industries in which you have experience
- how long you have been working (optional)
- the level of seniority you have attained
- your key strengths or skills
- some features of your interpersonal style

Here's an example:

A senior manager with expertise in applying leading-edge technologies to common business problems. Experienced in leading cross-functional project teams with the mandate to increase operational efficiency and /or reduce costs in a variety of areas, including internal audit, quality assurance and operations. Excellent credentials and 25 years' experience in financial services and manufacturing organizations. Able to motivate diverse specialists to contribute to a team effort in a collaborative and proactive working environment.

Use the following template to create a first draft of your profile.

A (adjective, e.g., results-oriented, focused) **title or professional category** (descriptive title for your professional area, e.g., lawyer, marketing manager, financial services executive, senior manager) with over (total number) **years' experience in** (type of work, e.g., financial analysis, recruiting or managing operations) **within the** (be specific, e.g., financial services) **industry. Key strengths** include (name three, e.g., cost reduction, developing new business and building teams). **Committed to** (comment on management, interpersonal or leadership style).

If your title or professional category seems misleading or inadequate for your purpose, substitute a more generic self-descriptor such as:

business leader	innovator	project manager
change agent	manager	risk-taker
communicator	motivator	self-starter
contributor	negotiator	specialist
executive	organizer	strategist
expert	planner	team builder
generalist	problem-solver	team leader
implementer	professional	troubleshooter

Additional ways to lead into strengths include:

able to	demonstrates	readily undertakes
adept in	emphasizes	skilled in
brings a ____ approach to	excellent knowledge of	solid grasp of
can be counted on to	excels in	takes pride in
capable of	experienced in	thrives on
combines (this) with (that)	expertise in	track record of
committed to	focused on	understands the value of
creates value by	proven ability to	willing to

You must be comfortable with every word and phrase in your profile statement. Ensure that your accomplishment statements substantiate it, and be prepared with an experiential story to illustrate every point.

Tip: Test your profile statement by sharing it verbally with someone who knows you and your industry. It should be a clear and appropriate description of you.

Additional Suggestions for Your Résumé

Keywords

Keywords are a crucial component of your résumé, regardless of its format. Both employers and search firms keep résumés on file in databases and retrieve them electronically using keywords. If you have developed a convincing, accomplishment-focused résumé, all the keywords pertinent to you and your targets should already be included. Nevertheless, it's a good idea to double-check.

GUIDELINES FOR CAPTURING KEYWORDS

- Include words that are specific to your industry or profession. Use functional descriptors and industry jargon, e.g., risk management, arbitration, procurement, market cap, ERP and CRM.
- Use the language of managerial and leadership excellence. If your organization has a list of competencies or stated leadership principles, borrow from it. Go back to Chapter 5 and ensure that the words you used to describe your style, skills and knowledge appear in your résumé.
- List your academic and professional credentials with your name at the top of your résumé.
- If you are bilingual or multi-lingual, name the specific languages.
- Scour job advertisements for keywords as you prepare your application. Revise your résumé to include any missing words that apply to you and repeat some of them in your cover letter.

Although computer searches will pick up keywords anywhere in a document, it's wise to position the most important ones front and centre. See Résumé Sample #4 for an example.

Common Résumé Problems

Many challenging questions come up as people write their résumés. Some of them involve titles that misrepresent responsibilities, work done under contract rather than as an employee, periods of unemployment, courses taken without completion of a degree and so on. Many of these issues are addressed in the sample résumés at the end of this chapter. Read the key points that precede each sample to see if your circumstances are reflected there. The most important principle to remember is that your résumé must represent the facts as clearly as possible.

Visual Appearance

Along with its content, your résumé's visual appearance will give readers an impression of you. In the next chapter, you will be invited to consider developing a consistent look for all of your written materials. Before making decisions regarding the font and layout of your résumé, read ahead and give some thought to the other marketing materials you might develop. Consider using your résumé as the first in a series of documents that will reflect your style and image. The samples on the following pages offer some options.

Electronic Dispatch

When you apply for advertised positions, you will forward your résumé to prospective employers online or by email more often than not. Internet job boards usually specify exactly how they want to receive your information. You must follow their instructions precisely. Failure to do so will cause your résumé to be discarded before it is ever seen by a human being.

> **Tip:** When sending your information by email, put your résumé and cover letter together into one document to ensure that the recipient sees both. Attach the document to a very brief covering email message with a meaningful subject line.

If you are an Internet neophyte, or have used the Internet only for email messaging, don't panic. There are many excellent resources that explain everything you need to know, including exactly how to use your computer technology. Thankfully, they are written for the layperson.

> **Tip:** For detailed, step-by-step instructions on formatting and dispatching your résumé electronically, see *The Riley Guide* (www.rileyguide.com), and go to the section entitled "Preparing Your Résumé for Emailing or Posting It on the Internet." The book *e-Résumés,* by Susan Britton Whitcomb and Pat Kendall (McGraw Hill), is also an excellent, comprehensive resource.

Your Next Move

Once you're satisfied with your résumé, ask people in your support network or your references to review it and offer feedback. Use good judgment when deciding whether to take or dismiss suggestions. Don't let résumé revisions become the focus of your efforts.

A training and development specialist made the mistake of asking 15 people to review his résumé. While spending weeks trying to incorporate all the feedback, he was so engrossed that he stopped checking job postings. He almost missed an excellent opportunity while he was revising his résumé.

That's it. With a final edit and careful proofreading of your résumé, you're ready to move on. If you've followed the steps, you should have an outstanding marketing document that describes in concise and compelling terms where you've been and where you want to go.

One of the real advantages of working through the résumé process is the tremendous psychological boost it gives as you begin to see, often for the first time, how much you have achieved and how marketable you are. Use this positive energy and enthusiasm to prepare some additional marketing materials that will help you stand out from the crowd. Turn to the next chapter and find out how to go beyond the résumé once you've read the sample résumés that follow.

Sample Résumés

Key Points to Note as You Read Sample Résumé #1

President, CEO and Director
Food Service Industry, Franchising

- The profile is concise and powerful. The reader is immediately aware of the writer's level of leadership, area of expertise and scope of experience.
- This is a chronological résumé with an effective variation on the standard format. The selected achievements are arranged in an order that exactly matches the chronological data. Brand names are mentioned in all but one point. Even though the dates of the achievements are not specifically indicated, it is immediately obvious to the reader which achievement relates to each position.
- At the CEO level, results tell the story. A one-page résumé is sufficient to relate the necessary information.
- The Situation—Action—Result formula is implicit in each achievement statement. The use of percentages implies the "before" picture.
- The style and formatting of this résumé is uncluttered. The use of bold type makes the impressive results stand out.
- Information on education and interests is omitted. With a track record such as this, added information is unnecessary.

Tip: One-page résumés are increasingly popular, especially among more senior executives. Brevity fits current communication styles and fewer words often make greater impact.

Sample Résumé #1

YOUR NAME

Address   Bus.tel.:
City, Province   Cell:
Postal Code   Email:

Leader, Persuader, Entrepreneur
A pioneer of franchising in Canada

Reputation for:
Successful multi-store business acquisition and restructuring
Excellent knowledge of Canadian, U.S. and international fast food industry

FAST CHINESE FOOD, LTD.	2001–2007
President, Chief Executive Officer and Director	
OFFICE SERVICES UNLIMITED, INC.	1999–2001
President, Chief Executive Officer and Director	
SUB SENSATIONS—MEGA FOOD SERVICES, INC.	1995–1999
President, Chief Executive Officer and Director	
BIG BURGER CORPORATION, LTD.	1992–1995
Executive Vice President, Chief Operating Officer and Director	
MAJOR MULTINATIONAL, INC.	1989–1992
Vice President and General Manager, Franchising Division	
STURDY TAIL PIPES, INC.	1978–1989
Vice President, General Manager and Director	

SELECTED ACHIEVEMENTS

Repositioned, energized and expanded FAST CHINESE FOOD restaurant chain in Canada (590 stores, $150 million in sales, 5000 employees)—**increased sales 72% and doubled the net profit**

Developed and expanded an international chain of service centres for small business owners through franchising—**realized increase in sales of 60% and net profit of 400%**

Expanded Sub Sensations restaurant chain in Canada (65 to 110 units) and in the United States (50 to 142 units). Opened 6 units in the UK—**increased sales 517% in the United States and 70% in Canada over four years**

Led the merger of four fast food outlet companies with distinct corporate cultures into Sub Sensations—international chain with $75 million in sales and 185 units

Launched Big Burger franchises in Taiwan, South Korea, Hong Kong, Philippines, Singapore, Malaysia, Thailand and Australia and opened units in the United Kingdom

Pioneered Sturdy Tail Pipes in Canada at 20 years of age. Led development from one storefront operation to 910 nationally with $48 million in sales by 1989

DIRECTORSHIPS

Relevant Industry Association	Canadian Franchise Association
Refrigerated Hauling, Inc.	Children's Charity
Fancy Fries Corporation, London, England	Jones International Limited, Hong Kong

Key Points to Note as You Read Sample Résumé #2

Executive Vice President and COO
Hospitality Sector, Travel and Tourism Industry

- The profile lets the reader know in a few words the level of seniority, breadth of experience and leadership qualities of the writer. The marks of an extensive and distinguished career are unmistakable. The claims made in the profile are substantiated by achievements in the body of the résumé.
- This individual identified more closely with the moniker "international hotelier" than with alternatives such as "COO" or "a seasoned executive from the hospitality industry." This concise descriptor creates an image befitting the individual.
- A role description is given immediately below the title, "Executive Vice President and Chief Operating Officer." It is more of a high-level strategy statement, which is very effective for understanding the organization and the seniority of the role.
- This is a chronological résumé.
- Achievements are at the strategic level. Accountability for results is a consistent theme and is often expressed in percentage increases, demonstrating a focus on the bottom line.
- The third bullet point confirms the extent of this individual's team-building activities.
- Because Eastview Management Ltd. would not be widely recognized, a one-line description of the company's business is included. The role description gives the well-known names of the hotels.
- Age can be a factor. Although it is clear that this individual joined Eastview Management Ltd. in 1978, specific dates are not mentioned for roles prior to 1987. The writer has not disclosed his age, but rather given the reader evidence of long-standing international experience.
- Roles prior to 1987 have been summarized by title and location on the last page of the résumé. This indicates that the individual's early experience was progressive in nature and laid a foundation for the senior roles that followed.

Sample Résumé #2

Your Name, C.H.A.

Address • City, Province • Postal Code • Tel: • Email:

Profile

An international hotelier with extensive experience in operations and strategic development at the executive level of two of the largest, global, multi-brand hotel chains. Achieved excellent results in portfolio growth, successfully developed strong brand relationships, substantially improved financial performance and selected and built outstanding management teams. An industry-wide reputation for integrity in all dealings with investment groups, developers, owners, franchise companies and joint venture partners. Mentor to many successful hospitality professionals.

Professional Experience

International Hospitality Inc.   2000–2007

EXECUTIVE VICE PRESIDENT & CHIEF OPERATING OFFICER

Directed the development and growth of the company's portfolio of full-service hotels under a variety of brands. $300-million revenue, 8,000 rooms, 3,500 staff.

- Negotiated conditions of the franchise agreement and management contract for the company's first Luxury Hotel in Canada. Produced higher margin incremental income with no equity investment by the company and laid the foundation for future development of Luxury brands in Canada.
- Established and nurtured a long-standing relationship with Distinguished Hotels & Resorts (Travel Suites, Royal Hotel and Squire Lodge) to secure the most attractive franchise terms and conditions.
- Raised the calibre of management at all levels throughout the organization. Selected and led a corporate executive team which included Senior Vice President, Operations; seven Regional Vice Presidents; Vice President, Sales & Marketing; Vice President, Food & Beverage and Directors of Revenue Management, Human Resources and Property Management. Recruited the best-in-class hotel managers throughout the portfolio.
- Developed a comprehensive five-year capital plan for all hotels to include pay-back analysis on all major capital investments, achieving aggressive corporate ROI targets.
- Directed sales and marketing activities of a multi-brand portfolio to achieve a 10% premium in market share over the competitive set.
- Established Regional Operations Vice Presidential role to more effectively support and coach hotel managers in every region of the company's operations.
- Initiated audits to benchmark every hotel's Food & Beverage operation and identify opportunities for increasing revenues and profitability.

Eastview Management Ltd.   1978–2000

North America's largest independently owned, multi-brand hotel management company.

SENIOR VICE PRESIDENT & CHIEF OPERATING OFFICER   *1987–2000*

Directed the development of the company's portfolio of 56 hotels under a wide variety of brands in Canada, the U.S. and Europe, including Caribbean Inns, Vacation Hotels, Guest Plaza, Les Suites du Roi and Independents and Resort Hotel Properties.

- Directed an executive team, which included four Regional Vice Presidents, three Regional Sales Coordinators, two National Directors of Sales & Marketing, two Directors of Design Services, a Director of Purchasing and two Food and Beverage Coordinators.

Your Name, CHA   **Page 2**

- Developed new contracts for the company, negotiated terms and conditions of all hotel management contracts and nurtured ongoing relationships with all owners, securing 27 new hotels contracts in a 10-year period.
- Developed relationships within the financial and real estate communities and acted as liaison for international hotel chains, potential joint venture partners, hotel owners and investment groups, creating an extensive network of investors for future growth opportunities.
- Formulated, developed and executed the operational decentralization of the company from a central hierarchy to four self-sufficient regions.
- Introduced effective ongoing strategic planning to cover all aspects of the company's growth including a national purchasing program, an awards recognition program and the introduction of executive floors in all full-service hotels.
- Introduced Food and Beverage troubleshooters to develop new concepts and turn around low-margin operations.
- Developed Regional Sales Coordinators' roles to maximize sales potential on a regional basis.

Additional Senior Roles Included:

VICE PRESIDENT, WESTERN/PACIFIC REGION, EASTVIEW MANAGEMENT LTD.
GENERAL MANAGER, RELAXATION INNS CENTRAL REGION
GENERAL MANAGER, PARADISE HOTEL, HONG KONG
GENERAL MANAGER, REVITA HOUSE, MADRID
SENIOR RESTAURANT MANAGER, PREMIER RESORT CORPORATION OF CALIFORNIA
RESTAURANT MANAGER, STONE MANOR, LONDON

Business/Community Affiliations

Director of a Number of Committees and Organizations Including:
Tourism Industry Association of North America.
Committee Member of International Association Luxury Hotels.
King Suites Promotion Committee.
California Hotel Association.
Eastern Seaboard Hotel Association.
Tourism Association of England.
Hotel Association of Canada.

Education

Catering Training College, Zurich, Switzerland.
Management Development Program, Paris, France.
C.H.A. (Certified Hotel Administrator), Educational Institute, AH & MA.
Luxury Hotel University Management Training Programs.

Interests

Skiing, Cycling, Cooking, Gardening, Live Theatre, Tennis, Travel.

Key Points to Note as You Read Sample Résumé #3

Vice President
Retail and Franchise Store Operations

- To illustrate capability in a breadth of functional areas, this individual chose the combination chronological/functional format.
- Notice the short description of the two companies. If your organization is not well known, or you want to emphasize the size and nature of the business, this is a good way to do it. Using bold type for the description keeps it as part of the heading.
- The description of your mandate or role provides a context for the reader. Results stand out against the backdrop of the mandate. In this example, the seniority of the role is explained simply by the statement, "Reported to the Chairman."
- If you are including one, the mandate or role description should be placed directly under your position title.
- Using bold type for the headings of the functions within each role allows the reader to scan for information and grasp the key components of each position quickly.
- This résumé is packed with quantified results. The writer's ability to deliver is unmistakable.
- At the end of the background section of the résumé, using the phrase "Roles Prior to 1989 …" alludes to greater experience without extending the résumé or giving away the writer's age. In such a statement, you can mention position title, companies, functional areas or any combination thereof.

Sample Résumé #3

Your Name

Address   Office:
City, Province   Cell:
Postal Code   Email:

PROFILE

A high-energy, strategic and bottom-line-oriented retail professional. Over 20 years of hands-on executive experience in store operations, merchandising, marketing and human resources. A motivator and team builder working with corporate and franchise managers and staff to develop and implement innovative programs for customer service and in-store merchandising.

BUSINESS BACKGROUND

WELL-KNOWN KIOSK CO.   **2004–2007**
The licensed operator for Sightlines Inc. managing 80 optical stores across Canada: 52 corporate stores and 28 franchised.

VICE PRESIDENT

Mandate: Plan and direct a reversed strategy for marketing and operations to return ABC Company to profitability within 18 months. Established proper staffing and service levels to ensure all stores achieved sales potential. Reported to the Chairman.

OPERATIONS

- Established sales, gross margin and salary budgets. Labour costs were reduced by 14.2%, sales increased 7.1% and gross margin increased 2.4%. Within first year of mandate, store contribution results were positive despite a significant loss in the previous year. Second year store contribution results increased 34.7%.
- Reduced lab "redos" by 25% and instituted quality control procedures at the lab by conducting random daily eyewear checks before shipping.
- Renegotiated terms and costs with most suppliers, resulting in a cost reduction of 25%, increase in terms to 180 days and new consignment deals. Cash flow improved as a result of honouring payment terms and commitments.
- Developed a Store Manager's Operations Manual and In-Store Checklist to increase efficiency and streamline administration.

PROGRAM INITIATIVES

- Set up a proto-store to test-market new strategies and serve as a merchandising model in order to standardize the planning process for promotional events and future expansion.
- Instituted a Store-Front Marketing Program to book doctor's appointments. Launched supplier Trunk Shows that doubled sales on event days. Used Board Management System strategy to merchandise the mix of frames on the boards.
- Began Monthly Payment Plan and Deferred Payment Plan for customers, in coordination with Sightlines Inc.'s legal, advertising, and credit departments.

DECORAMA LTD.   1982–2004

A national paint, wallcovering and hard window coverings specialty Canadian retail chain of 145 stores: 85 Corporate and 60 Franchised. Divisions included paint manufacturing facilities, wallpaper wholesale and warehouse. Sales in excess of $100 million with over 1,000 employees.

VICE PRESIDENT, OPERATIONS   1996–2004

Mandate: Manage all retail operations, providing leadership and direction to two Senior Regional District Managers, six District Managers, Manager Human Resources, Public Relations Consultant, Trainers, Payroll Department, six Shop-at-Home Sales Reps., and approximately 1,000 employees (including franchise stores). Reported to the Chairman.

PROFITABILITY AND COST CONTROL

- Identified the need to reduce out-of-stocks at store level to prevent lost sales. Created auto shipment program based on store volume, to anticipate peak sales periods and reduce out-of-stocks.
- Conducted research analysis and determined that average sales increased 10% when franchise stores were converted to corporate stores. Recommended and managed the conversion of 30 stores.
- Identified the need to create payroll system to control costs of $6 million. Developed methodology to measure stores with similar sales volume. Wage costs reduced 14%.

MERCHANDISING / MARKETING

- Identified need to improve general appearance of stores, store layout and merchandising practices. Executed monthly sales promotions and improved consistency and accuracy of information given to stores by District Managers. Sales increased 10%.
- Introduced merchandising programs, weekly manager meetings and bi-monthly videos to review current promotions: created standard displays, implemented checklists for customer service, general housekeeping, and merchandising, and developed photo albums for District Managers to take to stores.
- Developed long-term strategy to restructure and decentralize store operations to create an environment for stores to operate more independently, reducing the number of District Managers.

INFORMATION SYSTEMS

- Developed long-term information systems strategy that introduced a point-of-sale system to implement the following:
  - improve customer service by allowing inventory checking between stores
  - create an imaging system to restructure Head Office purchasing function
  - balance inventories within corporate stores

CUSTOMER SERVICE

- Identified the need to improve staff productivity and service levels. Instituted a "Customer Approach in 10 Seconds or Less" program.
- Identified with managers and staff, policies and procedures that were not customer friendly. Empowered staff to deal with customer complaints directly. Established new refund policy, instituted Head Office Policy of "Customer Complaints Handled Within 24 Hours."

TRAINING AND DEVELOPMENT
- Created a more effective method of training sales staff, store managers and owners, focusing on product knowledge, selling skills, and decorating advice to ensure that customers were always treated in a knowledgeable and courteous manner.
- Designed a Manager Trainee Training Program and produced educational videotapes to provide ongoing staff development.

VICE PRESIDENT, HUMAN RESOURCES   *1989–1996*
- Implemented and directed all personnel policies including compensation and benefit programs for stores, office, distribution centre and manufacturing division.
- Directed labour relations for 450 warehouse and factory personnel. Negotiated contracts and planned and coordinated strike coverage to prevent business interruption.

ROLES PRIOR TO 1989 INCLUDED *DIRECTOR OF HUMAN RESOURCES, MANAGER OF HUMAN RESOURCES AND TRAINING COORDINATOR*.

EDUCATION

University of Alberta, B.A., Economics & Sociology

INTERESTS

Basketball, karate, tennis, classical music

Key Points to Note as You Read Sample Résumé #4

Human Resources Manager
Business-to-Business Products and Services

- This résumé places keywords front and centre, drawing immediate attention to the individual's areas of expertise. This also accommodates computer scanning technology.
- Every one of the keywords is substantiated by an accomplishment statement in the body of the résumé.
- This individual's title does not reflect her true seniority. She has risen quickly to a level of responsibility appropriate for a Vice President, Human Resources. The role description explains the relationship of the incumbent to her boss in Chicago and her dotted-line relationship with the Canadian President to denote the true level of her role.
- When dates of employment are a puzzle, create a format that provides clarity. The employment gaps are obvious in this résumé and the individual would be prepared to explain them in an interview. Note that she is still employed at International Electronic Gadgets Inc.
- Overlapping roles and titles in 1997 are shown clearly on the second page.
- The phrase "fluently bilingual" would be assumed to refer to French and English by a reader. However, a computer scanner is not as quick to understand. Therefore, the word "French" appears in the education section.
- Aiming for full disclosure, this individual identifies her first job in the business world as a contract position. Clarity on details such as terms of employment is crucial.
- Human resources accomplishments are typically difficult to quantify since they often deal with processes. In this case, the number of employees and facilities shows the size of the organization. Impressive business results are quantified.

Tip: Mention on the first page the skills and functions that you most want to use in your next employment opportunity. Make sure that they stand out.

Sample Résumé #4

YOUR NAME, MBA, CHRP

Address   Tel:
City, Province   Cell:
Postal code   Email:

PROFILE

A fluently bilingual Human Resources generalist with over nine years' progressive experience in large national and international organizations. A strategic leader with a track record of linking HR initiatives directly to business objectives.

AREAS OF EXPERTISE

- Change Management
- Performance Management
- Total Compensation
- Labour Relations

- Employee Relations
- Benefits Design and Administration
- Policy Development
- HRIS

EMPLOYMENT EXPERIENCE

INTERNATIONAL ELECTRONIC GADGETS INC.   1996–1998 & 2004–PRESENT

DIRECTOR, HUMAN RESOURCES   *2004–PRESENT*

Reporting to the Vice President, Human Resources, Chicago, IL, and indirectly to the Canadian Regional President, responsible for the human resources function in Canada—approximately 2,200 employees in six divisions nationwide, with four collective bargaining units in distribution facilities.

Key accomplishments:
- Transformed a disjointed, decentralized HR function into a business-focused, proactive and coordinated team with shared vision and values. Reduced HR turnover from 35% to 9% and repaired HR's reputation with its client groups.
- Worked with the Canadian Regional President to restructure the national sales organization, leading to 15% year-over-year profitable sales growth. Developed a culture of accountability and changed sales roles from "order taker" to "business adviser." Restructured sales compensation to drive accountability.
- Initiated and completed detailed total cash compensation analysis for senior managers to address negative perceptions resulting from the integration of an acquired business.
- Led strategic labour negotiations for two collective agreements, which resulted in a 0% increase in their first year.
- Restructured the employee benefit program, resulting in an annual savings of $300,000 without any decrease in benefit coverage.
- Introduced the corporate office's performance management tool and process, ensuring it was successfully implemented.

- Managed numerous restructuring initiatives, including the closure of a 70-employee distribution facility in Montreal without incident.
- Handled issues and cases under employment law; mediated numerous settlements thereby reducing exposure and mitigating costs.

MANAGER, HUMAN RESOURCES   *1996–1998*

HRIS PROJECT CO-ORDINATOR   *1997*

- Supervised an HR Assistant, responsible for salary and benefit administration, meeting coordination and workplace health and safety.
- Facilitated an organization-wide working group of managers and executives to identify their information needs. Prepared an RFP and chose a vendor to implement a comprehensive HR information system.
- Developed, wrote and implemented a comprehensive HR Reference Policy Manual for national use. This included creating and delivering employee information presentations.
- Coordinated a French-language services audit and ensured that legislative requirements were met.

OFFICE SOLUTIONS OF CANADA LTD.   **1995–1998**

STAFFING CONSULTANT   *1996–1998*

HUMAN RESOURCES ASSISTANT (CONTRACT POSITION, INCUMBENT ON LEAVE)   *1995–1996*

- Initiated the restructuring of the recruiting team enabling closer contact with main clients.
- Designed and presented a new interview workshop for managers.
- Participated on cross-functional Risk Management and Corporate Communications Committees.

NORTH COAST SCHOOL DISTRICT, NB   **1984-1992**

ELEMENTARY SCHOOL TEACHER

EDUCATION

Master of Business Administration, University of Toronto, 1994
New Brunswick Teacher Certification, 1984
Bachelor of Education, Université de Moncton, 1984
Bachelor of Arts (French and Psychology), St. Thomas University, 1983

PROFESSIONAL DEVELOPMENT

Advanced Program in Human Resource Management, University of Toronto, 2000-2001
Active Leadership Program, 1996
Business Writing Skills, 1995
Targeted Selection (Behavioural Interviewing), 1994

Key Points to Note as You Read Sample Résumé #5

Director of Sales
Pharmaceutical Industry

- This is a chronological résumé. The writer's background lends itself perfectly to this format because of the steady progression up the ladder of responsibility and accountability. The layout of the résumé allows the reader to clearly see the writer's progress.
- This layout has appeal because it uses plenty of white space. The trade-off is that less space is available for accomplishment statements. However, the writer has captured her background clearly and concisely. The reader sees the career highlights of a capable sales manager headed for more senior management positions.
- Look at the content of the résumé. The first bullet point is more of a role description than an accomplishment statement. This works in this layout where the use of italics or bold type might be confusing.
- The inclusion of quantified facts gives the reader an understanding of this individual's level of responsibility. Her role revolved around the sales numbers, and without them, this résumé would be incomplete.
- The description of this individual's experience in her most recent role contains five bullet points. The previous role is described with four; and the one previous to that, only three and so on. This is an appropriate method of giving weight to more recent accomplishments, and it shows a progression of responsibility.
- Notice that the last section of the résumé refers to community involvement rather than interests. This reinforcing the claim in the profile statement. It's a good idea to place an important and convincing statement here. Readers who skim résumés will often read the last point.

Sample Résumé #5

YOUR NAME

PROFILE

A people- and results-driven senior sales director with over 13 years' experience in the pharmaceutical industry. Skilled in developing motivated teams that take pride in delivering organizational goals. Committed to fostering a professional work environment that values executional excellence and innovation. A self-starter who creates a strong business presence through active involvement in the community.

EXPERIENCE

Wexer Drugs PLC   **1992–Present**

Regional Director of Sales, Pharma Division   *2005–Present*

- Managed a $50-million, 11-product portfolio in Wexer's largest national region with 7 districts and 88 individual territories.
- Achieved 28% year-over-year revenue growth for fiscal 2005 and 2006, exceeding targets by more than 30%.
- Worked with VP, National Sales, to develop incentive plans for 2006 to help retain top talent. Plan was designed to be equitable among all regions and succeeded in reducing turnover from 18% to 9% in 12 months.
- Designed relaunch program of UniDet in Québec, which resulted in increasing monthly sales from $22,000 to $84,000. Program focused on intensive targeting of customers and pharmacy work.
- Coached and developed manager team through performance-related issues with field personnel. Facilitated course delivery and case study discussions.

District Sales Manager—Calgary, Alberta   *2000–2005*

- Expanded sales force from 10 to 20 in the district. Doubled sales volumes during tenure in the role.
- Drove the Heart Smart Health program to 200% of objective. This value-add program helped successfully launch a new cholesterol drug in district.
- Initiated the first Passports to Success program. This program helped new hires integrate quickly and effectively into the organization.
- Created District Manager Mentor program with manager sub-team. This program leveraged various skill sets within the management team to aid managers in their development.

Field Sales Trainer—Calgary, Alberta   *1999–2000*

- First incumbent FST for Western Canada (BC, Alberta, Manitoba and Saskatchewan). Created schedules, models and templates for new role.
- Facilitated training for three groups of hires and coordinated a five-tier training plan to span recruits' initial three years.

YOUR NAME   **Page 2**

- Coordinated development plans and follow-up for all representatives in Western Canada. Included work-related skills and personal development. Reviewed quarterly.

Specialist Sales Representative—Winnipeg, Manitoba   *1997–1999*

- Increased sales of Rhuematin by 50% within 24 months through the development of relationship with specialists in the field and patient groups.
- Identified local rheumatologist to coordinate Patient Partner in Arthritis in Winnipeg. Recruited a pool of trained patients to help our representatives deliver arthritis education to physicians.
- Developed Rheumatology Preceptorships and APMR Training for representatives to increase their product knowledge and credibility with customers.

Sales Representative—Saint John, New Brunswick   *1992–1997*

- Generated top 10 sales for territory for three consecutive years, 1994–1996.
- Achieved top Risorptin sales growth in country in 1994 (61%), 1995 (48%) and 1996 (21%).

EDUCATION

French Second Language Program, Université Concordia, Montréal, PQ, 1991
Bachelor of Arts, Mount Allison University, Sackville, NB, 1985–1990
John Worton Award Winner—for leadership and contribution to student life, 1990

AWARDS

District Manager of the Year, 2001, 2002 and 2004
Specialist Representative of the Year, 1998
Presidents' Club, 1995 and 1998

COMMUNITY INVOLVEMENT

Chaired Ride for Your Heart Fundraising Committee, 2003–2004
Breakfast Committee for Canadian Arthritis Foundation Stampede Event, 1999–2005
Chairperson, École St. Marguerite Fundraising Committee, 1992–1997
Saint John Silver Blades—figure skating coach, 1995–1997

Key Points to Note as You Read Sample Résumé #6

Information Technology Executive
Financial Services

- This individual has successfully made the transition from long-term employee to independent consultant. His up-to-date résumé includes accomplishments from his consulting work.
- The emphasis is on the alignment of technology with strategic business goals. Quantified cost savings, meeting deadlines and increased productivity are also key deliverables at the executive level.
- Where results remain unproven, indicate projections as shown in the third bullet point.
- Timelines add impact to accomplishment statements. For instance, the phrases "had been cancelled two weeks prior to implementation" and "implementation over 18 to 24 months" demonstrate the urgency involved.
- Spell out acronyms and demystify jargon. For example, in the third bullet point "SWOT" is clarified. In the fourth bullet point "Public Key Infrastructure" is mentioned, using upper case first letters for emphasis, and in the next point, the acronym "PKI" is used. This is a subtle and effective way of ensuring the reader's understanding.
- Ongoing professional development shows a commitment to being on the leading edge. This IT professional has chosen management courses to enhance his leadership potential.
- Sample biographies, an executive summary of the résumé and a sample brochure for this IT executive are included in the next chapter.

Tip: If your targets entail looking for contract assignments, let your résumé form the core of your marketing materials. Once you've written the résumé, the other pieces flow with less difficulty. At the end of every contract, update your résumé and all your additional marketing materials.

Sample Résumé #6

NAME
ADDRESS
CITY, PROVINCE POSTAL CODE
TEL: EMAIL: WEB SITE:

PROFILE

A visionary IT executive with proven expertise in aligning technical strategies to organizational goals. Applies intuitive and analytical skills to evolve programs of interrelated, realizable projects focused on the strategic vision. Successful in driving projects to implementation by building upon and extending existing foundations. Over 20 years' experience in financial services information technology software and hardware combined with extensive experience in project management of operational architectures for high availability, mission-critical systems.

PROFESSIONAL EXPERIENCE

John Smith, Principal
IT TECHNICAL AND STRATEGIC CONSULTING   2002–PRESENT

- Directed outsourcing of statement printing, selective insertion and mailing of customer statements. Project was planned and implemented to meet customer's schedule. Negotiated a competitive agreement with the preferred service provider valued at over $12 million.
- Resurrected a project to close a major data centre that had been cancelled two weeks prior to implementation. Working with the senior executive sponsor, and previous project participants from the involved companies, addressed the obstacles in the objectives, staffing, scope and schedule. As a result, the project was redefined and implemented on schedule and under budget.
- Contracted to translate a service organization's print business strategy and business improvement plans into a program of interrelated projects for implementation over 18 to 24 months. This program addressed three critical weaknesses—efficiency, service reputation and productivity as identified in the SWOT (Strength, Weakness, Opportunities and Threats) analysis. Cost savings will exceed $3 million annually.

TRADITIONAL BANK   1981–2002
VICE PRESIDENT, SECURITY RISK EVALUATIONS AND RESEARCH   2001–2002

- Led the team to design and implement hardware, software, secure network, operations, support and systems management for Public Key Infrastructure security used in online Internet banking and stock trading systems. The high-availability design allowed for hardware and software components to fail without any service interruption or on-site staff.
- Produced a technical strategy for security systems and secure networks using PKI. This foundation opened the secure and confidential delivery of services to customers through electronic channels and set up a virtual office for the Bank's global staff.

VICE PRESIDENT, TELECOMMUNICATIONS AND TECHNICAL SERVICES   1999–2001

- Developed the vision for strategic computer hardware and software technology for core Bank systems. Provided framework for major migration to new software, database and hardware platforms required to support expanding business needs. The strategy concurrently addressed Y2K requirements and new functionality. Further objectives met included asset preservation, technology and operations support, capacity and performance and availability and scalability.
- Implemented tactical planning processes into Telecommunication and Technical Services to provide structure. This effectively focused the efforts of 270 staff members on pre-determined strategic goals. The resulting

program of interrelated projects provided the clarity and knowledge to empower lower level decision-making. Results were higher availability and increased functional delivery.

- Refocused staff resources, creating a new support organization, without increasing the Department's $110-million budget. This provided hardware and software support for the Bank's centralized server complexes installed for data mining, Work Group support for global corporate bankers and commercial customer access to account information.

ASSISTANT GENERAL MANAGER, HOST PLANNING AND HARDWARE SERVICES   **1994–1999**

- Appointed a member of every Systems and Operations strategic architecture task force formed within the Bank over a 12-year period. Task forces included Operations Strategic Technical Plan, Efficiency and Effectiveness and the New Branch Platform Study. Contributed to the vision and technical knowledge regarding the hardware, software and database infrastructure that would facilitate the addition and extension of applications.

- Directed the project that integrated computer operations and technical support areas following the acquisition of Seaview Trust. The project exceeded expectations for transparency to the end users and compressed an eight-month schedule to five months. Savings were in excess of $8 million.

- Restored credibility to the forecasting, planning and control processes that provided the business justification to hardware, software and database assets acquisitions. The revamped methodologies introduced the concept of asset management to ensure that investments in infrastructure provided a business return to the Bank. Acceptance of the process by the Finance Department and CEO paved the way for major tape and print automation projects.

- Established closer relationships with vendors, specifically EMC, IBM, STK, Hitachi, Tandem and Amdahl, to understand their view of business drivers, and their future product directions. Advised and influenced vendors' development, sensitizing them to the needs of the Canadian banking system and Traditional Bank in particular. Scalability, high performance operability and cost effectiveness were critical as transactions migrated from paper to electronic formats.

ASSISTANT GENERAL MANAGER, SYSTEMS DEVELOPMENT RESEARCH   **1989–1994**

- Directed research into expert and knowledge-based systems, application development automation, and CASE (Computer Automated System Evaluation) systems. Result was the implementation of a $4-million investment in development automation and training. Accumulated annual increases in measured productivity ranging from 2 to 25 times the base.

- Led the design team of Bank and hardware and software vendors to solve the problem of the Bank's expanding network and database applications exceeding the technology's capabilities. The new design exploited the technology in an unprecedented manner. Project-managed a solution involving seven related projects to upgrade server, host, database, telecommunication and application system software without loss of availability or stability to 1200 domestic branches.

ROLES PRIOR TO 1989 INCLUDED A NUMBER OF MANAGEMENT POSITIONS AT TRADITIONAL BANK AND TECHNICAL SPECIALIST ROLES AT ESTABLISHMENT BANK.

PROFESSIONAL DEVELOPMENT

Myers-Briggs Type Indicator, Qualification Complete
Professional Management Skills, Quality Management Group
Re-engineering, Seaforth and Company

EDUCATION AND PROFESSIONAL ASSOCIATIONS

Member, Canadian Information Processing Society, CIPS
University of Waterloo, Bachelor of Mathematics, Computer Science

Key Points to Note as You Read Sample Résumé #7

Project Manager
Information Technology—Financial Services

- For IT résumés, the rules change. If the experience is relevant, the résumé may exceed the standard two or three pages.
- Career objectives are expected for IT résumés.
- The profile balances the technical content of the résumé by stressing customer service, management and teamwork skills, all of which are valued for progression to a leadership role.
- The summary of skills section uses a table format to list the individual's technical skills and organize them by type.
- The number of months of each assignment are noted for each position. IT employers want to know both how current and for what duration your experience with a particular technology is.
- This individual's accomplishments showcase a range of skills from troubleshooting and training to sales support and project leadership.
- In the education section, there is no attempt to hide the fact that the degree was not completed. Including your record of significant higher education is important even though you have chosen another route.

Tip: Do not be vague or misleading about education currently in progress or discontinued before the completion of the diploma or degree requirements. List all relevant education and use phrases such as "currently enrolled," "course completed" or "completed two years toward degree in."

Sample Résumé #7

NAME

ADDRESS, CITY, PROVINCE AND POSTAL CODE
RES. TEL: CELL:
eMAIL: WEB SITE:

OBJECTIVE

To contribute as a software engineer and project manager at a senior level.

PROFILE

An experienced, client-focused project leader, respected for delivering quality results on time and within budget. Manages and motivates people effectively, empowering individuals through positive reinforcement to be high-quality performers in demanding, multi-tasking environments. Recognized as a creative team player with unwavering commitment to quality and client satisfaction.

SUMMARY OF SKILLS

Management	Project leadership, technology implementation, customer service, vendor management, distributed software engineering, virtual development team management.
Technical	Client Server application development, User Interface design, Website and e-commerce design with Java J2EE, Database design, System Analysis and Design, Extreme Programming, document management and distribution system design.
Languages	C, C++, Java, VisualBasic.Net, SQL, Smalltalk, UNIX script, JavaScript, PHP, HTML, XML
Database	DB2, Oracle, MS Access, MySQL
Development Tools	Microsoft Project, WSAD, Visual Age, MS Visual Studio, Quick Test Professional
Operating Systems	AIX, Solaris, Linux, MS Windows NT 4.0/2000/XP
Networks	Ethernet, TCP/IP, routers, Windows NT 4.0/2000, UNIX, Linux
Middleware	Tibco Rendez Vous, Message Broker

CAREER HISTORY

Company 1   1993–2006
Project Leader — Client Access Systems   Jan. 2002–Dec. 2006

- Led a five-member team for support and integration of a vendor application for Trust and Securities clients. System was a successful amalgamation of both 16-bit and 32-bit products resulting in an application suitable for both WIN 95/98 and NT 4.0. Release featured several functional enhancements and was delivered two weeks ahead of schedule.

- Developed specifications for an enhanced client dial-up facility. Significant improvements made to speed of data transmission from Tandem hub to client workstation, thereby making the product viable for larger volume clients.
- Provided training, demonstrations and seminars for the support team on various product trouble-shooting techniques, to make the help desk and support areas more self-reliant.
- Provided technical support for product installation, help desk staff, and client training staff
- Performed analysis and code maintenance for PC-Investment Manager, an MS-DOS application, which was subsequently certified as Y2K ready. This allowed re-deployment of resources for the development of the NT replacement product.
- Developed application programs, Report Viewer, Automated Backup, Com. Stat using VB 5.0.

Senior Technical Analyst — Electronic Business Banking   **May 1997–Dec. 2001**

- Developed a Visual Basic client interface for Bank's 16-bit EBB communications platform.
- Created a broadcast message facility to relate important messages to the Bank clients, vis-à-vis daily data downloads.
- Converted a DOS data warehouse utility using an upgraded communication protocol. Application is certified as Y2K ready and will continue to be used into the next millennium
- Provided production support to the Bank's clients.

Technical Systems Analyst — Electronic Business Banking   **Nov. 1993–May 1997**

- Led development of PC Investment Manager, a DOS application written in MS C 6.0.
- Developed PC to PC file transmission utility for the EBB Umbrella.
- Converted PC Disbursement Auditor into a French-language version.

Company 2   **Feb. 1993–Nov. 1993**
Programmer

- Developed user interfaces for energy management and climate control systems using MS C 5.0
- Coded PLC communication components using FORTH and Motorola 6502 assembler.

Company 3   **June 1991–Feb. 1993**
Product Support Specialist/Software Engineer

- Provided product support for EASYL, pressure-sensitive digitizing tablet.
- Developed electronic correction algorithm-based on cubic spline quadrature, for digitizing tablet.
- Implemented algorithm in Motorola 68HC11 assembler.
- Developed graphical production control program for the EASYL using Lattice C for Amiga.

Company 4   **Feb. 1990–June 1991**
Technical Support Manager

- Supervised a two-person team, overcame linguistic and cultural barriers to deliver Japanese-engineered solutions to satisfy U.S. client expectations.
- Designed and developed PC/AT user interfaces for a pressure-sensitive digitizing tablet and signature verification system using, GW-Basic, dBase III and Paradox.
- Provided sales support and after market support.

Company 5   **June 1986–Feb. 1990**
Programmer/Analyst

- Designed and developed general financial and accounting applications using Business Basic on a Data General Eclipse S140.
- Created Lotus 123 macros for accounting staff on IBM PC/XT.
- Developed a remote dial-in facility allowing a Commodore 64 to emulate a Dasher D-100 terminal, thereby introducing full-screen editing to Data General programmers for the first time.

EDUCATION

Bank's Internal Courses

- Tandem Concepts and Facilities, Project Life Cycle, Managing Personal Growth and ABT Project Management.

Career Learning Centre   **1984–1985**

- Computer Programming and Systems Analysis (community college equivalent).
- Languages: COBOL, FORTRAN, RPG II, BASIC. Structured database design methodologies.

University   **1981–1984**

- Completed 11 courses in Applied Science and Electrical Engineering.

INTERESTS

Golf, tennis, music, guitar and MIDI equipment, Visual Basic computer graphics.

Chapter 11

Go Beyond the Résumé

Identify Your Brand and Communicate It Effectively

Once you've done your career assessment and written an accomplishment-focused résumé, you are as prepared as the next person to enter the competitive employment market. If you completed the work suggested in Chapter 8 and set your targets, you are ahead of the pack. Now give yourself a further advantage by identifying your unique brand and approaching your search as a marketing-driven initiative. If you invest the time and effort to define your brand and create materials that communicate it, you will truly have a competitive edge.

Marketing your capabilities by going beyond the résumé involves explaining and promoting the benefits of your potential contribution to an employer through well-prepared written materials that differentiate you from your peers. It does not mean that you will be using slick advertising methods or making exaggerated representations about your abilities. Marketing is an approach that may stretch you beyond your comfort zone, but when planned carefully and executed with integrity, it will be genuine. The marketing process begins when you identify your brand.

Tip: Using the concept of a brand can make some people feel as if they are being turned into a commodity. The intention here is simply to help you see and explain what makes you unique so that you can say, "I'm the one you should hire because ..."

Identify Your Brand

Your brand is the impression you leave in the minds of individuals in your target market. It positions you vis-à-vis the competition and helps decision-makers see why they should hire you. Your brand positioning is created by your value proposition and image. It communicates who you are, what you can do and what you want to do. Your brand should be positioned so that it is meaningful, memorable and believable.

Marketing professionals speak of brands as occupying space in the consumer's mind. The mere mention or sight of a well-known brand conjures up a wealth of stored information about the product or service represented by the brand. Your purchasing decisions are influenced by brands. You can put the same dynamic to work in your employment search. As you communicate with individuals in your target market, you want them to remember you by associating you with the information that would lead them to hire you. You need your brand to occupy space in their minds and give them good reasons for wanting to work with you.

Plant Your Brand in Your Target's Mind in a Way That Is Meaningful, Memorable, Believable

Value Proposition + Image = Brand Positioning

Your Value Proposition

One aspect of your brand is your value proposition. This refers to what you can do. It is how your skills and knowledge could address an issue or need in a specific market. It represents the potential benefit to the employer of hiring you.

Your value proposition will be somewhat different for each of your specific target markets, but the themes will be consistent. You started to identify the components of your value proposition in the accomplishment stories you recorded in Chapter 4 and in the strategic advantage you defined in Chapter 5. Your résumé is replete with evidence of what you can do. When you set your strategic targets and completed Worksheet(s) 8.4 you developed your value proposition more fully. Now your task is to package and communicate it in a memorable way.

One option is to find a concise descriptor for your value proposition, such as:

Turnaround Artist	Business Builder
New Ideas Generator	Implementer
Strategic Rule-Breaker	Customer Relationship Builder
Acquisition Specialist	Regulatory Specialist
Market Research Specialist	Operations Expert

You might already have such a descriptor in the Profile Statement of your résumé. If not, think about incorporating one for appropriate target markets. Use it in conversations to see if it delivers your message effectively.

Try a metaphor. Some people work well with words and phrases that symbolize their value proposition. If you are comfortable with the concept and can think of an appropriate image, use it. Here are two examples:

Explorer —A courageous, tenacious, self-reliant individual who dares to venture where others would not go. Often found in marketing departments, corporate development roles or the CEO's office.

Watchdog—A reliable and cautious monitor of the organization's activities. Could be an auditor, a regulatory expert or corporate counsel.

Your value proposition is the message. Memorable words and phrases exemplify one effective medium. More communication suggestions are offered below.

Your Image

An equally important part of your brand is your image. Your appearance, choice of words, tone of voice, energy level and charisma all play a vital role in creating your image. What others say about you also contributes to your image. It is crucial that your references, colleagues and contacts support your career direction and strategic targets. More will be said about the components of image in subsequent chapters.

Your written materials give you another opportunity to build a memorable and positive image. The nature and quality of the documents you distribute can make a lasting impression on your audience. Documents that contain a high-impact message, good grammar, error-free text and a polished appearance will make you look confident and professional. Sloppy work makes you appear uninterested or lazy. Be sure that you are conveying the image you want with every written piece you produce and distribute.

Develop a Look

For a very small investment of time and money, you can create an image that expresses your style and appeals to your target markets. It can be understated and conservative or a bit more creative and flamboyant, simply through your choice of paper, colour, type, layout and other elements of design. Once you have created your look, use it consistently on all of your written materials. The guidelines that follow will help you with your choices.

Tip: The availability of design software and colour printers allows most people to produce high-quality materials on their own. If you are not adept at using the software or are challenged when it comes to visual design, ask your support network for help before going to the expense of using a print shop.

GUIDELINES FOR DEVELOPING A LOOK

- Start by looking at other marketing materials. Collect samples of the items you need, and use the layout and design features that will work best for you. Business supply stores and print shops usually have catalogues of samples and off-the-shelf designs.
- Choose the colour and texture of your paper carefully. White is always safe because there's no problem finding matching envelopes, and it faxes and photocopies well. You can add colour with a logo or other printed design features. The texture and feel of your paper is important. High-quality paper is more expensive, but quality alone can do a lot to create an image.
- Different fonts create distinctive looks. Choose one you like and use it exclusively for letterhead design and headings. Vary your style by using (but not overusing) bold, italics and upper and lower case, but don't change the font. Be sure that your selection prints out crisply and clearly in small type for labels and footers.
- Good font choices include Times, Tahoma, Arial, Helvetica and Garamond. Inexpensive software containing extra fonts is available at any business supply store.
- If you want to incorporate colour in your text, use very dark colours in titles, logos and headings, but use only black for the main text to ensure readability.
- Ink colours look different when printed on coated, uncoated or coloured paper. Check a sample of your ink colour choices printed on your specific paper.
- Work with layout and type alignment. Specific elements such as name, date, page numbers, logo and slogan should always appear in the same place on the page. Be consistent with the use of centring and left and right justification.
- Be creative in your choice of other elements of style such as contrast, borders, lines, bullets and other symbols. Let the various design elements you choose become your signature by using them consistently.
- Having a logo is not necessary. If you decide to use one, have a graphic designer produce it. Homemade logos usually look unprofessional.
- Be sure that your design faxes and photocopies well.
- You might consider hiring a designer for assistance. Print shops and business supply stores usually provide referrals.
- If you use a designer, give them an idea of your style by showing them samples of letterhead, cards, brochures, ads or book covers that you like. Let them do their craft and then evaluate their concepts by asking yourself these questions:
  - Is the message clear to read?
  - Does it reflect my style and create the impression I want?
  - Is the content correct?
  - Is there anything else I should add before approving the design?

- Ask the same questions of individuals on your advisory board or in your support network.
- Whether you work with a designer or deal directly with a print shop, you are always entitled to see a proof. Remember that you are still responsible for content, proofreading and final appearance. Scrupulously check the layout, including a cut, trimmed and folded version of the final product if appropriate.

Tip: Never use design simply for the sake of design. Make sure that the message is clear, readable and worth reading. In the words of Shakespeare, use "more matter, less art."

Consistent use of your look starts with the most fundamental materials in your stockpile. Follow the suggestions below to develop basic materials that are consistent with your brand, and then turn to the last section of this chapter to see how you can market your unique qualities more boldly.

Cover the Basics

For traditional job seekers, business cards and a template on your computer for personal letterhead are the essential items. If you are looking for contract work or establishing a consulting practice, you will need an executive summary of your résumé and a biography for inclusion in proposals.

For individuals launching a business, the nature of the business and the marketing strategy will determine the need for materials. The range of possibilities is vast, and more elaborate marketing and advertising plans will likely benefit from professional help. However, for all businesses, standard stationery is a must, along with a web site. A brochure of some kind is probably also a necessary item. The principals of a business that provides professional service will need biographies.

Here are a few essential pointers for each of the communication and marketing pieces that you may decide to produce. Follow these guidelines to achieve results that will help your search.

GUIDELINES FOR DEVELOPING BASIC MARKETING MATERIALS

Business Cards
- Your name and contact information on your business card should match those on your résumé and other marketing materials. If your contact information might change during your job search, use a less expensive production option and plan to reprint your business cards.
- Consider giving yourself a title that explains something about your key skills or knowledge. For example, under your name you might print "Human Resources Consultant" or "Project Management." The concise descriptor of your value proposition could be a good choice, or you could use the metaphor that symbolizes it. Don't force this. If you are not comfortable with using some kind of title, stick with your name alone.
- Consider putting information, such as your mission statement or a concise outline of services offered, on the back of the card.
- Stick with the standard size. Choose a heavy stock, and use the design elements consistent with your other materials and stationery.
- Do not overcrowd either the front or back of the card.

Letterhead, Envelopes and Labels

- For most job seekers, creating personal letterhead with your computer software and using good-quality paper with a laser-quality printer is sufficient.
- White is the most cost-effective colour option. Matching envelopes are easier to find, and white faxes and photocopies well. If you choose a distinctive colour and quality of paper for printed letterhead, purchase an ample supply of the same paper for producing the subsequent pages. Matching envelopes are a must.
- Keep the design consistent on letterhead, envelopes and labels.
- Before having letterhead printed, check how it will look with an actual letter printed on it. Does it work well with the design elements and style you've chosen?
- For letter-size envelopes, use standard stock labels from a business supply store or print the labels on your computer. Labels for larger envelopes can be printed with your design, making your larger packages consistent with your look.

Executive Summary of Your Résumé

- Consultants, contractors, small business owners and many traditional job seekers often find an executive summary of their résumé useful. It can be an introductory piece attached to a marketing letter, a document that you walk through in a meeting or an enclosure with a follow-up letter.
- Design it to match your original résumé, and keep it to one page.
- Begin with your profile statement. Highlight only your key accomplishments and include employment information.
- Do not overcrowd the page.
- Do not use it when applying for an advertised position. To pass an initial screening process, your full history is essential.
- Use the sample further on in this chapter as a guide.

Biographies

- Biographies in various lengths are frequently required of consultants, contractors and some small business owners, for inclusion in their own and their clients' proposals.
- Write a full biography that is 300 to 350 words in length, keeping it to one page. Write a shorter version that is approximately 100 words and a very brief one, less than 50 words. Writing the shorter version is usually more difficult, but when you need these biographies, you will appreciate having done them in advance, even if revisions are needed.
- Put your one-page biography on your letterhead, or design a special page with the same elements of style used on your letterhead.
- Write in the style of a press release. Use the third person, as if you were describing someone else.
- Include your professional credentials and a synopsis of your background as it relates to the work you are seeking. Don't go into detail, but do include accomplishments in a concise form. Name any well-known organizations where you've worked, and mention your titles. Include professional associations and designations that add to your credibility.

- One of the shorter versions might be appropriate as text for your brochure.
- Use the samples at the end of this chapter as a guide.

Brochure Describing Your Services
- Design your brochure to highlight your key marketing points. Possible inclusions are the type of services you provide, benefits of the service, brief case studies, profiles of the principals, mission statement, quotes from clients and names of client organizations, with their permission.
- Contact information should stand out clearly.
- Writing your brochure can help clarify your thinking about exactly what service you are proposing to provide and what differentiates you from the competition.
- Draft the contents, design the layout and review it with your network. Consider having two formats, one on a single page to be dispatched by email, and another that contains more information and uses two or more pages to be produced in hard copy.
- A simple and effective hard-copy format uses a standard letter-sized page with a landscape page setup, printed on both sides and folded in thirds. Print it on heavy paper or light cardboard. Use the sample three-fold brochure further on in this chapter as a guide.
- Consider having your brochures printed professionally only after you have tested a prototype with a few clients.
- Keep the format clean, concise and consistent with your look. People are often tempted to be more creative with their brochure than they are with other marketing materials. Do not produce one that strays too far from your consistent image.

The samples of basic marketing materials on the following pages are derived from Sample Résumé #6 in Chapter 10.

Sample Executive Summary of the Résumé

John Smith

8910 Main Street

Toronto, ON M1X X1X

Business: (416) 555-1212   Fax: (416) 555-1212   email: jsmith@isp.ca

A visionary IT executive with over 20 years' experience in aligning technical strategies to organizational goals in the financial services sector. Expertise encompasses software, hardware, planning, project management and operational architectures for high availability, mission-critical systems. Employs excellent intuitive and analytical skills to drive programs of interrelated, realizable projects to completion. Committed to building upon and extending existing foundations while bringing insight to assessing the business value of new technologies in order to maximize return on investment.

CAREER ACHIEVEMENTS

- Developed the technical strategic vision for a $100-million centralized processing system and led the implementation team.
- Developed the plan for centralized support, systems management and operation of an advanced 1,200-branch client server banking platform.
- Directed the design and implementation of a fault-tolerant unattended operation for a secure Internet server complex that provided public key encryption for online banking and brokerage. Achieved 100% availability.
- Led the tactical planning team to re-evaluate effectiveness of line functions that resulted in 10% reassignment of staff to support new services.
- Contributed to executive task forces to set out strategies for systems management in change control, performance and capacity.
- Handled project management of data centre relocations, technology support integration, complex technology upgrades and automation.
- Forged strong vendor relationships for effective acquisitions and influenced vendor development directions to support the technical vision.
- Refocused and restructured the implementation of a faltering project to relocate the print, insertion, cheque and operations units to two new sites.
- Project managed a five-year outsourcing agreement valued at $12 million.
- Led design team of service-based organization to produce an 18-month program of interrelated projects to improve business operations with an estimated cost savings of $3 million annually.

CAREER PATH

John Smith, IT Technical & Strategic Consulting	2002–Present
Traditional Bank, Head Office	1981–2002
VP, Security Risk Evaluations & Research	2001–2002
VP, Telecommunications & Technical Services	1999–2001
AGM, Host Planning & Hardware Services	1994–1999
AGM, Systems Development Research	1989–1994
Prior to 1989, progressive management positions with Traditional Bank.	

Sample Full Biography

John Smith

John Smith's career spans over 20 years of broad experience in aligning technical strategy to organizational goals for the Financial Services—Information Technology sector. He successfully applies outstanding analytical and intuitive skills to drive complex, interrelated projects to completion. With an excellent track record of leading specialized teams, his diverse expertise encompasses software, hardware, planning, project management and operational architectures for highly available and mission-critical systems. Committed to leveraging existing technology, John provides crucial insight to the business value of new technologies and their best utilization to maximize return on investment. He brings an ability to foster vendor relationships that moves outsourcing to the level of synergistic partnerships.

With the launch of his consulting practice, John has provided expertise in IT solutions to Integrated Processors, Regency Limited and Paradigm International. Assignments have included an 18-month program of interrelated projects to improve operational effectiveness through technological innovation with a projected cost savings of $3 million annually. He also salvaged a five-year outsourcing agreement valued at $12 million, and project-managed a data centre closure that was at risk of cancellation.

As a Vice President at Traditional Bank, John combined his accumulated knowledge gathered from previous positions in line management, technical, strategic and executive responsibilities to lead the technical strategic vision for the $100-million centralized processing initiative. He also directed the design and implementation team for a fault-tolerant and secure Internet server complex for online banking and brokerage. In earlier roles he directed the integration of computer operations and technical support following the acquisition of Major Trust Co., delivering over $9 million in savings and exceeding expectations for schedule and transparency to end users.

John's quick grasp of an organization's priorities and challenges and his ability to negotiate, mentor and lead with finesse have made him an ideal choice to work with internal teams, vendors and senior executives in pursuit of key deliverables.

8910 Main Street, Toronto, Ontario M1X X1X

Bus: 416-555-1212   Fax: 416-555-1212   email: jsmith@isp.ca

Sample Abbreviated Biographies

John Smith, IT Technical and Strategic Consulting

With over 20 years' experience in aligning technical strategy to organizational goals, John's expertise encompasses software, hardware, planning, project management and operational architecture for highly available and mission-critical systems in the financial services sector. John is committed to leveraging existing technology and analyzing the business value of new technology to maximize ROI.

Consulting assignments with three major financial services companies have included a program of interrelated projects to improve operational effectiveness, delivering savings of $3 million annually; the successful management of an at-risk outsourcing project worth $12 million; and the refocusing of a faltering data centre closure. As a VP at Traditional Bank, John led a $100-million centralized processing initiative, implemented a secure Internet server for online services and led the technical integration of Major Trust Co.

John Smith: Visionary IT executive with over 20 years' experience in management and technical roles in financial services. Working with high availability and mission-critical systems focuses on strategic alignment of technology to organizational goals by implementing major initiatives including centralized processing, secure electronic banking solutions and acquisition integrations. Expert in leveraging existing technology and maximizing ROI from new technologies.

Sample Brochure

A professional-looking, three-fold brochure printed on both sides of a standard, letter-size page is easily produced using your computer software.

When folded for presentation or mailing, the contact information should be displayed clearly. Including a photograph is optional, but doing so adds a personal touch to the image and makes you look more established.

Pay attention to the order in which the reader will see your information. As the text unfolds, literally, a logical thought progression should roll out.

The following two pages show the layout of the brochure as it would come off your printer. Reproduce it two-sided and fold neatly.

JOHN SMITH

IT Technical and
Strategic Consulting

Business: (416) 555-1212
jsmith@isp.ca

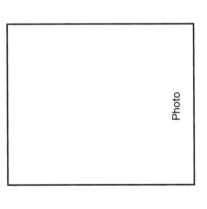

Photo

Address: 8910 Main Street
Toronto, ON M1X 1X1

Business: (416) 555-1212
Fax: (416) 555-1212
email: jsmith@isp.ca

PROFILE

IT EXECUTIVE EXPERIENCED IN ALIGNING TECHNICAL STRATEGY TO ORGANIZATIONAL GOALS. APPLIES EXCELLENT INTUITIVE AND ANALYTICAL SKILLS TO CREATE PROGRAMS OF INTERRELATED, REALIZABLE PROJECTS FOCUSED ON THE STRATEGIC VISION.

SUCCESSFUL IN DRIVING TO IMPLEMENTATION PROJECTS THAT BUILD UPON AND EXTEND EXISTING FOUNDATIONS IN TECHNOLOGY AND ORGANIZATIONAL STRUCTURE TO REALIZE BUSINESS SOLUTIONS.

JOHN HAS BROAD EXPERTISE IN SOFTWARE, HARDWARE AND PLANNING, WITH EXTENSIVE EXPERIENCE IN PROJECT MANAGEMENT AND OPERATIONAL ARCHITECTURES FOR HIGH AVAILABILITY, MISSION-CRITICAL SYSTEMS.

BACKGROUND

John Smith's career spans over 20 years in the Financial Services Information Technology sector, advancing to executive responsibility for the support, architectures and strategies for operating software, databases and national networks of a $250-billion Canadian bank.

John's broad experience encompasses:

- applying emerging technologies for business benefit
- management of operational support for mission-critical systems
- strategic planning for transaction delivery systems
- organization integration of IT technical support and operations
- project management of complex initiatives

Recent research has involved:

- development productivity
- secure networks
- public key cryptography
- secure electronic transactions (SET)
- advanced systems management

SERVICES OFFERED

☑ Development of technical strategies for centralized systems supporting business directions.

☑ Articulating strategic directions for IT systems management and operation.

☑ Directing the planning, organization and implementation of hcomplex technical projects.

☑ IT program development of interrelated initiatives to support business and IT strategies.

☑ Leadership in developing technical operational architectures and designs for mission-critical systems.

☑ Development and direction of projects to integrate IT operations, data centres and support organizations, following mergers and acquisitions.

☑ Outsourcing projects and developmeofthe service management relationship processes.

GUIDING PRINCIPLES

Information Technology strategy serves the purpose of providing a business with a vision of how technology assets will support the corporate goals.

Information Technology strategy supports business solutions by enabling sound investments in technology assets that provide full value for their expected economic life.

Information Technology strategy is successful when it leverages the skills of the organization to manage, operate and support the delivery of the business function.

Availability and extensiveness of technologies are becoming critical success factors for businesses in achieving their financial and corporate goals. These vital systems require architectures, robust designs and skilled support as components of any strategy.

Go Beyond What's Expected

Think creatively about different ways to make your brand occupy space in your contacts' minds. People usually need to receive a message more than once before they remember it in full. Your task is to illustrate your value proposition to your contacts in as many ways as possible while enhancing your image. Every communication must be valuable to the recipient. Your message must be meaningful and its delivery appropriate.

Do the preliminary work now. Develop additional marketing materials that exemplify your brand. As you meet prospective employers or clients and develop an understanding of their issues and concerns, you can tweak your materials to specifically address topics that are relevant to them. Once the original work is completed, it is easy to make adjustments. When your schedule fills up with networking sessions and interviews, your stockpile of materials will stand you in good stead.

Use some of the following suggestions to create additional marketing materials that go beyond the résumé and communicate your brand.

Write Case Studies

A powerful way to communicate your value proposition is through case studies. Use the accomplishment stories that you have already recorded and transformed into bullet points on your résumé. Choose the stories that most clearly illustrate what you want to do next and develop several of them more fully. Write each case study using a visual layout that will engage your reader and make your key points clear.

A Director of Learning and Development from a government agency took one of his accomplishment stories from his résumé and created a case study from it. This is how the accomplishment story appeared on his résumé:

> • *Rebuilt leadership training as a multi-faceted curriculum that incorporated practical functions linked to corporate objectives as well as self-development and leadership theory. Designed programs on consistent foundational principles, tailored to the different needs of executives and managers. In-sourced training, reducing cost by 20% while allowing twice as many people to participate.*

The case study that he prepared as a separate handout is presented on the next page. Notice how the compelling title, the outline in the left-hand column and the highlighted results make the content clear and engaging.

HEADACHE #1
Disconnected, Inaccessible and Expensive
Leadership Development Program
In Need of Transformation

The Challenge	• The head office of this government agency outsourced one-off leadership development training to an expensive external supplier. Only executives and a small, select group of senior managers were eligible, leaving frontline and middle managers with either no training or limited access to in-house workshops that were ad hoc and dated. • None of the training opportunities were linked to the others; nor were they linked to the organization's objectives.
The Obstacles	• Championing leadership development as part of succession planning. • Securing the involvement of busy executives. • Cost constraints. • Securing feedback from busy participants and their supervisors.
The Actions	• Created a leadership development program—*The Leadership Advantage*—that was consistent, current and employed the same foundational pieces for executives and managers alike. • Built client support for a comprehensive learning curriculum. • Rounded out leadership development to include not only self-development and leadership theory but practical everyday management skills so that development was linked to business objectives. • Pioneered the involvement of senior executives in design, delivery and dialogue. • Tracked success through evaluations before, during and after delivery.
The Results	• *The Leadership Advantage* **scored excellent evaluation results—4.5 out of 5 on overall feedback from 100 participants.** • **Training costs were reduced by 20 % and twice as many people were able to take advantage of the training.** • Direct impact on the business. To quote one key leader: "I learned how to change the way we work by creating a common goal for a project and improving the communication between team members. This led to the creation of a new production methodology that **brought our next project in at 15% below budgeted expenses and on time for the first time in 5 years."**
The Lessons	• Getting the attention of senior executives requires bold but astute behaviours. • Having a framework is critical. The CEO and all executives must buy into the leadership principles. • Metrics are essential. Leadership development must be tangibly linked to business results. **Metrics are easy to create but challenging to implement, requiring processes that demand discipline and tenacity.** • To deliver training efficiently, be judicious. Research best practices for each endeavour. Eliminate the middle person where it makes sense.

Develop a List of Relevant Activities

If your work involves a series of activities, the size and scope of which define your level of competence, list them on a separate document that you attach to your résumé or dispatch separately. This could be a list of acquisitions, ads, new products, publications, presentations, board appointments, financial transactions or anything else that relates to your value proposition. Such a list can powerfully illustrate the quantity and scope of your experience. Some or all of these activities will also be mentioned in your résumé, necessitating the use of good judgment regarding the distribution of the list.

Create a format for the list and use it consistently.

A banker developed a list of deals such as these:

$115 million — acquisition financing for the purchase of a licensed laboratory by a provincial health ministry	*2006*
$950 million —facility for the construction of a shopping mall	*2005*

Create a Portfolio

Portfolios are most often used by people whose product is better appreciated visually. They are a necessity for some job seekers as well as some contractors and consultants. Samples of writing, web sites, art, training materials, drawings, design boards, print ads and the like should be collected and displayed online, on a CD, or in a binder of photographs or print materials.

The standards for portfolios are usually well known in the fields or professions where they are commonly used. To develop yours, follow these guidelines:

- Develop your portfolio with your audience in mind, and include a broad sampling of items. You might be surprised by what interests them.
- Know what's in your portfolio and have a plan for how you will walk your prospective client or employer through it.
- If presenting your portfolio requires the use of any technology, arrive at your destination early and make sure that everything works.
- Display every item in the best possible way. Don't take shortcuts in presentation.

A CIO who was very active in industry associations and had received a significant amount of public attention for her excellent work created a unique portfolio. She compiled a booklet with six separate sections containing written materials describing her accomplishments. The sections were: case studies written by vendors, press releases, client testimonials, industry presentations, newspaper and magazine articles and awards. This booklet, which she entitled "Industry Profile," strengthened her brand positioning.

Display Your Awards

If you have won one or more awards, prepare a document that shows them off. Use the logos of the award-granting organizations and include dates, the title of the award and a very brief description if necessary. Use colour and make the document as artistic as possible. Convert it to a PDF file so that it transmits without alteration. Don't forget to put your name and email address somewhere on the document.

Design a Creative Introductory or Leave-Behind Piece

An unexpected, eye-catching marketing piece might be appropriate for you. This could take the form of an item that you send in advance of a meeting or leave behind as you say goodbye. It could be something sent by email or delivered. If you use this medium, make it meaningful. It must communicate your value proposition and be consistent with your image.

A marketing executive created a small laminated piece, the appearance and size of a playing card. One side of the card displayed the number "7," and the letter "X." The other side contained this marketer's seven points for building "X-traordinary Value." This card was an effective means of reminding contacts of the key points the marketing executive made during their conversations.

An experienced salesperson who constantly used metaphors in conversation would follow up meetings with contacts by emailing them a personalized cartoon that would serve as a reminder of their conversation. For example, if the job-seeking salesperson had compared the market to a jungle and the successful sales manager to a lion hunter, he would dispatch a note containing a picture of his face superimposed on a character dressed for a safari complete with pith helmet and rifle. The message regarding his potential contribution to the organization was clear.

This type of marketing material is not for everyone. If you use it, be sure that it does not come across as contrived.

Consider a Web Site

The value of having a web site varies dramatically from one industry to another. It also differs given various roles within industries. Your return on investment and the expectations and viewing habits of your target audience should be the deciding factors. You need to constantly stay in touch with your market niche and find out what your competition is doing. If your competitors have web sites, you need one.

For most traditional job seekers, designing a web site is not an efficient use of time and energy. That said, web sites are a must for web developers, multimedia designers or for those in other occupations where having a personal site is a means of demonstrating the ability to create one. Many IT, communications, public relations, advertising and marketing specialists need a web site as a venue for displaying their portfolios.

Tip: Recruiters and potential employers will probably check you out online. What they find, or don't find, contributes to your image. A personal web site that showcases your accomplishments can be a powerful marketing tool.

Anyone considering an entrepreneurial venture—whether it's establishing a consulting practice or starting a business—should have a web site. It's tantamount to being in the phone book. For businesses, the high expectation of quality and interactivity makes it difficult to know what level of investment makes sense. Seeking expert advice is a prudent step.

The varied need for web sites is exemplified by two next-door neighbours who operate sole proprietorships from their home offices. One of the entrepreneurs, a financial counsellor, has only her contact information and service offerings on a very simple web page that was created at minimal cost. She is convinced that her site is sufficient for her needs. If she were to provide a value-added service for her clients on her web site, she would need to develop inordinately expensive interactive models, which would undermine her commitment to personalized service. In contrast, her neighbour, a real estate broker, could not do his job without a top-quality web site. He needs real-time information and the best virtual touring capabilities to work effectively with his clients in the timing-sensitive environment of residential real estate. Fortunately, his wife has a talent for technology and is constantly upgrading her design and programming skills along with her husband's site.

Tip: The design and programming of web sites has shifted from something that everyone was doing to a very sophisticated skill. If you create a web site, ensure that its quality is good.

Send Handwritten Notes

Handwritten notes are a refreshing alternative to email messages and formal business letters. This form of correspondence is not for everyone, but if you are comfortable with it, handwritten notes are noticed and appreciated. They are particularly useful for brief thank-you notes or as an attachment to an enclosure.

Blank, single-fold note cards from any greeting card store are sufficient for this purpose. Similar cards with the words "Thank You" are also an appropriate choice. If you want to go one step up, have your name and/or the name of your operating entity printed on the front of a note card and on memo pads. The design should be consistent with your look, and you'll need matching envelopes for the note cards. You will probably need to find a specialty printer for this job. Give them samples of your other materials and check the proof carefully.

A woman who had extensive experience managing manufacturing facilities found the perfect combination of two of the marketing strategies mentioned above. She came across a greeting card with a reprint of a cartoon from The New Yorker *that depicted her independent style and reputation for getting things done. It also subtly acknowledged the fact that she occupied a role that was unusual for a woman. She bought as many of the cards as she could find and judiciously used them to send handwritten thank-you notes to her contacts.*

Tip: When sending handwritten notes, write briefly and legibly. Address the envelope by hand to ensure that it does not get discarded as junk mail before it's opened. Small envelopes bearing an address label and delivered by regular mail often contain unsolicited correspondence.

Consider carefully the mediums that are appropriate for you and choose wisely from the communication options that have been suggested.

During a frustrating period of unemployment, a database manager rented a large billboard at a busy intersection in the business district, advertising his skills and contact information. An out-of-work training specialist stood at an LRT exit, handing out flyers that asked for help with his employment search. Another anxious job seeker walked around the downtown core wearing a sandwich board outlining his project management capabilities. None of these tactics is recommended. They create an image of desperation.

You will find many opportunities to hand out or send copies of your materials as your job search progresses. They will become invaluable when you need to make additional contact with the people in your target market. You will be glad that you took the time to write them and produce them with a look that suits your image.

Chapter 12

Interview for Success

*It is not always the most qualified person who gets the job;
it's the one who does the best job in the interview.*

Everything you have done to this point in the career transition process is going to be put to the test during interviews. Preparing thoroughly for interviews affords you the opportunity to see if the way you describe yourself and your accomplishments substantiates your targets. It also gives you a checkpoint to test whether you are headed for an opportunity that fits your ideal. Once prepared, you can go into any interview, confidently expecting it to be the culmination of all your efforts.

When you have been selected for an interview, be assured that you have met the hiring organization's preliminary skills and experience requirements. As you enter the interview process, the audience is on your side. The interviewer is hoping that you will be the right candidate for the position so that they can successfully conclude their search and bring a qualified and well-suited person on board. The interviewer's goal will be to verify that your qualifications and experience meet the hiring specifications, and that your style, personality and other attributes will be a fit with the chemistry and culture of the organization.

Interviewing is a two-way street. While the interviewer is judging your suitability, you will be evaluating the position, the organization and the people. As you move through the interview process, you need to ascertain whether or not the content of the job meets your criteria. Both the position and the organization must also meet *your* needs and expectations regarding values, interests and career goals.

Preparation for the Interview

The prerequisites for doing well in interviews include knowing your strategic advantage, having clear criteria for your ideal job, preparing an accomplishment-focused résumé and doing thorough research. If you have given any of these areas short shrift, go back and work on them now. If you have done your homework so far, you're ready to prepare your verbal presentation.

To be completely ready to interview with confidence, you must understand the process and anticipate the interviewer's objectives and questions. You need to plan and practise your responses. This can present a challenge if you're out of practice. Many people haven't been interviewed for a job outside their organization for years. Even if you have changed jobs within your organization, those interviews are often merely friendly formalities.

Be cautious of being overly confident if you are experienced at interviewing others. Switching to the other side of the table requires a different mindset. There are numerous styles and approaches to interviewing, and you need to be flexible, attentive and prepared. Questions that you would never think of asking might be posed, and an unfamiliar format might be used. Don't let false confidence lead to a lack of preparation and a less-than-excellent performance.

The Five Sound Bites

An excellent way to prepare for interviews is to create and practise a five-part script that answers the questions most frequently asked of job seekers. This five-sound-bite method requires you to organize your thoughts and deliver your key points thoroughly yet concisely. You will plan how to present your career history, choosing which accomplishment stories to include so that every claim you make about who you are and what you can do is backed by a statement of proof from your past. Your five-sound-bite script will include your reasons for previous job changes and significant career transitions. It will dispel concerns about your current motives for seeking a new opportunity and explain how your experiences, interests and values create the rationale for the next career step you are planning to take. The five-sound-bite script offers a format for making the elements of your story congruent and therefore trustworthy. It will be most useful when you are asked, "Tell me about yourself."

Tip: The five sound bites cover most, but not all, of the topics that you must be prepared to discuss in an interview. Be sure to also read Guidelines for Special Interviewing Challenges and Inventory of Interview Questions at the end of this chapter to be completely prepared.

Although you will develop the five sound bites as an uninterrupted monologue, you will more often take the script apart and deliver its parts as stand-alone pieces when needed. By preparing and practising your sound bites as a cohesive script, you will be ready to handle an open-ended invitation to introduce yourself in an interview, and you will have a format for your opening dialogue in networking meetings and other informal conversations. The five sound bites create a mental checklist of the key points you want to cover whenever you have a chance to talk about your career plans. The sound bites include:

• Capsule Profile	30 seconds
• Key Strengths	15–30 seconds
• Career Review with Accomplishments	5–7 minutes
• Leaving Story	30 seconds–1 minute
• What Now?	1–2 minutes

Capsule Profile

This is the conversational version of the profile statement you wrote for your résumé. It includes your most recent position title, plus a very brief explanation if your title would be misleading or confusing without it. The capsule profile also states your number of years' cumulative experience, the types of industries where you have worked and, if well known, the names of specific companies. It concisely describes your functional areas, level of seniority and depth and breadth of experience. Round it out with a statement of your uniqueness or a brief description of your value proposition as a segue to the next sound bite.

The capsule profile should be developed verbally. Do not write it out first! Try different ways of phrasing it, and keep working on it out loud until the words flow naturally. Then write down what you've said: sentence fragments, vernacular, pauses and all. Rehearse frequently without looking at your notes. This sound bite should be practised frequently so that it is virtually committed to memory.

Tip: To prepare the next four sound bites, jot down only the key points. Do not write them out in full and try to deliver them from memory. That will make you sound stilted and ill at ease. Remember the outline of each sound bite and rely on verbal practice to increase your comfort level. You will find patterns of speech and phrasing that are natural and easy for you.

Key Strengths

Name three or four of your most significant strengths in concise, bullet-point form. This is your opportunity to incorporate the work you did to identify your brand. Highlight in one brief sentence how your particular combination of strengths, skills and experience work together to deliver value. Include a statement about your style or values. Focus on what you most want the interviewer to remember.

You might open with a phrase such as, "My key strengths include…" or "I excel at…." Use single words or very short phrases to fill in the blanks (e.g., "listening and understanding my client's needs, problem solving and cross-functional team leadership"). Do not give details, explanations or substantiation of any kind. You are going for impact here, and supporting examples will follow in the career review bite.

Tip: When you use the "key strengths" sound bite out of the context of the full presentation, offer brief supporting examples at the same time.

The capsule profile and the summary of key strengths need to be delivered together and should take no more than one minute in total. These two sound bites are a vital part of making a good first impression. They make a claim about who you are and what you can do.

Career Review with Accomplishments

This sound bite substantiates what you have said in the first two segments. It offers proof to support your claim. Introduce it by telling your listener where you're headed. Say, "Let me give you a brief overview of my career highlights. I'll concentrate on the last few years." Proceed chronologically, from earlier days to today, and walk briefly through the last 10 years of your career, touching on the dates, names of organizations, position titles, roles or mandates, key accomplishments and reasons for moving on. Do *not* use reverse chronological order; it's confusing to the listener.

Tip: As you explain your career history it's very important to bridge each move by giving a credible reason for it. This answers the unasked question, "Why did you leave that job or role?" It builds trust and holds the interviewer's attention.

Prepare for the career review by dividing your history into chapters. What determines chapter breaks is arbitrary. You could choose different organizations, jobs held within one organization, periods of time or separate projects. The first chapter should begin about 10 years ago. Mention earlier experiences only to the extent that they were significant in the formation of your core skills, interests or goals and are therefore meaningful today. Keep your listener oriented by giving dates and the names of organizations or departments.

Within each chapter, talk about accomplishments. Mention fewer from the beginning of the chronology unless they better exemplify what you would like to do next. Choose the stories for each interview carefully. Let the research you have done on the audience guide your selections. Tell the stories in their abridged form. Move from chapter to chapter quickly and lightly, like a stone skipping across the water. Let the interviewer choose where a more detailed explanation or discussion would be helpful.

For each accomplishment, use the Situation—Action—Result formula. If you do a good job describing the situation by including the starting point, mandate, challenges, issues, deadlines, magnitude, risks, etc., the rest of the story will flow. Ground your story in a solid rationale for action, so that the steps you took seem logical and prudent. Quantify the results whenever possible. Also include non-quantifiable results such as "improved communications," "model was used for other units," or "earned maximum bonus." Mention any feedback that you received and subsequent results. If you are struggling to identify results, the alternative is to explain what you learned from the experience. Keep this segment down to seven minutes, maximum.

Tip: Take the time to fully describe the situation as you tell an accomplishment story. Mention what might have happened if you hadn't acted. Paint a vivid "before" picture, allowing the listener to appreciate the extent of your contribution and the value of the "after" picture.

Leaving Story

For many people, explaining why they left their previous organization is a very difficult task in the career transition process. It can touch the most sensitive nerve, causing a recoil so obvious that your chance of success in the interview is ruined. The remedy involves preparation and strategic presentation.

There are three important guidelines with regards to your leaving story:
- Prepare it with utmost care.
- You broach it.
- You be comfortable with it.

The interviewer will take their level of comfort from you, and they will be relieved when it's out of the way. Most interviewers relax noticeably after you've put your leaving story on the table with an appropriate amount of detail. You have given the impression that you have nothing to hide and they don't have to worry about asking. Including it as one of your sound bites gives you a distinct advantage.

Depersonalize the story by setting it in an understandable and verifiable context. Refer your listener to well-known facts about the organization, industry, region or whatever makes sense. Talk about trends, changes in strategy or the new management focus that eroded your enthusiasm. Explain the mismatch between the organization's needs and your strengths. Work hard at making your leaving story sound like an understandable business decision that is completely acceptable to you. Keep it brief, but not too brief.

A marketing executive was hired by a highly bureaucratic, traditional organization to implement an aggressive new strategy. After three years of feeling like a pawn in the battle taking place above him, he was criticized for not fulfilling his mandate and his employment was terminated. Notwithstanding his lingering bitterness, he told his leaving story this way: "I was brought in to create a brand for the Telecom Company. We worked on several strategies based on my earlier successes with 'Brand One' and 'Brand Two.' As yet Telecom has not chosen to move forward on any of the options. It became clear to me and to them that my approach did not match their vision. We agreed that it was best to part ways."

Invest time in developing your leaving story. Every word of it must be true. Your tone must not contain innuendo or underlying animosity, and it must not belie the positive words you've used. Practise telling your story out loud to someone from your board of advisers or support network. It is often wise to vet it through your former employer and those who will be giving references.

Never allow your leaving story to just hang there alone. After a brief but comfortable pause that implies, "You don't have any questions about that, do you?" move directly into "What now?" By sounding confident and leading your listener into your desired future, you virtually ensure that there will be no further probing or discussion of the leaving story.

What Now?

Use the final moments of your presentation to describe what you see yourself doing next. Depending on the circumstances, you can choose to stay general, speaking in terms of the skills, style and knowledge that you would like to contribute, or be specific. If you know your target precisely, mention the job title, type of organization, mandate or role you hope to find and relate them to your value proposition.

In an interview, make "What now?" sound remarkably like the opportunity at hand and refer back to what you have done in the past that proves you could add value in this situation. To be specific in a networking meeting, mention the mandate or role you seek and offer one or two hypothetical examples. Your research will allow you to tailor this sound bite to the needs of the organization and the interests of the interviewer.

Rehearse

Practising out loud is the only way to become truly comfortable with the five sound bites. After you've developed the content, put the sound bites together and rehearse them as a 5- to 10-minute presentation.

Use a video camera, tape recorder or your own voice mail as you practise and critique your delivery of the sound bites, especially your capsule profile and leaving story. You can have great conversations in your head, but when you actually say the words, your best approaches and phrases are easily forgotten.

Once you've done this, you will find it easy to use each piece separately in answer to specific questions. Some interviewers will expect you to be able to talk about yourself unprompted and uninterrupted. Most will give more direction, asking targeted questions and moving the discussion through their agenda. Regardless of what the interviewer does, with the five sound bites, you are well on your way to being prepared for any interview. You are also better prepared for networking meetings and informal chats. The sound bites, used judiciously, can pack enough useful information into any encounter to interest the listener in continuing the conversation.

Tip: Allow enough time to prepare thoroughly every time you have an interview. Do not overlook these steps or leave them to a last-minute run-through in the interviewer's reception area.

WORKSHEET 12.1
Prepare the Five Sound Bites

Capsule profile (30 seconds)

_____

_____

Key strengths (15–30 seconds)

_____

_____

Career review with accomplishments (5–7 minutes)

_____

_____

_____

_____

Leaving story (30 seconds–1 minute)

_____

_____

What now? (1–2 minutes)

_____

_____

Tip: What many people call an "elevator speech" is a condensed version of the Capsule Profile, Key Strengths and What Now sound bites combined. To prepare yours, think about how you would abbreviate these three sound bites and deliver them in an informal or spontaneous setting. Be creative with the order of the phrases and precise with your choice of words. Practise out loud and get it down to less than 30 seconds in length.

Having the sound bites developed and rehearsed is the best general preparation you can do, but you still need to anticipate and prepare for other questions. Use the following guidelines to focus your preparation for a specific interview.

GUIDELINES FOR INTERVIEW PREPARATION

- Keep working on the research. If you haven't done so already, find out everything you can about the organization. Develop a wealth of knowledge on its products, services, strategy, structure, culture, challenges, opportunities and people.
- Get as much information about the job as you possibly can. If there is a search consultant or external recruiter involved, ask them your questions. If the interviewer makes the appointment personally, keep them on the phone for a few minutes and ask some questions about the job. Get a copy of the position description if at all possible. Be creative and determined in your research.
- Use your network to find someone who holds a similar position. Ask them in detail about their responsibilities, challenges and opportunities, as well as the key characteristics necessary for success.
- Know your audience. Search executives and external recruiters will conduct the first round of interviews for their client. Human resources staff from the hiring organization might conduct a screening interview. In some cases you proceed directly to the hiring manager. Use your research and networking techniques to learn something about each person you will be meeting in the interview process. If you can discover what's important to them, all the better.
- Plan your approach. Armed with all of the information you've collected, do the following:
  - Anticipate the key skills, knowledge and personal characteristics that could be required for the job. Think about the elements of your strategic advantage that match the requirements, and bring to mind an accomplishment story that would illustrate your expertise and attributes on every point. This takes some time.
  - Include the stories arising from your work on the previous point, and refresh your memory on at least 10 to 12 unique stories from your past. Practise telling them and keep them top-of-mind, even though you may not need to recount them all.
  - Create a brief outline of the key points you want to get across in the interview. Jot them down.
  - Go through the questions found at the end of this chapter, and plan your responses with this specific opportunity in mind.
  - Think of at least three questions that you could ask each interviewer. The individual's role will determine the suitability of the questions. Jot your questions down for review immediately prior to the interview.

- – Think of at least three reasons for your interest in the opportunity and three compelling reasons for the organization to choose you for this role. Jot them down.
- Find out exactly where you're going and plan your travel route. Think about parking, walking distance and bad weather options. You don't want to arrive late or frazzled.
- Think about the dress code for the industry sector and organization. Plan to dress one step up. If in doubt, opt for conservative business dress.
- On the night before the interview, check your outfit and accessories, consume only healthy foods and beverages and get a good night's sleep.
- Take extra copies of your résumé and your jot notes for a last-minute review. Do not weigh yourself down with an over-sized briefcase.
- Do something to control your nerves and emotions before the interview. Go for a walk, do deep breathing exercises, meditate, listen to calming music if you're tense or energizing music if you're feeling low. Call someone from your support network and have them talk you into the right frame of mind.
- Remind yourself that one of your goals is to make the interviewer's job easy for them.
- Visualize yourself doing well.

Tip: If you have trouble coming up with three convincing reasons for wanting the job, it's probably not the right one for you!

During the Interview

To gain perspective, put yourself in the interviewer's shoes. The pressure of selecting a good candidate to fill a vacant position is tremendous because hiring mistakes are costly. Choosing someone who will work well and fit comfortably with the existing group is no small task. Aside from personality issues, there's a mandate that needs to be filled, and the interviewer has limited evidence regarding your abilities and potential for the role. Perhaps reminding yourself of what the interviewer is experiencing will help you stay calm.

Interviewers have different styles, attitudes and levels of skill in conducting interviews. They also have varied knowledge of the job, the key issues and the people involved. You won't know how much information, experience, training or support the person you're meeting has. There may have been plenty of time to do adequate planning, or they might be operating on-the-fly. The interviewer might disagree with the hiring approach, or it could be their pet project. They could be a seasoned veteran at conducting interviews or a complete novice.

All of this is going to have an effect on the interview, and all you can do is be alert for clues and be prepared to adjust to the situation as it unfolds. The more calm and confident you are, the better it will go. Your body language, voice quality and ability to think improve dramatically when you are relaxed. It also helps to put your interviewer at ease and reduce tension. Remain focused on the interviewer and listen carefully to the questions. Stay in the moment by concentrating fully.

Tip: Regardless of the interviewer's level of experience and effectiveness, the responsibility for explaining your qualifications and convincing the interviewer that you are the best person for the job rests on your shoulders.

In an interview you are evaluated on much more than what you say. Some communications specialists say that body language and appearance convey well over 50% of the message. Eye contact, handshake, posture, walk, facial expressions, hand gestures, nods and shrugs count. Pay attention to clothing, accessories, grooming and general health. Nervous habits such as coughing, blinking, fidgeting and throat clearing detract from the message, just as a confident, courteous, friendly and poised demeanour enhance it. How you speak is important; this includes tone, volume, diction, inflection and pace. The content of your message is of primary importance, but how you say it and the disposition you project are also crucial.

Tip: When under stress, your breathing typically becomes limited to your upper chest, making it shallow and more rapid. You can counteract this, reduce your stress level and clear your mind by taking slow deep breaths.

GUIDELINES FOR CONDUCTING THE INTERVIEW

- Turn off your cell phone and pager!
- First impressions count. Greet the interviewer with good eye contact and a firm handshake that does not inflict pain. Smile and offer a pleasant greeting. Stand tall, walk with confidence and be attentive. The first 30 seconds of your interaction with the interviewer will do a lot to set the tone of the meeting.
- Break the ice by complimenting or commenting on something. The helpful staff, the decor, the location and the view are all possibilities. If none of this suits your style, try a point of common interest or experience such as the weather, the traffic, the parking, the local team's win or the headlines, as long as it is not controversial.
- As the interview proceeds, be direct and specific in your answers. Vague generalities and unsubstantiated claims are not good enough. Offer bullet-point explanations, top-line summaries, examples from experience and informed opinions. Unless it would breach confidentiality, include factual data in your examples.
- Be concise, but don't say too little. Outgoing people often say too much, and those who are too reserved need to make an effort to provide more information. Answers to most interview questions should vary in length from 30 seconds to 4 minutes. The most important thing is that they refer strictly to the question.
- Take cues from the interviewer. If they appear bored or uninterested, condense your answer. Their interest invites you to answer fully. Make slight adjustments in your energy level, gestures, tone, volume and pace to mirror the interviewer. Don't mimic.

- Sell your skills and abilities as they relate to the job by talking about accomplishments using the Situation—Action—Result formula.
- If you are concerned that an answer hasn't hit the mark, check it out. It's acceptable to ask the interviewer, "Did I answer the question?" or "Is there anything else that you would like to know?"
- The interviewer might be taking detailed, even verbatim notes as you speak. This can be very disconcerting, but understand that it is often part of the process. If your answers are to be scored, the interviewer will need to defend the scores with specific quotes from you.
- Keep thinking about inflection, expressions and body language as you speak. Don't slouch or assume too casual a posture in the way you sit.
- Listen for expressions, phrases and recurring themes. Pick them up and use them judiciously in your answers. Overuse will sound contrived.
- Look for opportunities to insert evidence of your research into your answers.
- Do not ask about remuneration. The interviewer will raise the topic when they are ready. The only exceptions would be if you suspect that you are well out of their range or you have another written offer with a deadline for response.
- Remember your agenda for the interview. If the interviewer's questions have not provided an opportunity to get your points across, mention them before the interview ends.
- As the interview closes, try to find the opportunity to summarize your key strengths and qualifications, and restate your interest in the job.
- When the interviewer makes it obvious that time is up, stop talking! End with a thank-you, and ask what the next steps are and in what time frame.
- Stand up when the interviewer stands. Smile, shake hands and leave.

Tip: One of the most common mistakes made in interviews is forgetting to smile. Smiling eases tension, conveys enthusiasm and indicates genuine interest. Very few people overdo smiling.

Debrief after the Interview

Before you do anything else, head for the nearest coffee shop and take the time to debrief by writing down notes about the interview. If you wait until you've made the trip home, the details of the meeting could be lost. Capture your thoughts and impressions while they are fresh in your mind. Use the following worksheet to debrief thoroughly. Your notes will help you compose the thank-you letter and will provide a valuable refresher when you return for a subsequent interview.

WORKSHEET 12.2
Debriefing after the Interview

- What did I learn about the position, the manager, the organization and the industry?

- What important details were mentioned? Sales targets? Project mandates? Relationships?

- What do the key qualifications for the role appear to be?

- How well does the position fit my skills and interests?

- What aspect of my skills, experience and knowledge appeared to be of most interest?

- Was there anything that seemed to concern the interviewer?

- What did the interviewer say about the organization's strategy, opportunities and challenges?

- What else do I need to know about the position, manager, organization or industry?

- What went particularly well in the interview?

- What aspects of my interviewing technique need more work?

- What questions did I have difficulty answering?

- What questions were new to me?

- What questions did I ask and what were the answers?

- What was my impression of the interviewer? The position? The company?

- What questions could I ask the next time I interview at this organization?

- What are the next steps? When do I expect to hear from them and when should I call?

Follow Up

Write a thank-you letter immediately. Ideally, you should send it within 24 hours of the interview. This gesture can make a significant difference in your chances of landing the job. Busy interviewers will be surprised and appreciative of your efforts, and by writing you can reinforce or add important information. You could enclose one of your case studies to emphasize your suitability for the role. Guidelines for writing interview thank-you letters are offered in Chapter 13.

At the end of the interview and in your thank-you letter, expectations have been established regarding the next steps in the process. Call the external recruiter where appropriate or the interviewer on the date that was agreed, or in the absence of a specific date, call in about one week's time. Restate your interest in the position and ask how the selection process is going. If necessary, you can leave a voice mail message. Keep all anxiety and impatience out of your voice. Use a friendly and upbeat tone. Make a diary note to do a further follow-up if necessary.

Tip: By following up with tactful persistence you offer the potential employer concrete evidence of how interested you are in the job. Careful follow-up efforts will demonstrate that you are self-reliant, thorough, courteous and organized. Calling too often makes you look desperate. Use your best judgment.

Six Different Types of Interviews

Skilled practitioners identify several types of interviews or formats for conducting interviews. The six most commonly used are described below. However, rather than adopting one particular format, most interviewers use a combination. For example, a structured interview may include some behavioural or situational questions. By understanding each format individually, you will be well equipped to handle any shift in questioning style.

The Behavioural Interview

Behavioural interviews are designed to solicit specific and detailed examples from your background that are relevant to the position being discussed. This interview format is based on the premise that past behaviour is the most accurate predictor of future behaviour. This concept and method of interviewing has become fundamental for evaluating candidates.

An interviewer's preparation for behavioural questions involves analyzing the requirements of the position and noting the skills and attributes of individuals who have excelled in this or similar positions in the past. Doing this establishes a benchmark for each of the behaviours selected for review. Questions are designed that will draw out illustrations of how the candidate has used these skills and attributes. The questions will cover a broad spectrum of topics and will begin with phrases such as:

- "Tell me about a time when …"
- "Give me an example of …"
- "Have you ever had to deal with …?"

The behavioural interview is the perfect venue for your accomplishment stories. As you would with any interview, anticipate the requirements for the job and bring to mind the stories from your past that demonstrate your qualifications on each point. Every accomplishment story can be told in a way that emphasizes the particular skill or style being questioned. You can use a story more than once by referring to it and highlighting a different aspect. The challenge is remembering and telling the stories clearly, succinctly and with sufficient detail to make your point.

Tip: In this format in particular, the interviewer will expect you to take a few moments to select, recall and think through your answer. Take the time you need. It will make a substantial difference in the quality of your answer.

In behavioural interviews that are well planned, you might encounter questions that seem to be asking for the same information repeatedly. This could indicate that the interviewer is looking for a mix of both recent and long-standing behaviours that would hold the greatest predictive value. Questions that seem repetitive might also be probing for contrary evidence. To get a balanced view of your competence, a skilled interviewer will look for both positive and negative experiences or a variety of methods and approaches to situations. Be patient with the process and vary your examples.

A sampling of behavioural questions includes:
- "Tell me about a time when you had to use your political savvy to advance a controversial project."
- "Tell me about an experience in your career that you found to be particularly frustrating."
- "What role do you typically assume when working with a team of peers? Give me an example."
- "Please give me an example of your persuasiveness."
- "Tell me about a time when you had to deal with a subordinate whose performance was below standard."
- "Please describe the most disappointing experience of your career."
- "What was the most significant decision you had to make in this past year? Tell me how you made it and what the result was."

Tip: When answering behavioural questions, be clear about why the situation was important to the organization. Explain the context, issues, obstacles and dynamics concisely yet thoroughly. What would have happened if you hadn't acted? Doing this will hold the interviewer's attention and allow them to appreciate the result.

The Situational Interview
The situational interview is based on the premise that intentions are the best predictor of future behaviour. The questions in a situational interview are constructed using hypothetical, but very specific, job dilemmas, situations or case studies. You are asked to think through a problem and explain specifically what you would do under the circumstances.

Situational interviewing shifts the focus of the interview from what you have done in the past to how you might apply your knowledge and experience in future situations. If situational interview questions are well constructed, there should be no apparent correct answer, thereby limiting the risk of the candidate saying only what they think the interviewer wants to hear. You have to put yourself in the situation and be completely honest. This technique enables the interviewer to uncover a wealth of information.

The process of designing the cases used in the situational interview format is often very intensive for the organization. Several critical requirements of the job are selected. Realistic scenarios are then developed by asking experienced employees how they would respond in these situations. Their answers will elicit the qualities and skills that interviewers will be looking for in an answer. A scoring system is established to evaluate how close each candidate's answer comes to the benchmark response.

Preparation for situational interviews is difficult because the potential scenarios are innumerable and unpredictable. Sometimes they are completely unrelated to the job itself. They are designed to assess style, values and motivation as well as specific skills. Solid research, analysis and understanding of the requirements of the job are imperative. It's also helpful to review your accomplishments with a focus on how you prefer to work and which situations you are most comfortable in. The key to success is an honest, straightforward description of what you would actually do in the situation described.

GUIDELINES FOR ANSWERING SITUATIONAL INTERVIEW QUESTIONS
- As you begin your answer, state your desired outcomes.
- Be clear about any assumptions that you are making.
- Explain as clearly as possible the steps that you would take or what you would say.
- Detail how you would mobilize people and resources, if appropriate.
- Outline some of the obstacles you would expect to encounter or different directions the situation might take and explain how you would deal with them.
- Explore alternative solutions along with your primary answer.
- Give your rationale for the moves that you would make.
- Sum up your solution and explain how you would take action to prevent the situation from happening again, if that is appropriate.
- Mention any follow-up that you would do.

An early-retired bank branch manager decided that he would take a shot at fulfilling his lifelong dream of becoming a tour bus driver. He got his licence and did his research. When he had identified a company that was hiring, he landed an interview and began to prepare for it in earnest. His career transition consultant challenged him with this scenario to prepare him for situational questions: "You are returning to Ottawa along Highway 417 with a full load of passengers. It's after midnight and suddenly your bus breaks down. The passengers begin to get panicky, spurred on by one individual who feels short of breath and mentions chest pains. How would you handle the situation?"

After working through his responses to this and several other scenarios, he went into the interview with confidence. A situational question similar to the breakdown story was posed, and he handled it with ease. He got the job!

The Structured Interview

Structured interviews use a pre-selected series of questions that solicit an overview of your style and background. In an effort to be equitable, every candidate will be asked the same questions in the same order. Some interviewers using this format will pose carefully constructed questions based on the job description and others will use a random sampling of their tried-and-true favourites. The structured interview could include conventional, behavioural and situational interview-type questions. A consistent characteristic of structured interviews is that the interviewer takes control of the session, leaving you little independent opportunity to deliver your convincing points.

A sampling of conventional questions includes:
- "Tell me about yourself."
- "What sort of opportunities and challenges are you hoping to have in your next role?"
- "What are your strengths?"
- "What are your weaknesses?"
- "Why did you leave your last position?"
- "Where do you see yourself in three years? In five?"
- "How would you describe your management, leadership or team style?"
- "What interests you about this position?"
- "What do you know about the organization or the position?"
- "Why should we hire you?"

You have a two-part challenge in structured interviews. First, you need to be prepared to answer the conventional questions. Your reflective work and research plus your advance preparation of the five sound bites should make this easy. Second, you must be able to interject sufficient information to prove your suitability for the position if the questions posed do not offer the opportunity. The preparation of your accomplishment stories should stand you in good stead. Use them whenever you can. If you are frustrated in your attempts to put your points forward, your chance might come when the interviewer asks a question like, "What have I missed?" or "What else should I know about you?" Another opportunity could arise when you are invited to ask questions. At that time, first make your points using a concise, bullet-point style and then ask your questions.

The Unstructured Interview

In an unstructured interview, the interviewer asks only a few pre-selected questions and offers minimal direction while you do most of the talking. The interviewer might start with a conversational approach such as, "I'll let you start by telling me about yourself," or "Tell me about your work over at Environmental Company." They might pick up on elements of what you say and use them as the basis for further questions, or they might remain silent after you have stopped speaking to see where you take the conversation. It can be a daunting experience.

Another mark of the unstructured interview is the stroll down tangential avenues. The interviewer might chat about people or events that are interesting but bear no apparent relevance to your qualifications or to the available position. The interviewer might also talk too much, making it difficult for you to get a word in edgewise. However, this could prove helpful, especially if they describe the organization or the position in depth and this interview is one of a series within the organization.

Sometimes very skilled interviewers will test your ability to perform under pressure and adapt to unexpected circumstances by using an unstructured format. They could also be using the format as a calculated method of assessing your level of preparation, research or genuine interest in the position. Unfortunately, unstructured interviews are also popular with interviewers who haven't had the time or training to prepare properly.

The challenge for you is recognizing when you need to bring some structure to the session and determining how to do that. When it appears that things won't get on track without your intervention, offer to tell the interviewer about something you believe to be pertinent. For example, "Would it be helpful if I summarized my experience at Environmental Company?" You could also use one or more of your sound bites, watching the interviewer carefully for their reaction.

Another technique for handling the unstructured interview is for you to ask the key questions and then, upon hearing the answers, offer evidence from your past that qualifies you on those points. For example, ask, "What are the major human resources challenges facing the client group at this time?" When the answer is "Retention," tell your story about implementing recruiting and orientation policies to reduce turnover by 25%.

Other questions that you might pose in your efforts to discover the salient points include:
- "What do you see as being the key mandate for this role?"
- "If I were successful in getting this job, how could I add the greatest value to this organization?"
- "What are the important characteristics needed to be successful in this job?"
- "What leadership, management or team style do you think would be the most effective in this role?"
- "What will the roadblocks be for the person who accepts this mandate?"

In each instance, use the answer as a lead-in for one of your main points and accomplishment stories. Be vigilant in watching for signs that the interviewer wants to reclaim control of the process. You don't want to hijack the session.

It is not easy to take control of an interview that seems to be disjointed, but the responsibility to present your background and skills is yours alone. You need to persuade the interviewer that you are the ideal candidate for the position by giving factual data to prove your qualifications, even when it is not solicited.

The Panel Interview
Panel interviews involve more than one interviewer meeting a candidate at one time. There might be a large number of interviewers or as few as two. This format was once limited to use by the public sector, institutions, non-profit organizations and boards of directors, but it has become much more widespread. Panel interviews are efficient for the organization and effective in providing an equitable venue for job candidates. They also create more internal support for the successful candidate.

The challenge for you is to determine who will be on the panel, their titles and their roles. Use your network to learn something about each member's priorities and focus, and identify the decision-makers and most influential members. It will take a lot of digging, and you may not be able to get complete information. Often, the person who is organizing the interview is an excellent source of information, regardless of the seniority of their position.

Tip: Do not let the number of interviewers on the panel affect your poise and concentration. No matter how many interviewers you face, you will still answer only one question at a time.

Sometimes you will not know in advance that you will be in a panel interview. In other circumstances you may be given a package of material about the job and the organization. You might be asked to prepare and present something for the panel. Do your homework thoroughly.

Unless they are structured solely around your presentation, panel interviews ideally use a carefully constructed series of questions, asked in turn by pre-selected members of the panel. The organization should have appointed someone as a moderator to keep the process moving smoothly. The reality is that panel interviews are not always well planned or moderated. They can easily become disjointed as individual panel members show off their interviewing styles, ask their favourite questions and pursue their own agendas. As always, prepare by anticipating the organization's needs and have your key points in mind.

Once you are in the interview, do your best to create rapport. Time will be limited and the group may want to dispense with the informalities. Use your best judgment. The questions will not differ from those used in any of the other interview formats. The following guidelines will help.

GUIDELINES FOR A PANEL INTERVIEW

- Prepare in the same way you would for any other interview, with the added task of learning something about each panel member, if possible, and preparing a presentation if required.
- Don't start the interview by making jokes about how intimidating the situation feels. Be confident and your confidence will show.
- Try to commit the names and positions of the panel members to memory before the interview. When you are introduced at the start of the session, do everything you can to remember who's who, including jotting down names as the interviewers are introduced, if that seems appropriate.
- As you answer questions, it's very impressive to call a panel member by name, but do this only if you have all their names clearly in mind. Don't make mistakes! Err on the side of caution.
- When a question is being posed, look at the person speaking as if they are the only one in the room, and begin your answer by speaking directly to them. As you speak, make eye contact with every other person, finishing with the original questioner.
- If you have done your job in discovering the panel members' individual priorities, and you have been able to catch who's who in the room, look directly at the person to whom the question really matters when you know you are dealing with a sensitive issue.
- Don't be thrown by panel members' neutral expressions. They might have been told to try to control their expressions so as not to lead or influence you in any way.
- You might see signs of internal politics and power plays as panel members vie for air time and react

to one another. Take mental note of the interactions, but don't let them distract you. Remain calm and focused. Take care to continue addressing the panel members with equal eye contact.

- Do not hesitate to ask questions when invited to do so. Address your question to a specific person by looking at them as you speak.
- Don't forget to smile!
- Thank the panel as the session ends. Unless it's a very large group, close the interview by shaking hands with each person.

The Non-Interview

Outside of preparing for formal interview situations, it is crucial to understand that you are always on stage. Whether you are considering a career change or not, your colleagues, superiors and external contacts are constantly collecting information regarding your competence and style. When you are confident with who you are and what you're doing this should be an encouraging thought.

The best preparation for the ever-present non-interview is to be working at something that suits your strategic advantage and make personal and professional development a lifelong quest. Be continually conscious of how your words and actions affect others, and be clear and honest in putting your ideas forward. Even in the most challenging circumstances, you can say what you think as long as you separate the people from the issues and substantiate what you say. You don't have to be right all the time, but you do need to base your stance on solid experience, research, analysis and judgment.

Special Interviewing Challenges

Telephone Interviews

- Hiring organizations and recruiters are increasing their use of telephone interviews because they are an efficient means of screening applicants for a position, and they are practical when a candidate lives at a distance. They are often conducted by someone other than the hiring manager.
- Your primary goal in a telephone interview is to be invited to an in-person interview.
- If you are called unexpectedly, don't hesitate to ask to reschedule the interview at a more convenient time if taking the call means you might be rushed or interrupted.
- If you can take the call, give yourself a moment to collect your thoughts by asking the caller to hold for a moment while you move to another phone or close your office door.
- When a telephone interview is scheduled, prepare for it just as you would for an in-depth, face-to-face interview. Any of the six different types of interviews could be used. Your advantage will be the opportunity to have your preparatory notes in front of you during the call.
- Conduct the interview in a calm, quiet place that is free of distractions. Focus completely on the interview. Do not multi-task.
- Keep in mind that without visual clues, the interviewer is relying entirely on your tone of voice, diction and speed of conversation to get a sense of your personality and level of interest in the position.
    - Make a conscious effort to sound upbeat and enthusiastic.

- Put a smile in your voice by actually smiling. It works.
- Stand up to increase your confidence and sound more powerful.
- Don't smoke, chew gum, eat food or drink anything but water, and that only as needed, not out of nervousness.
- Relax. Breathe deeply and speak clearly and purposefully.
- Get the correct spelling of the interviewer's name and contact information.
- Debrief following the interview and dispatch a thank-you letter just as you would for an in-person interview.

When to Broach Your Leaving Story

- Be aware that the interviewer might already know your circumstances through conversation with the search firm or a few well-placed phone calls before the interview.
- If the interview starts with an open invitation such as, "Tell me about yourself," or "Tell me about your work at Entertainment Inc.," use your sound bites as prepared and rehearsed, including your leaving story.
- Don't give the impression that you are still working if that is not the case. It would be awkward to correct this misconception later, and you need to stay in control of this crucial piece of information. You do not want the interviewer to learn the truth when you are not present to explain your leaving story.
- Before the conclusion of the first interview, your leaving story must be told. Offer it at the end of the session if no better opportunity has presented itself.
- Be sure that you are comfortable with your leaving story through careful preparation and practice, and always include your plans for the future before you stop talking.

Questions about Weaknesses, Disappointments and Failures

- Skilled interviewers know that there is much to be learned from exploring the less successful aspects of a person's experience. Be prepared!
- Every point you make about your weaknesses, disappointments and failures must include what you've learned and how you prevent this from being an ongoing problem.
- Since most weaknesses are overused strengths, go with this premise. Reiterate one of your strengths and talk about what it's like when used in the extreme.
- Don't mention weaknesses that will ruin your chances for the job. Based on your research, decide which three to five areas you are willing to discuss. Choose characteristics that are the antithesis of the job requirements. For example, a business developer might admit to impatience and boredom with detail-focused, isolated tasks.
- Along with the preparation of accomplishment stories, think about the disappointments and failures that have advanced your learning. Be prepared to give specific examples of the difficult times, focusing on what you culled from the experience.

A general manager from an operations environment took pride in his tight control over the quality of work in his area. He would delegate responsibility reluctantly and always with excessively detailed instructions. He was often criticized for keeping too much administrative and supervisory work on his own plate. In describing his weakness, he said, "I pride myself on the quality of the output from my division. I delegate cautiously and check on my subordinates' work frequently. The result is that I'm probably slower to delegate than others. However, when my mandate changed to include both developing my subordinates and focusing my attention on business strategy, I learned to be less directive and give increasing responsibility to my people."

Handling a Series of Interviews with One Organization

- In a long series of interviews with an organization, the greatest challenge is staying fresh, enthusiastic and interested. You need to go into each interview as if it were the first one.
- Have plenty of accomplishment stories on hand. Tell the most pertinent ones repeatedly, and try to use a new story in each interview.
- Don't wear the same outfit or suit too often. Have copies of your résumé with you. Learn the names of support staff. Greet people cordially and begin to act as if you belong.
- Remember that you must make a good first impression with each separate interviewer. Be confident and relaxed. Think about how you can put them at ease by establishing rapport.
- Don't assume that the interviewers have spoken with one another, and don't take shortcuts with your answers. Be consistent and thorough.
- Know your various audiences. Before each session, use your notes to refresh your memory on the next interviewer and where they fit in the organization.
- Debrief following each interview. If you are in a series of back-to-back meetings, at the very least quickly jot down the pertinent names, facts and details that have been mentioned. Do a thorough debrief at the end of the day.
- Remember the names of previous interviewers and the distinguishing points of your conversation with them. Drop this information into subsequent interviews, demonstrating your growing enthusiasm for the opportunity.
- To aid your understanding of the position, the organization and the key issues, ask the same questions to a number of interviewers, such as "What do you see as the major challenges facing the person chosen for this position?"
- Write a thank-you letter to every interviewer. Make them specific to each conversation, because they might be circulated among the entire group.

Tip: If you are involved in a series of interviews with one organization and you have an interesting opportunity emerging with another, begin now to slow down the process with the first organization. Very carefully delay the scheduling of meetings to buy time.

Raising Your Questions

- Having thoughtful and pertinent questions to ask of your interviewers is an excellent way to demonstrate your interest in a position and gather information on which to base your evaluation of the opportunity.
- Your research should uncover areas of interest that you want to explore further. Don't hesitate to ask your questions, prefacing them with an acknowledgement that the interviewer might not be free to disclose some things.
- In an initial interview, wait for the invitation to ask your questions unless an obvious entry point presents itself. In subsequent interviews with the same person, you will be expected to have cogent questions. Do not go in unprepared.
- If the process appears to be moving toward the offer stage, and you have not had the opportunity to ask your questions and satisfy your concerns, call the person in charge of the process and ask for a meeting in which you can raise your questions.

Discussing Remuneration

- Do your homework first. It's usually possible to determine the approximate base salary range and total compensation package for the position you hope to land. The search firm or placement agency and your network are the best sources. Salary surveys will give you a general idea of the level of compensation specific jobs command in various industries.
- The interviewer will probably raise the issue of remuneration well before you are given a concrete offer of employment. However, if salary is very important to you and the issue of remuneration has not come up after several interviews, ask. It won't do either of you any good to keep the conversations going if the organization is not able to meet your needs.

A senior manager with expertise in hazardous waste management was in a series of interviews with an international firm. Both parties were excited about the obvious fit and the prospect of working together. The organization's process entailed eight interviews, several requiring officers of the company to fly in from Europe and Asia. Unfortunately, neither the candidate nor the organization mentioned remuneration during any of the interviews. When the process was complete and a written offer was delivered, the base salary was set at $65,000. The candidate had been making twice that amount and could not consider taking less than $115,000. The transaction ended in disappointment for all concerned.

- If you are asked what your salary expectations are, the interviewer is looking for an indication that you and the organization are in the same range. Don't evade the question.
  - Offer a base salary range varying by approximately 10% from top to bottom and indicate your flexibility in looking at the total remuneration package.
  - If bonuses or commissions are involved, state a range from the midpoint of your expectations up to the highest level that is reasonable for your industry.
  - Keep the conversation open by stating your interest in the position and the contribution you believe you can make.
- If you are asked point-blank what you are currently making, be honest and be sure to include everything from the excellent pension plan and the strike price of your stock options to your

club memberships and parking spot. Express your flexibility in terms of the overall structure of the remuneration package and your interest in the position.

A corporate finance executive was interviewing with a major investment banking firm. His remuneration expectations were well within the range of what the hiring organization was willing to pay, and he was not looking for a significant increase. His interest was in working for the firm itself. When asked about his current remuneration package, he dodged the question, expressing confidence that whatever would be offered for the prospective job would be fair. He was immediately taken out of the running. The interviewer already knew what he was making and thought that if he was not prepared to be forthcoming on the issue of pay, he might be hiding something else.

Tip: Don't lie about your compensation. A surprising number of candidates do this and ruin their chance of landing a job. What you say can be verified by companies checking references.

References

When the organization is ready to extend an offer of employment to you, their last step before doing so should be a thorough reference check. This can often delay the process, but it is very important to the organization. See Chapter 18 for a thorough discussion of how to manage your references well.

In Conclusion

To be thoroughly prepared, go through the following inventory of interview questions. Some of the questions relate to your previous experience and can be answered the same way in any interview. Others are directed at the prospective opportunity, and require a specific and thoughtful answer.

An Inventory of Interview Questions

Position-Related

- What did you enjoy most (least) about your last position?
- What would you like to have done more of in your last job?
- What are the three most important things you look for in a job?
- Describe your understanding of what is required to fulfill this role.
- What objectives would you set for your first 12 months in this position?
- What aspects of your current job do you consider to be most critical to your success in this role?

Working Environment

- How would you describe the culture of your current (most recent) organization?
- What would you consider to be an ideal organizational culture?
- After working with the same organization for as long as you have, what obstacles or challenges do you anticipate in trying to adapt to a new organization?

Leadership Style

- How would you describe your leadership style? Please give an example of a specific action you have taken that would illustrate this style.
- How do you stay current on what your team or work group is accomplishing?
- In what ways has your leadership style changed as you have gained experience?

Operating Style

- Please describe how you handle the following activities and give examples to illustrate:
  - organizing your time
  - managing your priorities
  - bringing new ideas forward
  - communicating with others—subordinates, peers, senior managers, clients
  - managing issues
- Tell me about a work experience you have had that you found to be particularly frustrating. How did you deal with it and what was the outcome? How could you have handled it differently?
- What has been the most difficult management responsibility you have handled?

Team Skills

- What type of people do you work with best? Why?
- How do you handle conflict with co-workers? Please give me an example.
- Tell me about a time when you were on a team that was successful in accomplishing a particularly difficult task. In what ways did you participate and contribute to this achievement?
- From your experience in working as a team member, tell me about a time when the team objected to your ideas. How did you attempt to influence or persuade them to accept your views? What results did you achieve?
- Looking back on your team experiences, have you ever assumed the role of team leader? How did you act when you were the leader on various projects?

Negotiating Style

- Please give me some examples of different approaches you've used in persuading someone to help you accomplish a work priority.
- How would you approach and prepare for dealing with a complex issue requiring you to negotiate with one or more people? Please give me an example.
- Please describe a particularly successful negotiation in which you took part. What did you do to contribute to that success?
- Please describe a negotiation that did not produce the results you wanted. What went wrong and what would you do differently next time?

Decision-Making Style

- Please describe the process that you generally follow to make decisions.
- To what extent do you provide opportunities for your subordinates to participate in making decisions?

- Describe a poor decision that you made. What might you have done differently to produce a successful result?
- Tell me about a time when you changed a decision you had made or an opinion you had held because you were persuaded that you were wrong.

Accomplishments

- What would you consider to be your most significant career-related accomplishment to date? Why?
- Name three or four of your proudest achievements.
- What would you consider to be the biggest disappointment or failure in your career to date? How did you handle it? What did you learn from it? What should you have done differently to produce a more satisfactory outcome?
- How do you define and measure success?

Personal Characteristics

- What characteristics would you say are the most important for a good manager (sales executive, senior economist, CFO, etc.) to have? Can you describe some of the accomplishments that would demonstrate how you have displayed these characteristics?
- How do you react to criticism?
- How do you handle pressure on the job? Stress?
- What did you think of your last boss? Your last organization?
- What would you consider to be your three strongest assets? Please give me an example of a time when you demonstrated these strengths to achieve successful results.
- How would you describe yourself? Tell me about some of the people or events in your life outside work that have had the greatest influence on you.
- What makes you unique among your peers?
- What areas of your skills and abilities do you feel need more work in order for you to become more effective in your career?
- How do you stay plugged in to what's happening in your current organization?
- How do you stay current on new developments in your area of expertise?
- Tell me about a time when you had to take a stand on an unpopular position or issue.
- Have you learned more from your successes or from your failures? Please give examples.
- Describe three elements of your personal code of workplace ethics.
- Why have you changed jobs so frequently/infrequently?

Chapter 13

Create Meaningful Correspondence

If I had more time,
I would write to you more briefly.

Well-written, appropriate correspondence plays a critical role in your job search. It is significant not only for its content, but also for the impression it creates. Written materials provide concrete evidence of your skill as a communicator and convey a wealth of information about your attitude, thinking skills and judgment. Career transition correspondence, whether delivered by email or regular mail, falls into five categories:

- cover letters responding to ads or job postings
- networking letters used to introduce yourself to a potential new contact
- marketing letters for contract work, consulting services or a small business
- thank-you letters to interviewers and networking contacts
- "I've Landed" letters announcing your new position

Tip: Many people use broadcast letters with attached résumés as a means of introducing themselves to a large number of prospective employers. *This one-size-fits-all approach is a poor use of your time.* Unsolicited résumés are often ignored or discarded. At best they are scanned for key words and their information is filed electronically.

Use the following guidelines to ensure that every letter you write is an effective communication piece.

GUIDELINES FOR ALL CAREER TRANSITION CORRESPONDENCE
- Allow enough time to compose and proofread each letter carefully.
- Address every letter to a specific person. Use your research skills and find out the name of the person to whom you are writing to avoid using the "Dear Sir/Madam" salutation.
- Keep every letter to a single page.
- Limit letters to four paragraphs of no more than eight lines each.
- Balance short and long sentences for variety.

- Let your personality shine through and keep the tone of your letters positive yet professional.
- Limit the use of the first person, especially the use of "I" at the beginning of sentences.
- Do not use trite phrases such as "strong communication and interpersonal skills" or other words that have lost their effectiveness through overuse.
- Use either your personal letterhead or the heading from your résumé on every letter, so that your contact information stands out.
- Close each letter with your commitment to follow up and make a diary note to do it.
- Be meticulous about grammar and spelling. Do not rely on "Spell Check." Proofread your letter carefully.
- Keep copies of your letters where they can be easily retrieved. Use them for reference when you follow up.

GUIDELINES FOR FORMATTING A LETTER

For proper layout and paragraph formatting, use a template in your computer software or follow these rules:

- The top margin will vary according to the letterhead design. The bottom margin should be at least half an inch. Side margins should be equal and no narrower than three-quarters of an inch.
- All text should begin at the left margin.
- Place the date one or two lines down from the letterhead. Leave two to four blank lines before the inside address. Leave one blank line after the inside address before the attention line, and one blank line before and after the salutation.
- When using a reference line, centre it in bold after the salutation, leaving one blank line before and after.
- Do not indent paragraphs. Leave a blank line between paragraphs.
- Leave one blank line before the signature line and approximately four lines for your signature.
- Leave one blank line before the enclosure or cc line.

Cover Letters

A carefully written cover letter should accompany your résumé every time you respond to an ad or job posting. If it is brief, relevant and to the point, your letter can have more influence on the reader's decision to interview you than the enclosed résumé. Recruiters often give more credence to your cover letter because, unlike your résumé, which could have been written by someone else, it will have been authored by you. The cover letter forms the first impression of you in the reader's mind. It builds a bridge between your past experience and the future opportunity. It should be sufficient on its own to convince the reader that you are a qualified candidate for the advertised position.

Tip: Email has not changed the importance of writing cover letters. Recruiters report that many people who use email are skipping this crucial step, but those who do make the effort significantly increase their chances of being interviewed.

Every good cover letter starts with thorough research. In addition to traditional resources, try to get a copy of the full job description. Contact your network to learn about the key people and the culture of the organization. This unpublished intelligence is often the most valuable.

Next, analyze the ad or job posting carefully. Use the worksheet that follows to record the requirements of the position, and compare them with your skills and abilities. Consider what you could bring to the position or the organization over and above the requirements mentioned in the ad, and describe it succinctly. This added-value statement will give you a distinct advantage because most people reply only in terms of the requirements mentioned in the ad.

Tip: Your cover letter should tell the reader that you read the ad or posting thoroughly, you gave it careful thought and you have a good reason for applying.

WORSHEET 13.1 The Cover Letter	
Key Points in the Ad or Job Posting Professional and Functional Skills	**Corresponding Points Describing You** Professional and Functional Skills
• • • • •	• • • • •
Personal Characteristics and Values	Personal Characteristics and Values
• • • • •	• • • • •
Relevant Industry and Corporate Information You've Learned through Research	
• • •	
Added Value You Would Bring to the Position and the Organization	
• •	

In the heading of your letter, clearly identify the ad, posting, reference number, project name, file number or position title for which you are applying. If your application is going to an external recruiter or the human resources department, this information should stand out to ensure that your material is sorted correctly.

Tip: Suspend the use of informal email etiquette for cover letters. Most hiring managers will be put off by "Hi Susan" from someone they've never met. Stick with formal salutations, good grammar and perfect spelling, even in the casual milieu of email.

Compose a compelling opening. You want to do more than refer the reader to the ad and your enclosed résumé. Here is an example of what you should *not* write: "Enclosed please find a copy of my résumé in response to your ad in *The Globe and Mail* on May 4th for the position of Purchasing Manager." This opening generates little interest, and shows a lack of originality and effort.

Contrast the following opening to the one above: "As an experienced Purchasing Manager with a track record of consistent cost reduction and quality standards maintenance, I am very interested in the position you have advertised. Industrial Parts Company's reputation in the widget industry is second-to-none, and I would like to be a part of your service-focused team." Assume that the writer picked up the phrase "service-focused team" from a networking contact.

In the body of the letter, point out the information on your résumé that substantiates your qualifications. Highlight one or two convincing accomplishments and mention quantified results, adding explanations of their relevance if needed. Use crisp, powerful phrases and persuasive points to sell your style and skills. Express enthusiasm for the position. Explain the added value you offer and close by stating your commitment to follow up. Make a diary note so you remember to do this important step.

Tip: Don't be tempted to rewrite your résumé to fit each ad or job posting. A résumé that targets your ideal employment opportunity and a well-written cover letter should be adequate for almost every opportunity. Don't let résumé revising become the focus of your job search energies.

Do not make the mistake of using the same cover letter repeatedly, and don't compose a generic one. If a letter is tailored to one ad, it will not be appropriate for another. Customize your letter to reflect the contents of the specific ad or posting and the additional information that you collect through research. Certain phrases and sentences may transfer well from one letter to another, but avoid copying whole paragraphs without making suitable changes.

A market research specialist from a multinational consumer packaged-goods company wanted to explore opportunities with other organizations. Her interest was in either advancing her career in research or switching to a marketing role with a broader focus. She saw two ads run by a major retailer, one for a research specialist and the other for a more junior position as a marketing generalist. Her dilemma was that both opportunities appeared to be well worth pursuing. After struggling with the idea of submitting separate applications, she decided to write one straightforward cover letter that explained her interests and stated the contribution she could make to each job. She asked to be considered for both opportunities and successfully landed both interviews.

GUIDELINES FOR WRITING COVER LETTERS

Opening Paragraph

- Write a compelling opening to capture the reader's attention. Refer to the ad or job posting.
- Explain why this opportunity appeals to you.
- Write a comment that illustrates your effort to learn something about the organization.

Second Paragraph—Skills Match

- Demonstrate that your skills match those mentioned in the ad or posting by briefly highlighting one or two accomplishments.
- Describe the added value you would bring to the position.

Third Paragraph—Personal Style

- Describe your competencies and characteristics in terms that mirror the ad or job posting.
- Indicate your interest and enthusiasm for the position.

Closing Paragraph—Follow-Up Commitment

- Indicate your desire to meet for an interview.
- Thank the reader for considering your application.
- Commit to following up on a specific date.

Look at the sample that follows. It illustrates good technique and the application of the principles that will help you find the work you want.

Tip: It's not easy to critique your own work. *Grammatical and spelling mistakes are inexcusable.* Have someone else proofread your cover letters before sending them.

The sample cover letter on the next page responds to this ad.

VP Marketing and Sales
Reference # 81349

Using current and emerging marketing and promotional tools, you will be responsible for expanding market share and profitability for our major consumer product lines. Your mandate will be to continuously develop, improve and manage strategies to outpace the competition and advance our relationships with major retailers. You are skilled in direct marketing, project management, media effectiveness and business analysis. You are strategic, conceptual and analytical in your thinking and you thrive in a fast-paced, team environment.

Multi-Household Products Co.
Address
City, Province   Postal Code

Sample Cover Letter #1

YOUR NAME
Address
City, Province   Postal Code
Telephone   / Fax   / Email

Date

Donna O'Rourke
Vice-President, Human Resources
Multi-Household Products Co.
Address
City, Province   Postal Code

VP Marketing and Sales
Reference #81349

Dear Ms. O'Rourke,

Your recent ad for the position of Vice-President Marketing and Sales is of great interest to me. I believe that Multi-Household Products Co.'s strong national presence in household paper products provides the ideal platform for launching your recently announced global expansion plans. The emerging Asian markets and their potential for high-volume sales hold particular promise, and I would like play a leadership role in your aggressive marketing strategies and dynamic sales initiatives.

My marketing experience began with Classic Established Co., where I spent four years in new product development in addition to several product management and sales assignments. The move to Smaller Co. as National Sales Manager in 2002 afforded me the opportunity to establish excellent relationships with senior managers at the major retail accounts in Canada. I was able to negotiate both additional shelf space and better advertising support for our household product line with Tight Co.

As Vice-President, New Products Division, for ABC Company my contributions have included the increase in specialty products sales from $750,000 to $2.5 million and the aggressive driving of Ultra-Pack Tissues to capture market share in excess of 50%. Strategies have included maximizing the emerging potential of B2B commodity buying with major international accounts.

My management style can be best described as energetic and hands-on. I thrive in a results-oriented environment that is focused on growth and profits. I take pride in motivating and inspiring individuals to higher achievements and building committed teams founded on mutual respect.

I trust you will find my qualifications well suited to your requirements. I will take the initiative to touch base with you next Thursday to discuss your needs in greater depth.

Sincerely,

Name

Encl.

Networking Letters

Conducting an active job search sometimes involves writing introductory letters, known as networking letters. Their sole purpose is to aid the process of arranging meetings with individuals to gather information, leads and advice. More is said about the networking process in Chapter 15.

A networking letter introduces the writer, explains the reason for the contact, requests a face-to-face meeting and promises to follow up by telephone. Without a follow-up phone call, networking letters are ineffective. Few people will take the initiative to phone you and set up a meeting in response to your letter.

Use this type of letter only if it helps you gain comfort with the networking process. For some people, picking up the phone and asking for a meeting without first having sent a letter is daunting. If you are one of those people, use networking letters as part of your strategy, but remember that writing them creates a significant amount of extra work and delays your direct contact with people who are probably willing to help you. Measure the effectiveness of your networking letters by keeping track of the ones that result in meetings.

Tip: Networking letters can be used as a last resort when all other attempts to make contact have failed.

Use the following guidelines to increase the effectiveness of networking letters. A sample follows the guidelines.

GUIDELINES FOR NETWORKING LETTERS

- Target each letter to the recipient. Generic networking letters and broadcast mailings are not effective.
- In your opening sentence, mention the person who referred you. When there is a personal connection, people pay attention; their willingness to help increases and their curiosity is piqued.
- Be clear about your intention to request a meeting and state your agenda for the meeting. You should be looking for information and advice on something specific. Do not say that you would like to know what opportunities are available at the recipient's organization.
- Consider enclosing a topical article. This could form the basis for your discussion in the meeting.
- Another option is to put forward a hypothesis or mention an issue you would like to discuss.
- In some instances, a summary of your targets or one of your case studies might be appropriate.
- Do not enclose your résumé. You are not applying for a job with the recipient; you are asking for a discussion, information and advice.
- Close with the commitment to call and schedule a meeting. Make a diary note and follow up.

Sample Networking Letter

YOUR NAME
Street Address
City, Province   Postal Code
Telephone   / Fax   / Email

Date

Name
Title
Organization
Division
Address
City, Province Postal Code

Dear First Name,

Fred Smith, Vice-President at Enterprise Inc., recently told me of your new role as Director, Vendor Relations for Interprovincial Trains Ltd. Congratulations on your success. Although we have not spoken in some time, you may recall our brief contact while I was Manager of Operations at Start-Up Inc. prior to the acquisition. My role there came to an end in May, and I am currently exploring new career options. Fred suggested that I get in touch with you.

Because of my diversified background, which includes senior roles at Marketing Plus and Stellar Inc., I am researching a range of options that include operations or project management within a pharmaceutical, health care or biotech environment.

With this in mind, I would appreciate the chance to speak with you briefly. Any information or comments you have regarding potential areas of growth within these industries would be helpful. I will call you toward the end of next week to see when a short meeting might be convenient. I'm looking forward to speaking with you and hearing about your new responsibilities.

Yours truly,

Your Name
Encl.

Marketing Letters

Marketing letters might form a part of your strategy if you decide to pursue contract or consulting work. These letters introduce your services and offer a few persuasive points highlighting the potential benefits of retaining you. Their objective is to prepare the way for a phone call requesting a meeting, ideally as the result of a specific referral. Develop a generic edition of the letter at the outset of your marketing efforts and plan to customize it for each recipient. The content of the letter will evolve as your consulting or contracting practice grows.

An indiscriminate mass mailing of marketing letters is usually a waste of effort and money. You know what happens to the unsolicited mail that you receive. A personal referral provides the most compelling reason for writing, but where you don't have a referral, use a focused approach that shows you have made an effort to learn something about the person or organization.

Review the guidelines for writing networking letters. The same tips and techniques apply to marketing letters. A quote, a copy of an article or a hypothesis based on your research are ideal ways to introduce the potential issues and challenges for which you propose to provide solutions. Include a brief description of a few of your relevant accomplishments either as part of the narrative or in bullet-point form. Do not include your résumé. You are not applying for a job, but rather making contacts that might lead to work opportunities.

Other ways to generate interest with marketing letters include enclosing your brochure or samples of your materials. However, you might prefer to reserve these for use in the marketing meeting. You could include a list of your clients or relevant quotes from clients, with their permission. Another possibility is to include an invitation for the reader to visit your web site. If you do this, be sure that your site adds something to what you have said in the letter.

Tip: Write an article for a trade journal or industry newsletter that addresses an issue where your expertise could be applied. Buy reprints of the article, reference it in your letter and attach a copy.

Sample Marketing Letter

YOUR NAME
Address
City, Province   Postal Code
Telephone   / Fax   / Email

Date

Name
Title
Company
Address
City, Province Postal Code

Dear Name,

Mark Steiner suggested that I contact you to introduce myself. My background in driving major organizational change may be helpful to you and your firm.

The leading companies in the Canadian insurance industry are undergoing some very costly, risky and potentially beneficial changes. These changes include: acquisitions and divestitures in Canada, the U.S. and internationally; outsourcing of information technology; outsourcing of business processes; and the launching of new products and services to increase revenues. These changes can be very complex, spanning multiple business functions, covering broad geographies and including both business and information technology functions.

I believe that I could assist you and your executive team in meeting these challenges by drawing on my capabilities in:
- Driving multi-million-dollar change initiatives.
- Defining quantified business cases for major organizational change and clearly articulating the benefits.
- Determining when and how information technology is appropriate to business needs.
- Turning around major projects that are not meeting expectations.
- Developing strategies and implementing them.
- Working with complex multi-business-units organizations.

I have enclosed a brief summary of my achievements at XYZ Insurance Co. and ABC Consulting Co. I will call you next week to see if we might find a time to meet.

Sincerely,

Name

Encl.

Thank-You Letters

As you search for your next opportunity, whether it is a full-time job, consulting assignments or starting your own small business, you will have many occasions to thank people for their help. A simple and effective way to show your appreciation is to put your thanks in writing. It's best to do this within 24 hours of a meeting or phone call, but don't let tardiness stop you from writing. Even if your letter is dispatched months later, it's better to send it rather than entirely neglect this important piece of correspondence.

You will want to thank every networking and marketing contact plus the person who provided the introduction. It is also important to thank every interviewer at every stage in the process, and the people who provide references on your behalf.

Thank-you letters and notes don't always need to be formal business letters. You could send a handwritten note on a blank card or businesslike stationery. Some people buy single-fold note cards with their name printed on the front. In many cases, email is appropriate. Your choice of paper, print and delivery channel is a matter of your style and your evaluation of the recipient's style. What's most important is that you thank people every time the opportunity arises.

Tip: One drawback with using email to write thank-you notes is that most people will read the note and then delete the message rather than print it. A letter or a note is more likely to be kept in a file and looked at later.

You can show your appreciation in other ways, too. You might be able to provide useful information, leads and referrals for those who have helped you. For exceptional assistance and support from a networking contact, consider sending or delivering flowers, a gift basket or some other token of appreciation. Once you have landed, you might want to celebrate by taking a key contact to lunch.

Networking Thank-You Letters

In the networking process, thank-you notes and letters are the simplest and most appropriate way to stay in touch with the people who give you their time and support. Immediately following every networking meeting, write a thank-you note or letter. Be specific, mentioning what you learned that was new or helpful. If you can, offer concrete proof that you have taken advice given to you in the meeting. This might mean commenting on a recommended article or web site, or on rare occasions enclosing a revised copy of your résumé. Forwarding a revised résumé is especially important if your contact has mentioned an available position at the same time. Reiterate your intention to pursue the leads you were given and indicate when the recipient can expect to hear from you again. Be realistic with these commitments. If you say you'll do something, you must do it.

A young woman seeking an entry-level role in the human resources field kept her ever-increasing network of contacts informed every time she met with a person who was suggested by another. Her handwritten thank-you notes sat on her contacts' desks and bookshelves, reminding them of her interests and goals. What's more, her job search became the topic of conversation for a group of eight women in human resources roles who supported her efforts. It took over a year, but finally someone heard of the perfect opportunity and personally arranged the interview that led to the break she needed. Without the flow of thank-you notes, her networking contacts might have forgotten her.

Tip: Very few people are diligent about thanking their networking contacts when the advice or referrals received open more doors. You will distinguish yourself by letting your networking contacts know that their help has advanced your search.

Sample Networking Thank-You Letter

YOUR NAME
Address
City, Province   Postal Code
Telephone   / Fax   / Email

Date

Name
Title
Company
Address
City, Province Postal Code

Dear First Name,

Thank you again for taking the time to meet with me two weeks ago. I am pleased to update you on the status of my contact with Pat Chan and Gary DeNova. I was able to meet with each of them this week to discuss my interest in moving into the e-commerce sector. They were very helpful, and I appreciate the introductions you provided.

As you had mentioned, they have vastly different viewpoints on the challenges facing start-up businesses and it was enlightening to hear both sides of the issues surrounding growth and financing. Gary was especially helpful and I will be meeting with his Manager of Special Projects, Ghitu Das Gupta, to explore the possibility of contract work. I would welcome a short-term assignment. It would give me a first-hand opportunity to assess my fit with the culture of a high-tech environment like theirs.

I'll let you know how this next meeting turns out and in the meantime, please accept my thanks for all your efforts on my behalf.

Regards,

Your Name

Thank-You Letters for Interviews

After each interview, follow up immediately by writing a thank-you letter. This will remind the interviewer of the discussion you had and refresh their memory of your qualifications for the job. It will also differentiate you from other candidates, since writing thank-you letters following interviews is a relatively rare practice, despite the consistent advice of experts to do it.

Use your debriefing notes, and make specific reference in your letter to points that were discussed in the interview. Express your appreciation for something you learned as well as any advice or direction you received. Reiterate your strengths and relate them to the job requirements. If there is something important that was not mentioned during the interview, include it in your letter. It could be a convincing point that is necessary for your success. As you debrief you might think of things said in the interview that you would like to correct or clarify. Use the thank-you letter to revisit points that were not addressed adequately in person.

Take this opportunity to go beyond what's expected and send one of your case studies along with your letter as proof that you would be able to make a valuable contribution to the organization. Respond to an area of interest or challenge mentioned during the interview by doing some research to find the needed information. If appropriate, spend some time developing a possible solution and propose it in a written attachment to the thank-you letter. If you can add value at this early stage of the game, you will no doubt significantly increase your chances of landing another interview.

Finally, allow your interest in and enthusiasm for the job and the organization to show in what you write. Restate the follow-up steps that were set out. If nothing was said about next steps, indicate when you plan to initiate contact again. Make a diary note and do it.

Sample Interview Thank-You Letter

YOUR NAME
Address
City, Province   Postal Code
Telephone   / Fax   / Email

Date

Interviewer's Name
Title
Company
Address
City, Province Postal Code

Dear Name,

I enjoyed the opportunity to meet with you again this week. Thank you for making the time to meet for breakfast on Tuesday morning.

As I mentioned in our subsequent telephone discussion on Tuesday evening, I very much enjoyed meeting with Messrs. Brazeau and de Selliers. I found their perspectives on the development, priorities and future opportunities for the Caribbean Bank tremendously interesting and exciting. I especially appreciated their insights on the scope of some of the challenges that are emerging for the human resources function.

Lorraine, I feel most fortunate to have had the opportunity to pursue these employment discussions with you and your colleagues at the Caribbean Bank. Everyone I have met has been most enthusiastic about the Bank's mission and achievements and about the prospects for the future. I believe that my 10 years' experience in international recruiting in the financial services sector plus my recent experience with implementing world-wide compensation policies for Global Mutual Funds, Inc. would enable me to contribute significantly to the Bank's future plans.

Thank you again for your time and for facilitating my interviews with your colleagues. Please be assured of my very keen interest in the Bank and in the position of Director of Human Resources. I will look forward to hearing from you over the next few weeks.

Yours truly,

Your Name

"I've Landed" Letters

When you land that next position, whether it's a permanent, full-time job or an interim contract or consulting assignment, be very careful to let the contacts you've made during your job search know where you are working and what your new role entails. Sending an "I've Landed" letter is a professional courtesy that you owe to those who have helped along the way. By closing the loop, they gain a sense of satisfaction from assisting you, and you can offer your future assistance in return. Unfortunately, in the excitement of beginning a new job, many people neglect this important step. If you have your new business cards, enclose one with the letter. If not, follow up again by sending your card in a later note. These simple courtesies are very much appreciated and they often lead to ongoing networking relationships and perhaps future business.

A senior sales and marketing manager accepted a three-month assignment with a media company that was experiencing significant growth. He wrote to each one of his networking contacts, telling them what he was doing and indicating that he would continue his search for a full-time job at the end of the contract. Two weeks before he wrapped things up with the media firm he dispatched another batch of letters, saying that he was back in the job market and would be in touch shortly. During the first week of his resumed full-time search, he made a phone call to every person to whom he had sent a letter.

Tip: It's never too late! Even if you have allowed months to pass by in the excitement of landing and starting your new job, it's still appropriate to send a letter announcing where you're working. People appreciate hearing the news.

Sample "I've Landed" Letter

YOUR NAME
Address
City, Province   Postal Code
Telephone   / Fax   / Email

Date

Name
Title
Company
Address
City, Province   Postal Code

Dear First Name,

I'm very pleased to let you know that I have joined Communications Consultants, an international human resources consulting firm with offices in Montreal, Toronto, Vancouver and over 175 locations worldwide. In my role as Director here in Montreal, I will be conducting activities primarily related to professional development for executives.

My decision to join Communications Consultants was influenced in large part by their substantial experience in managing the human side of organizational change, working with leading corporations. In particular, I was impressed by their success in the areas of leadership and organizational development. I believe that my experience in assessment and coaching will complement the firm's reputation for excellence in working with executive teams.

I would like to thank you for your assistance and encouragement during my transition, especially since Trailblazer's initiatives have placed such a premium on your time. As you know, your introduction to Michel Remy was particularly helpful. His advice on 360° performance reviews paved the way for my early discussions with Communications Consultants. I hope that I will be able to repay your kindness in some way.

I will look forward to keeping in touch.

Yours truly,

Your Name

Move into Action

Opportunity is found
where good luck and hard work intersect.

Objectives

This step involves being organized, staying focused on your priorities, building momentum, maintaining motivation and refining your targets as you search for employment. It demystifies the use of networking and provides a process for conducting effective networking meetings. The chapters in Part Four cover:

• Putting your targets in priority order.
• Allocating time to maximize effectiveness.
• Networking effectively.
• Using search firms and placement agencies.
• The importance of newspaper and trade journal ads.
• The Internet and your job search.
• The advantages and challenges of an active job search.

Rules to Follow

• Try not to worry; never be bitter. Although it is hard to do, make sure that you are able to hide your negative feelings while you are networking and interviewing.
• Go for the buy-in. As this book and others will tell you, being out there talking to people is imperative.
• Keep asking questions aimed at clarifying your targets.
• Set up a record-keeping and diary system that works for you. Efficient information retrieval and timely follow-up are critical to the effective job search.
• Trust that the vast majority of people are pleased to be helpful. As long as you approach them in an appropriate way, they will respond positively and supportively.

Moves That Can Set You Back

- Allowing yourself to remain isolated and inactive.
- Spending countless hours on the Internet. It's the most effective black hole for time that's come along in quite a long time.
- Making networking calls or attending a networking meeting without doing your research and planning your approach.
- Failing to plan time to take care of yourself. You need to do whatever it takes to keep your energy and spirits up.
- Thinking that the only measure of success is landing a job, rather than giving yourself credit for every positive step along the way.

Chapter 14

On Your Mark, Get Set…

Plan your work and work your plan.

You are almost ready to launch an active search for employment that will require you to reach out and talk with a large number of people. To increase your confidence and help you do your best, there are a few more preparatory steps to complete. You need to prioritize your targets; give them time frames and align the resources you have developed with each of your intended targets. Finally, you need to create a sales plan, establish a good record-keeping system and get yourself organized. With these steps complete, you'll be ready to go.

Refer to Appendix A: Strategic View of Targeted Employment Search Process. You are in the communication and sales planning phases.

Set Your Priorities: Targets A, B and C

Return to the targets you set in Chapter 8. If you have only one target, stretch your thinking and create at least two more. If you already have more than three targets, narrow your focus to only three for now. Pursuit of these targets will direct your initial forays into the marketplace. Prioritize them based on your current market knowledge and interests.

Your top priority, Target A, could be the role and market where you expect to achieve the quickest results. Alternatively, your first priority could be the target that would involve moving to your preferred geographical location, or starting your own business. It could also be the target that you are most compelled to pursue because of personal interests. Choose Targets A, B and C using the criteria that make sense for you. As your search progresses, you will refine, revise and re-prioritize your targets.

Use your strategic targeting worksheets from Chapter 8 (Worksheet 8.4) and label them A, B or C according to your priorities. Briefly state your rationale for the priority ranking you have given to each target.

The SVP-IT described at the end of Chapter 8 had set three targets: a more senior role in the sector where she had recent experience, a switch to IT consulting in a different industry and a significant change that involved both a new role and a new market. She made the third target, becoming an executive director of a non-profit organization, her first priority, or Target A. She was very committed to helping children with challenges similar to those of her niece and she wanted to either quickly eliminate the possibility of finding this sort of work, or decide to pursue it exclusively for several months. Target B became consulting on IT issues in the health care industry, which she believed to be somewhat close to her primary interest. Target C, her most accessible option, became staying in the industry she knew best to seek a more senior role in a smaller company. The priority order of her targets was driven entirely by her personal interests.

In contrast to this story, many people take a more narrowly focused approach to setting their targets. Some are successful with a singular focus, landing a good opportunity without having to expand their range of possibilities.

A risk management expert with experience in implementing fraud prevention software needed to replace his income immediately. He saw his severance package as an opportunity to get out of debt, and he knew that he could land another job quickly. For him, Targets A, B and C involved approaching different companies in the market he knew very well, and accepting the highest offer available in the shortest period of time. Job content, title and future direction took a back seat to maximizing earnings and minimizing transition time.

Allocate Time to Each Target

Use Appendix B: Sample Search Activities Project Plan to create a detailed project plan and track your progress. Review the number of weeks left before your desired re-employment date, and plan the amount of time you can spend in pursuit of each target. Do you have the luxury of taking several weeks or even months to assess each target, or do you need to evaluate and revise your targets quickly? For each target, set a start date for actively and aggressively pursuing it. Also set a date when you will evaluate its viability and revise, drop or continue pursuing it.

A lawyer who handled supplier contracts in the legal department of a large automobile company wanted to make a major career change. When she did her self-assessment, writing emerged as the skill she most enjoyed using. In fact, she had often thought about writing a novel and made this Target A. Her personal circumstances allowed her the luxury of taking two years to complete her transition. Allocating six months to the pursuit of Target A, she took a creative writing course, began her novel and approached publishers. At the six-month mark, she decided that being a fiction writer would not provide a sufficient income. She moved to Target B, which was enrolling in a public relations and business communications course at a community college. This generated an abundance of well-paid freelance assignments, allowing her to pursue the novel as a hobby for the present and as a career goal for the future.

Most people pursue several targets concurrently. Allocate a specific percentage of your time to each target each week. For example, you might spend 90% of your time pursuing Target A in the first two weeks of your search, and later reduce the allocation to 60%, while increasing the amount of time you spend on Target B or C.

Make a commitment to yourself regarding the amount of time per week you will dedicate to your search for employment. Looking for work is a full-time job. It's wise to devote 30 to 40 hours a week to it. If you need a temporary break, take one, but don't fritter your time away through the weeks that are allocated to the search.

Record your weekly time commitment and time allocation plans on each of your strategic worksheets.

Tip: The deadlines you set and the amount of time you devote to exploring each target are matters of personal priority and circumstance. Some people need only a few days to determine if their most compelling idea is feasible. Others might have a vision that will take years to develop, and their targeting work will help them identify the steps toward their ultimate goal.

A sales and marketing executive in the pharmaceutical industry worked with multinational organizations during the early years of his career. A brief opportunity to run the Canadian division of an offshore company gave him the vision of owning and managing a small company. His Target A was to immediately identify and purchase a small company; however, he recognized that his operational skills were in need of development. Consequently, he placed equal priority on Target B, a lateral move to an operational role in a medium-sized company. An opportunity aligned with Target B came along first and he accepted it, which proved to be a valuable interim step toward his ultimate goal. Five years later, he landed the employment opportunity of his choice, heading up a spin-off organization from one of his former multinational employers.

Align Your Communication Resources with Each Target

Think carefully about how your résumé communicates your fit with each target. Take one target at a time and review your written resources. Do you need to tweak or revise your résumé? Do you need additional marketing pieces such as case studies or a biography for a particular target? Be judicious about this. Don't have more variations of materials than the diversity of your targets requires.

Tip: Ideas for effectively tailoring written resources to different targets will emerge from research and conversations with people in your network. Listen, learn and improve your materials as you go.

Your verbal pitch in networking meetings and interviews must be consistent with the target you are pursuing. Go back to the five sound bites (Chapter 12). For different targets, you will need to change some of the content or simply adjust your emphasis. It is crucial to try out your pitch on a few people whose opinions you trust.

Consult your support network, board of advisers and, as appropriate, references. Ask them if they think each target is realistic and suitable for you. Are your thoughts too narrow and concrete, or is your thinking so broad and open that it won't be understood? Fully explain your thinking to help them understand why you are interested in a target that might surprise them. Tell them how you think you can make a contribution. You need to know if they will refer and recommend you to others for each target you plan to pursue. A first revision of your targets often comes from receiving this input.

You will often be discussing more than one target with a networking contact. It's important to be able to articulate how all of your targets incorporate a common thread. Even if they seem disparate, your targets arise from your unique history and present circumstances. When you explain your rationale clearly, openly and fully, others will understand your targets.

For each target, align your communication resources and aim them directly at the target. The figure below illustrates the process. Refer to Appendix A to chart your progress.

Alignment of Communications Resources with Employment Target

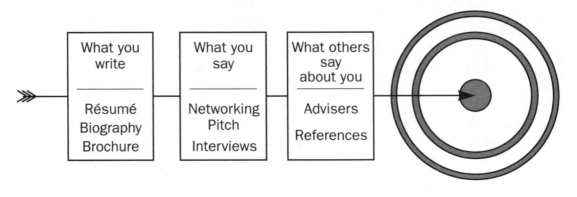

Tip: Many people begin their search with a generic networking pitch that includes their vision of their ideal employment opportunity and their preliminary market assessments. Conversations with others help them identify potential targets that are aligned with what they say and what they have written.

Create a Sales Plan

Return to your market assessment worksheets (Worksheet 8.3). Add to the lists of organizations in your target markets and key people you want to meet by doing thorough research using publicly available information. These lists will expand further as you network. Incorporate the input from your support network, and plan how you will pursue each target efficiently. Which organizations are highest on your list? Who in your network might know a board member or someone who works there? Which contacts are likely to provide valuable insights to your targets? How can you arrange to be introduced to key people?

Once you know what you want to learn about an industry or organization and who you need to meet, networking will get you there. The next chapter deals exclusively with how to network effectively and appropriately.

Establish a Record-Keeping System

Once you are actively networking, your search for work will become a numbers game. The more face-to-face meetings you have with your networking contacts and those to whom you are referred, the closer you will come to your goal. A good system for keeping track of your activities is essential.

Choose a diary or calendar that you will use and visualize it filled with appointments. Organize your address book now. Don't get behind in recording contact information for everyone you intend to contact plus every new person you meet while networking.

Develop a method of keeping notes from each meeting. Consider using contact tracking software. On page 214 is a sample networking tracking sheet, which you can set up to merge with your address book for efficiency. Develop a way to measure your weekly activity level.

Sample Networking Tracking Sheet

Contact Name:			

Title: _____   Business Phone: _____

Company Name: _____   Cell Phone: _____

Address: _____   Business Fax: _____

_____   Email: _____

Referred By: Name: Title: Company:

Business Phone: Cell Phone:

Date:	**Status/Comments:**	**Follow-Up Plans**

It's a Dynamic Process

You have now completed the preparation phase for launching an active search for employment. Refer to Appendix A. You have reached the implementation phase. As you move forward, you will receive valuable information about your targets, learn more clearly where your strategic advantage meets marketplace needs, revise your targets, reallocate your time, set new targets, ask for more input and keep the process going until your hard work uncovers an opportunity that is right for you.

The process is not linear. It will require you to loop back to your market assessments and targets many times. You will also fine-tune how you describe your style, skills and knowledge as you get feedback in the marketplace. You will need to remain flexible and open to new possibilities as you build momentum and become more widely networked.

An international consultant specializing in business process outsourcing recognized the need to accommodate his family's priorities and reduce his overseas travel. In his preliminary search for domestic opportunities, he discovered that one of his ex-employers was selling its Canadian operation. His Target A very quickly shifted from business development in Canada to exploring the possibility of purchasing this company. The idea of being a small business owner had been on his list but relegated to the distant future. Suddenly, it was Target A and he was into full exploration mode. The purchase eventually went to another bidder, and finding domestic assignments returned to Target A status.

Chapter 15

...GO!

Make Networking
the Focus of Your Search

You seldom get what you don't ask for.

Networking is the way to access your most valuable resource—people. Networking is an organized process whereby you arrange and conduct a series of face-to-face meetings with your colleagues, contacts and individuals they have recommended as you pursue your targets. Cold calls are not part of an effective networking process.

The objectives of networking include acquainting people with your background and targets, and exchanging information, advice, leads, opinions and, most importantly, referrals. Networking does not involve asking for a job, nor is it always a one-sided encounter where you are the sole beneficiary. Through networking, you often have the opportunity to share your knowledge and insights and build valuable relationships you will take into the future.

Tip: "I'm looking for work" is an unspoken message in networking meetings. Gathering information and advice about your targets should always be the formal agenda. If you plan your presentation carefully and ask pertinent questions, your networking contacts will have the opportunity to help you without feeling pressured to talk about specific job opportunities.

Success Rates of Job Search Methods

The most convincing argument for networking is that over 80% of people seeking employment find their next opportunity through their network. For those at the most senior levels of organizations, networking probably represents a 95% success rate, and for anyone pursuing a new role in a new market, it likely accounts for 99% of success. The only alternatives to networking are using search firms and placement agencies or answering ads for posted positions. Your options look like this:

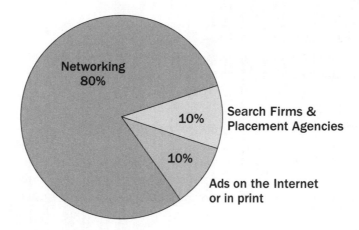

Tip: An active job seeker should divide their time and energy in proportion to the success rates of the various methods.

If you are not convinced by the success rates, consider the many additional benefits of networking. First, networking keeps you up-to-date on events, issues, ideas and opinions. It's the best way to keep track of people on the move in your target organizations and industries. Knowing what's happening is crucial. You need to become a sponge, soaking up information and opinions, reading and talking constantly about what's new.

Second, networking can give you an early advantage for an employment opportunity. When you discover an opening through networking, you may have an earlier entry into the selection process, potentially less competition for the job and the advantage of having been referred by someone known to the organization. Many job opportunities go to effective networkers without ever being advertised or posted, and networking sometimes results in an organization creating a position to accommodate an excellent candidate.

Another benefit of networking is the longer-term value of being connected to a large number of people in a wide variety of occupations and industries. The explosion of information and the fast pace of the workplace have caused managers and executives alike to take a more collaborative approach to work. Therefore, maintaining a healthy network is important for ongoing success. Networking not only enables you to gather information and advice for on-the-job decisions, it is also invaluable if you decide to change employers, careers, industries, or even launch your own venture at some point in the future. The networking process you begin now will be an important resource for you throughout your career.

Finally, networking helps to prevent you from becoming isolated and despondent during your search. People who actively network usually have less difficulty staying motivated because they are busy and externally focused. There are phone calls to be made or returned, emails to be sent, letters to write and upcoming meetings that require preparation. Networking is a way to keep going when optimism wanes. People who network diligently find work.

Networking Is a Mutual Exchange

The information you gather through networking can flow both ways. Even in the short term, your own experience and the knowledge you gain as you network can be of great benefit to others. As well, your ever-expanding list of contacts might contain a key name for someone else. If the employment opportunities that are mentioned are not suitable for you, perhaps you know someone who would be a qualified candidate. In the long term, you will have the chance to return the favour for some of the people who helped you.

If you are no longer employed, you have the unique advantage of being a free agent. Most people will be more generous with their information because you are not representing anyone except yourself. They will tend to talk about their organization, its strategies and challenges with less reserve, while at the same time you will be free to discuss many topics more openly.

Tip: Be careful that you do not betray confidences or give away sensitive information in networking meetings. If you are indiscreet about a person or organization, you will be seen as untrustworthy. When discussing confidential information or highly competitive subjects, talk only about information that is in the public domain.

If you are unemployed, you have the luxury of time to read. Most busy people have a stack of magazines and trade journals weighing down their briefcase. If you can point out the useful and interesting pieces in recent literature, you will have done your networking contacts a favour. Be prepared to give a synopsis of the articles and books you are recommending. Get reprints of exceptional material.

A change management consultant who was in the process of building her own practice read a pivotal article in Harvard Business Review *about communicating change to front-line employees. She made a point of mentioning the article in networking and marketing meetings during the first six months of building her venture. She also purchased a supply of reprints and found that almost everyone who heard her synopsis and accompanying interpretation wanted to read the article for themselves. Sending a reprint gave her another welcome point of contact and a topic for further discussion.*

Steps to Effective Networking

The secret to effective networking is targeted planning and a singular focus on each person you intend to meet. Everything must be tailored to the individual, from deciding when you are ready to make the contact to planning the telephone message, arranging the time and venue for the meeting, planning how you will open the meeting, how much of your background you describe, which targets you mention and what questions you ask. It's obvious that you would handle a meeting with your boss from 12 years ago differently than you would handle one with an industry expert or key decision-maker you have not previously met. There is no universal plan, agenda or script that works for every networking meeting. You must plan and use your judgment for each one separately.

Develop a Comprehensive Networking List

This list is broader than the one you compiled in the market assessment and sales planning exercises. It captures *everyone* you know, including the names of key people you previously identified as being valuable contacts. Do not exclude anyone assuming that you could never get a meeting with them or that they couldn't help you. First, they might surprise you, and second, they might be able to introduce you to others who could be helpful. Use the Personal Network Chart on the next page to jog your memory and think as broadly as possible. For the moment, don't make judgments or do any analysis; just record as extensive an inventory of names as you can.

A career transition consultant was working with a group of warehouse workers in a light industrial park. These men were very skeptical about the value of talking with everyone they knew about their need to find work. However, when each one was asked how he got his most recent job, it was networking all around. Shortly after this discussion, a woman who operated a catering truck arrived. Having heard that the warehouse was closing, she wanted the men to square their accounts with her. They jokingly asked her if she knew of any job openings. The next day she returned to tell the group that a warehouse down the road was hiring. Several applied and two men landed jobs through that serendipitous networking opportunity.

Tip: Consider contacting people who have successfully completed a search somewhat similar to yours. They might have information, contacts and leads they would be glad to share.

Personal Network Chart

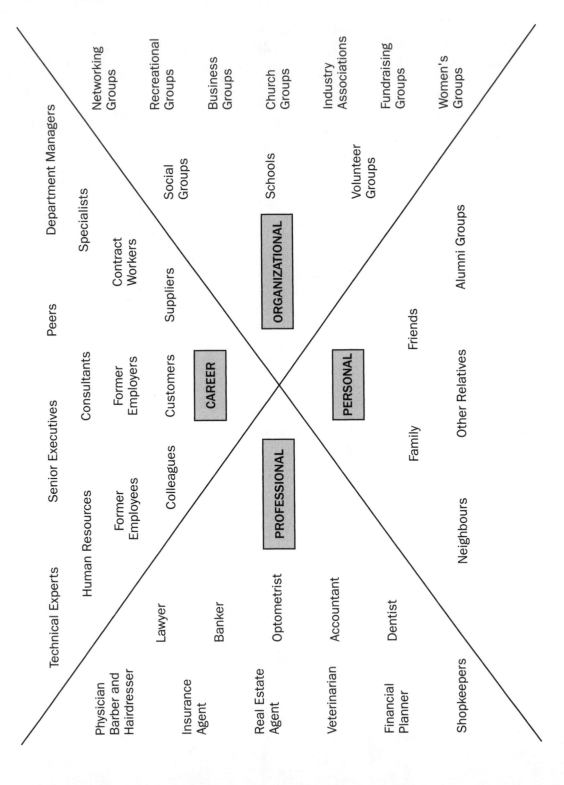

Categorize the List

To make your list manageable, you need to sort the names. These three categories are usually sufficient:

Category 1   Include the people you know well and feel comfortable approaching. This will include your original support network, board of advisers, references, colleagues from the workplace and perhaps some additional friends and family members. These are the people you will contact first, as you gain comfort with the networking process.

Category 2   These are people less well known or less accessible to you. Also include people who would know *of* you and might be willing to meet with you without an introduction. You will contact the people in this category as your confidence and competence at networking increase.

Category 3   Include people you know are beyond you in seniority or expertise, making them seem inaccessible to you. Also include people you know who seem busy, aloof or otherwise unapproachable, and those you haven't met, for whom you need an introduction or referral.

Return to Your Targets and Plan Your Calls

Deciding on what order to make networking calls is not a random or haphazard process. You want to pursue your targets as efficiently as possible while increasing your confidence at networking. At the outset, call only people from Category 1. Tell them that you want to talk about your targets and search plans, and ask their advice on both. Later in the process, when you are calling people from Category 2 or Category 3, you will need to be more specific in your approach.

Tip: Match your list of names to your targets. Approach people from Category 1 who might advance your pursuit of Target A first. Move to other categories and targets as your confidence grows and your clarity regarding specific targets increases.

Being fully prepared before making a call is a large part of networking success. You don't want to make key calls too early in the game, yet you can't wait too long after having been offered a referral before making the contact. Also, it is important to consider the appropriateness of the referring person. It is best to be referred to key decision-makers and influential people by someone they respect. Sometimes it's prudent to intentionally arrange one meeting ahead of another, based on your expectation of what you might learn, and how that information could be useful in subsequent meetings.

Before you pick up the phone, use these guidelines to be sure you're ready.

GUIDELINES FOR PREPARING TO MAKE AN INITIAL CALL

- Focus on one person at a time.
- Decide who to call next based on the following:
  - Your readiness to meet with them, including how comfortable you have become with the networking process and where you are in pursuing your targets.

- Your level of confidence that the person who referred you is the best one to provide the introduction.
- How recently their name was suggested to you. It's better to make the call while the suggestion is fresh so that you can let the referring person know that you are following their suggestion.
- In what way you anticipate the contact to be helpful.
- Once you've chosen a name, do your research. Review what you learned about this person from the referral source or from the context in which you know them personally. Research their organization, the industry or anything else that will give you clues as to what you might discuss with them.
- If they are from an industry less familiar to you, get copies of recent issues of newsletters or journals from their industry to see what topics are current.
- Surmise what might interest them from your experience, knowledge and research.
- Before planning what you will say on the telephone, create a preliminary agenda for the networking meeting.
- If you know them, how will you bridge the gap from the last time you've spoken with them?
- If you don't know them, what will you say about the person who referred you? Why did this person suggest that you make this call?
- Why are you asking for this meeting? What is it that you want to learn from them?
- In the meeting, what key questions might you use to invite them to take the floor?
- Script the telephone call to set up the meeting.

Tip: Remember that you are not making cold calls but rather following up on the leads given to you by someone else in your network. Contacting people you know and using their referrals is the best way to network.

A communications and public relations specialist was looking for a new job when market conditions were particularly slow. She asked for a networking meeting with the VP of Communications at her husband's firm. In that meeting she was given the names of contacts at four organizations that were suppliers of communications services to the firm and who valued their relationship with the VP of Communications. She called the contacts and found that using the VP's name was magical. Meetings were immediately arranged with the four contacts, and she was able to offer them valuable insights into her husband's firm's culture. Although there were no immediate openings at the suppliers' firms, she was given 14 new leads. Three months later, one of those leads resulted in a contract assignment that eventually led to a full-time job.

Tip: Don't feel that arranging networking meetings over lunch is necessary. It's usually easier to schedule a brief meeting in the contact's office than to arrange a lunch date. Also, a series of networking lunches can become very expensive. If you suggest lunch, you need to be prepared to pay.

The Phone Call

The purpose of your telephone call is to arrange a face-to-face meeting that will last approximately 15 to 30 minutes. It seems very short, but this is the amount of time that most people are readily willing to commit. In stating the reason for the meeting, be honest, brief and enthusiastic. Do not attempt to conceal your purpose in an effort to intrigue them and do not hint at potential benefits they might glean from the meeting. You are asking for information, advice and leads regarding a specific occupation, industry or organization. If your contact receives any immediate benefit from the meeting, it will be a bonus.

Tip: Face-to-face meetings are much better than meetings conducted over the phone. In person you will usually receive more information. You also significantly increase the likelihood of getting additional leads and referrals, and have a better chance of being remembered by your contact.

GUIDELINES FOR REQUESTING THE MEETING

- Make your initial calls during regular business hours. However, if you do not connect after a week or so, try calling either before or after hours when it is more likely that the person you want to meet will pick up their own phone.
- Stand up while making the call, to help you sound more confident and businesslike. Smile and it will transmit through your voice. Speak more slowly than usual, especially when you give your name and phone number.
- Use the feature that allows you to review and re-record your message.
- Have your diary in hand and be prepared to suggest a few dates and times.
- Be prepared for each of these three possibilities:
  - Speaking directly with the person you hope to meet.
  - Leaving a message on their voice mail.
  - Speaking with your potential contact's administrative assistant.
- Use the same basic script, adjusting it slightly for each different audience. Practise out loud before placing the call.
- Clearly state your name and the name of the person who referred you.
- Indicate that you would like to arrange a brief meeting, no more than 15 to 30 minutes, and then explain the purpose of the meeting in one or two sentences. Plan your wording carefully. Don't be vague and don't say too much.
- If you reach the contact person directly, try to avoid having the meeting on the phone. Reiterate your willingness to come to their office and be prepared to schedule the meeting for the distant future if the individual is exceptionally busy. If they are insistent about having the discussion on the spot, you'll have to comply. Go through your abbreviated sound bites, ask your questions and ask for referrals.
- If you get voice mail, explain your reason for requesting a meeting as briefly as you can, suggest a time that would work for you and close by saying how much you would appreciate their willingness to meet. The message should take 30 seconds, maximum.

- After leaving a voice mail message, make a diary note to follow up within a week. The second voice mail message should simply remind them of your name, the referring person and the request for the meeting.
- Speaking with the person's administrative assistant can often be the best alternative. Although it is their job to act as a gatekeeper, you might be able to get to know them and make them your ally in arranging a meeting. You can ask them when your chances would be best to speak with their boss.
- If you are having trouble connecting either through voice mail or the administrative assistant, persist by trying once a week. Don't harass, but sound upbeat and confident of the fact that arranging the meeting will happen eventually.
- When a meeting is arranged, restate the time and place as a means of confirming the commitment. Make sure you know exactly how to get there before you hang up.

A successful networker used a telephone script that went like this: "Hi, Mr. Radomski, I'm Janet Newman. I met with Frank Cheng yesterday to talk about the retail investment business, and he suggested that you would probably be able to help me. I spent the past 12 years with Worthy Asset Management Company, where I held a series of positions focused on internal controls and policy. I am currently exploring possibilities for my next career step. My expertise is in risk management and I am interested in understanding how different organizations manage compliance issues. Would you be able to meet with me briefly at your convenience? I am available every afternoon for the balance of this week and anytime next week."

Most people are willing to schedule a networking meeting if they are approached in a straightforward manner and the proposed agenda is credible. Chances are they know first-hand about the challenges of a job search, either because they've been through it or they know someone who has.

Tip: Every time you leave a voice mail message for any reason, make it a habit to slowly and clearly state your phone number right after your name at the beginning and again at the end of your message, allowing the listener to pick it up at either point.

Further Research and Preparation for the Meeting

Now that you have the meeting scheduled, celebrate! You've leaped over a high hurdle. Move on to prepare thoroughly for the meeting.

Note anything that was said in the phone call, and review what your referral told you about the individual you are going to meet. Knowing their role, priorities, issues and challenges will help you plan an effective agenda for the meeting. Develop realistic objectives for the meeting that will advance the pursuit of your targets.

Think about what you will say about the person who referred you. Be exact in your plans for describing yourself and your background. Remember that you have a short time to accomplish a lot. Practise the four-minute version of your sound bites using a timer. It's easy to talk too long. Formulate three to five open-ended questions that you can use to invite your contact to take the floor. These are called "over-to-you" questions. An inventory of suggested questions is found at the end of this chapter.

Continue your research on the industry and the organization, including a last-minute check for press releases on an Internet newswire. If you have up-to-the-minute information about your contact's organization, they will be impressed with your level of preparation and realize that you are serious about your networking efforts.

A marketing specialist who became an expert networker made a habit of checking for press releases on the newswire immediately before leaving for every networking meeting. Many times, doing this enabled him to direct discussions to current topics. Once, he was able to initiate an animated conversation about revolutionary marketing approaches following the recent change in government regulation on the advertisement of specific products. His contact was unaware that a press release on the topic had been issued by his organization. The networker reported that his "over-to-you" questions were so up-to-the-minute that he sounded like a soothsayer. The meeting resulted in introductions to several more networking contacts.

The following worksheet is similar to the one used for preparing your five sound bites in Chapter 12. For networking, you need to add information explaining what you are doing to pursue your Targets A, B and C, plus the "over-to-you" questions. It's crucial that you invite dialogue. Finally, every meeting should end with your request for additional referrals. The worksheet offers a sample dialogue as a guide.

WORKSHEET 15.1
Prepare a Networking Meeting Dialogue

Build Rapport (30 seconds–1 minute)
Greetings, handshakes and card exchange should be accompanied by a very brief conversation aimed at breaking the ice. "I appreciate your taking the time to meet me. I understand that (refer to a point of common interest or the person who introduced you) _____
_____."

"I asked for only 15 minutes of your time, and I want to stick to that, so let me get right to the point."

Capsule Profile and Career Review (3–4 minutes)
"If I may, I'll give you a quick overview of my background and current interests as a means of explaining why I wanted to meet with you. I'm a (title or professional designation) _____.
I've spent the last ____ years in the _____ industry. In the past 10 years, I have worked with or in (name the organizations, projects, people or whatever makes sense for this context) _____
_____
_____.
Most recently, I was (title)_____ of (division or area) _____ with (name of organization plus explanation of its business, if necessary) _____
where I (role or mandate) _____. One highlight for me
was (mention a significant achievement relevant to this meeting and include the result) _____
_____.
I also had the opportunity to (mention more relevant achievements or experiences) _____
_____and _____."

Leaving Story (30 seconds–1 minute)
"My role at _____ came to an end as a result of _____
_____."
Or: "I'm looking for other opportunities because _____."

What You Are Looking For (30 seconds)
"Ideally, I would like my next role to entail or utilize (describe the aspects of your targets that are relevant to this meeting) _____,
and I'm also looking at _____.
Another option would be _____."

What You Are Doing about It (1–2 minutes)

"What I've done so far is (mention research, networking activities, and interviews)_____
_____ and _____ .
"I would appreciate your advice on _____ (or your opinion of) _____
and some feedback on my approach to _____."

Three to Four "Over-to-You" Questions (10 minutes)

"I understand that (lead into your questions by mentioning the referring person or something from
your research) _____ and (ask your most pressing "over-to-you"
question)_____?"
(At this point listen and watch the time. Ask your subsequent questions only if time allows.)
"_____
_____
_____?"

Optional: Ask for Feedback on Your Plans (1–2 minutes)

"How plausible do you think (reiterate Target A, B or C) _____ is?"
"How would you suggest that I approach _____?"
"Is there anything else you think I should keep in mind?"

Ask for Additional Referrals

"Who else do you think I should be talking to?"
"What is your relationship to them?"
"Please tell me more about them."
"Why do you think that they would be a good contact for me?"
"Would it be appropriate for me to mention your name when I call?"

Closing

"I'll stay in touch and let you know how things go. You've been tremendously helpful and again, I
appreciate the time you've given me."

Tip: This is one time it's not advisable to telephone ahead and confirm the meeting. Doing that opens up the possibility of a cancellation.

Conduct the Meeting

Review the advice on preparing for an interview. Many of the principles apply to networking meetings as well. Put yourself in the shoes of the contact person, and be aware that they are probably unsure of how they will be able to help you. It's important to think of ways to put them at ease. Being well prepared and willing to take over the agenda is the best way to do this. This does not mean that you do the talking. You ask the questions and listen.

During the meeting, take responsibility for the time. If you asked for 15 minutes, you must try to stick to it even though it's a very short amount of time. Mention the originally agreed time limit up front, allowing your contact to either confirm that the meeting must end within the allotted time or invite you to stay longer than originally agreed. If the time can be extended, you can relax a bit and explain your background, skills and interests in more depth. However, if you have prepared well, you should be able to turn the floor over to the other person within 5 minutes and have enough time to get answers to your key questions before time is up.

Every networking meeting needs to be handled as if it's the most important interview you will have in your job search. You never know which meeting will be the one that generates the lead to the ideal employment opportunity for you.

Tip: Do not hand your résumé to your networking contact during the meeting unless it is requested. You are not asking for a job or even job leads. Some people don't take a copy of their résumé along to ensure there is no risk of appearing to be asking for a job. The résumé can always be enclosed with the thank-you letter, if requested.

Ask for Referrals

Every networking meeting should include your request for suggestions of people who might be able to offer information and advice. It's best to ask toward the end of the meeting, after you have explained your background and targets. Sometimes you will be comfortable asking for a specific referral, for example, "If you know Fernando Circosta at International Design, I would appreciate an introduction to him," or "I'm interested in finding out more about Town Travel Corporation. Is there someone there you could suggest?"

When you are given referrals, record the names and contact information. Try to find out enough about each person so that you understand why they are recommended and in what way your contact expects them to be helpful to you. Ask if you can, use your contact's name when you call. Express your gratitude for these leads and commit to keeping your contact informed as you make the new contacts.

A general manager who was quite introverted found himself in the job market during the worst years of a recession in which his industry was particularly hard hit. He realized that he would have to make networking the central focus of his job search activities, and there was almost nothing he could have dreaded more. His career transition consultant had assured him that before he conducted his 200th face-to-face networking meeting he would find the work he wanted. The general manager discovered that thinking of networking as a "numbers game" helped to keep him motivated, and he measured his success by the number of new referrals he was given. To keep track, he kept a growing stack of contacts' business cards, which he counted regularly. At any given moment, he knew exactly how many cards he had in his "meeting completed" pile, which had grown to 168 by the time he got an excellent job offer. His success was the result of persistently being out there talking with people.

Debrief and Write a Thank-You Letter

After every networking meeting, debrief in writing as you would following an interview. Use the Sample Networking Tracking Sheet from Chapter 14 to record the relevant facts. Write a thank-you letter within 24 hours if possible, and mention something specific from the conversation that was particularly helpful to you. Close by stating your intention to follow up, and as always, make a diary note to do it. File the information in your record-keeping system so that you can retrieve it for future meetings, interviews or other opportunities.

Follow Up

As soon as you can, contact the people whose names you have been given. If you don't feel ready to make some of the calls, use your judgment, but remember that it often takes a long time to set up a meeting. If you plan the phone calls very carefully, make them and arrange a meeting, your confidence will probably build by the time you have the meeting.

Every time you contact someone to whom you have been referred, thank the person who referred you. Send a brief email message, handwritten note or letter, or leave a voice mail message. This simple courtesy accomplishes three very important things:

- It demonstrates that you value the leads given to you.
- It lets the referring person know that the contact has been made.
- It keeps your name top-of-mind with the referring person, thereby increasing the likelihood that you will be remembered when additional networking opportunities or job leads arise.

Tip: When someone gives you permission to use their name as a reference for a networking call, they *want* to know when the contact has been made. Your career plans often become a point of mutual interest between the referring person and the new contact. You must keep your contacts up-to-date on your activities and thank them not only after the first meeting, but every time their advice and referrals help you.

Once you have had an initial networking meeting, followed up on all of the leads given to you and expressed your gratitude appropriately, you need to find more ways to stay in touch with your networking contacts. Think of how you can become a blip on your contacts' radar screens! It doesn't take much. A 30-second voice mail message giving a quick update on your progress will do it. An email asking for a very specific piece of information is an excellent option. A greeting card during the holidays or verbal regards delivered by a mutual acquaintance also works. Use the following guidelines to generate more ideas.

GUIDELINES FOR STAYING IN TOUCH WITH NETWORKING CONTACTS

- Make your networking follow-up efforts unique to each individual. There is no universal plan that dictates the frequency or form of subsequent contact.
- For your original support network and board of advisers, monthly contact is probably a minimum. For others, the minimum could be as long as six months. Use your judgment.
- Use voice mail, email, handwritten notes or letters to stay in touch. Brief messages are best.
- Do not put all your networking contacts on a mass mailing list using your email software. Do not assume that using the bcc function makes this form of communication acceptable. Your contacts may be annoyed to receive regular messages that are not personally relevant.
- When you have heard an interesting speaker or read an informative article or book, send a quick message about it to those who you know would be interested.
- If there is a speaker you would like to hear, think of inviting someone in your network who would be interested in attending with you.
- When you write a new case study, create a portfolio or develop a new biography or brochure, send it to appropriate contacts, asking for their feedback.
- When you have an upcoming interview or networking meeting and you know that someone in your network could provide valuable input, phone them and ask specific questions. Most people respond to questions such as, "I'm meeting with Heather Speigle next Tuesday, and I wonder if you know how long she's been at Engineering Consulting Company and where she worked before joining them?"
- Send your congratulations when you learn of a contact's promotion, transfer or change of employers.
- Similarly, if a mutual acquaintance receives a promotion or changes jobs, check to see if your networking contact has heard the good news.
- Remember personal details that are mentioned in networking meetings. If you know that a contact has just returned from vacation, ask about it in your next message or conversation. Try to keep track of family concerns and special occasions if your contact has confided in you.
- Schedule the occasional breakfast or lunch with your key contacts, if your budget can handle it.
- Most importantly, keep your contacts up-to-date on your job search activities, especially if your targets change.

Tip: The year-end holiday season and July and August are excellent times to have networking meetings. Because so many people are away, those who remain in the office often have more time and are less likely to feel pressured than at other times of the year.

Make Networking a Way of Life

Don't make the common mistake of neglecting or forgetting your network once you've landed. Stay in touch at least twice a year and look for opportunities to be helpful. Be proactive in offering your time and talents in some way that you know would be appreciated. Lead a seminar in an area of your expertise for your contact's direct reports, contribute to a fundraising effort, suggest candidates for a job opening and introduce others from your network. There will be many opportunities if you look for them.

Raise your industry profile by joining and participating actively in professional associations. By becoming involved in committees and special projects, you will be able to work with and get to know people that you would not otherwise meet. Accepting a position on the executive will also expand your range of contacts and develop your reputation.

Consider volunteering for a charitable, recreational or political organization that reflects your values. When you contribute your time to a cause or activity that means something to you, you usually meet like-minded people. Get to know the organizers and executive boards of these groups. Contacts from your non-working life can be more valuable than your work-related network when you need advice and assistance for problems on the job or during times of career transition.

Attend business and social functions. Become more active in your community. Take courses, attend conferences and sign up for workshops and seminars. Be proactive in introducing yourself in these situations. Ask questions of people you meet and learn what they do. Share your own background and look for areas of mutual interest. It's a small world, and you'll often be surprised by the connections you share with the people you meet.

Tip: How many times in your life have you made the effort to contact someone and then thought, "I wish I had waited three more weeks before I made that call"? More often, you wish you had made the call sooner. Don't procrastinate.

GUIDELINES FOR SPECIAL NETWORKING CHALLENGES

When Someone Offers to Take Your Résumé to Someone Else

- Occasionally a networking contact will offer to take a copy of your résumé and pass it around for you. At best, this offer is well-intentioned, and the individual will do what they say. At worst, it's a brush-off. Regardless, there is no assurance that your background, skills and career plans will be introduced properly by what someone else says about you.
- When someone is passing your résumé around, it can be a deterrent to your networking efforts by causing awkward overlaps that make you appear desperate.
- Letting someone else hand out your résumé precludes your opportunity to follow up.
- It's better if you maintain control of the process. Thank the people who make such offers, and ask if they would be willing to give you the names and allow you to make the approach.
- Sometimes there will be a good reason to let a contact go ahead and pass your résumé around. More often, you will be given a list of referrals for follow up.

- Ask if you might use the referring person's name. Try to find out as much as possible about each potential new contact.

Breaking Out of Concentric Circles

- Once you have been actively networking for several months, you might find that you're beginning to hear the same news and the same names repeatedly. This means that your networking is moving in concentric circles and you need to break into other networks.
- To expand your horizons, explore an entirely new idea with your existing contacts to see if additional referrals are available.
- Contact people in organizations who supply the industry that interests you.
- Take a trip to another city and network there for a week. This takes careful pre-planning and a willingness to relocate.
- Choose another industry that holds your interest and ask your existing networking contacts to introduce you to someone in that industry.
- The executive directors of industry associations are often quite generous with information and referrals.
- Ask your stockbroker to provide an introduction to an industry analyst. They have in-depth knowledge of the influential people within an industry.

Getting in Touch with Category 3 Contacts

When you sorted your inventory of names, you put some people in Category 3 either because you didn't know them or you thought that they were inaccessible to you. Also, as you conduct networking meetings, you are given more Category 3 names.

- Make it a goal in your research and networking conversations to find out as much as possible about these individuals and their organizations.
- If one of them is speaking at a conference or making a public presentation, make every effort to be in the audience. Ask a thoughtful question from the floor if the opportunity arises.
- Find out who knows them, and try to arrange meetings with their acquaintances.
- Think strategically about who would provide the most persuasive referral. If you can use the name of someone who is very important to the person you want to meet, your chances of being granted a meeting are much higher.
- Be direct in telling your networking contacts and board of advisers that you are looking for an opportunity to meet these people. When you know that someone has the ability to introduce you, ask them if they would feel comfortable doing so.
- Even though some people seem so distant that they are barely on your radar screen, someone you know will know them. That brings you closer to the opportunity to be in touch.

After researching recent changes in health care, a facilities and technology manager from a large urban school board wanted to see if his skills might transfer to the health care sector. To assess his marketability, he set up a networking meeting with a senior manager at a large urban hospital. He used the meeting to verify what he had learned and gather more specific information about the impact that changes within the health care industry were having on his area of specialty. During the conversation, he received excellent advice on repackaging his experience to align it more closely with the health care industry. He then drafted a résumé using this advice and forwarded it to his contact for feedback. The contact was impressed with both the résumé and the serious interest of the facilities manager, and offered several valuable leads for contract and consulting work.

An Inventory of Questions to Ask in Networking Meetings

These questions are intended to direct your thought processes, not to be rhymed off without considering the specific individual and the circumstances of the networking meeting. Your best questions will arise from your research. When you preface a question with a statement such as "I read about your recent acquisitions in Chile," your contact will be more inclined to give you useful information.

- Review the research questions on trends, industries, organizations and people listed in Chapter 9. They are excellent networking questions.
- Ask your networking contact to describe their background and experience:
  - What is your history in this organization?
  - What were your previous roles?
  - Where were you before you joined this organization?
- Ask about your contact's current role:
  - How is the organization structured and where does your department fit?
  - How is your department structured?
  - What is your mandate?
  - What issues do you think you'll be tackling in the next 18 months?
  - What might be a next step for you?
- Ask about the industry and the market:
  - How would you define your organization's competitive advantage?
  - Where do you think _____ is headed?
  - What is your attitude toward _____?
  - What skills are most in demand in this industry … in your organization?
  - Are there any books or management theories that are popular in this organization or industry?
  - What search firms and placement agencies does your organization use?
- Ask for feedback on your plans:
  - Do you think that my skills and experience would be seen as transferable to _____?
  - What do you think of my prospects for moving into the field of _____?
  - What sort of position might someone with my background aspire to in this industry?
  - Who else should I be talking to?

Chapter 16

The Internet, Ads and Search Firms

*Passive search techniques
add value when used effectively.*

Notwithstanding the importance of getting out there and talking with people, you must also search the Internet for postings, look for ads in print media and approach search firms and placement agencies. You need to understand how to best employ these methods and include them in your search strategy. They cannot be ignored, but invest your time in them only in proportion to their effectiveness. Do not become discouraged if they don't generate quick results.

Using the Internet
The Internet is a powerful tool for corporate recruiters and executive search professionals, giving them the ability to collect many more résumés than traditional methods allowed. The cost efficiency of online postings, email receipt of information and electronic filtering for first-level sorting has caused the Internet to eclipse conventional newspaper advertising. The huge benefit to the job seeker is the increased number of advertised positions in the public domain and the efficiency of electronic matching technology.

The Internet has not, however, magically transformed the arduous task of the job search into a cakewalk. There are no guarantees of effortless success, especially for those who have reached more senior levels or work in specialized, non-technical areas. However, you must not overlook the opportunity to see what's out there. Using the Internet as an effective part of your search requires selectivity and discipline. You must stay focused on your targets; otherwise, the vast array of information and advertising can be distracting and very wasteful of your time.

There are thousands of job search sites in cyberspace, some claiming to have hundreds of thousands of advertised positions. There are sites covering all industries, professions and levels. They may be Canadian, North American or global in scope. There are also specialty sites devoted to specific fields such as IT, biotech, the arts and non-profit organizations. Most industry and professional associations have career sections on their sites. It can be overwhelming. Make the initial, albeit substantial, investment of time to identify the ones that have a number of postings at your level, in the industries and locations that interest you.

Select a few sites that are relevant to your search, and register using their notification service called "job alerts," "career alerts" or "agents." These electronic agents are search engines within the site that you create using keywords and job titles that apply to you. They locate matches between your information and their job postings, emailing their findings to you on a regular basis. Open a separate, free email account for this purpose to protect your privacy. At the end of your search, you can cancel the email account when you delete your search agents.

Creating effective job alerts requires yet another substantial investment of your time. The major job boards invite you to have multiple alerts. Discovering which job titles and keywords generate appropriate responses may take a few weeks of intuitive work. You need to check the postings emailed to you against your independent search for relevant postings on the site. This way you will discover if the information you registered captures the right postings. Persist! This feature of the Internet job search repays your effort tenfold.

An architect who moved into general management and advanced to the executive level in a major real estate company discovered that listing the word "architect" with Internet job search agents was not helpful. The information technology industry has usurped the word, using it to describe the creators of systems and programs. Through trial and error, he discovered that using the words "executive" or "leader" in combination with "real estate" generated the desired matches.

The careers sections on corporate web sites are designed to attract qualified candidates and promote the organization. By visiting the web sites of your target organizations you can view the list of posted positions and apply directly using the specified protocol. This will allow you to avoid the technical glitches that sometimes occur when applying through a job board. Another advantage is the glimpse you get of your targets' overall hiring needs. You can learn a lot about the challenges and opportunities facing an organization and glean valuable information for planning your approach in networking meetings and in preparing for the interviewing process.

Tip: The career sections on corporate sites do not necessarily list all of the positions available in an organization. More senior positions are seldom posted and opportunities in the planning stages are never posted. Networking is the only way to find unadvertised opportunities.

The proliferation of job postings on the Internet has created a niche for the application of spider technology to the employment market. Job search sites that rely exclusively on spider technology pick up postings from other web sites rather than directly from the original source of the posting. Their goal is to provide a one-stop service to job seekers who subscribe for a fee. Once you sign up, you will establish your search criteria just as you did for the job boards. Powerful spider software will then retrieve relevant postings for you from thousands of other sites including the major job boards, corporate sites and search firms' sites. Before subscribing, be sure that you understand the scope of the spider's search. The managers of this type of job search site dictate how far and wide their technology reaches. Their criteria must be as broad as yours for the service to be worthwhile for you.

Tip: Once you have done your research, selected the job seach sites that are appropriate for you and registered several job alerts, do not spend more than 10% of your ongoing search time and energy on Internet job boards. Let the technology take care of the search for you, emailing you information about possible matches. You should carry on with your networking activities.

Internet job boards also offer you the opportunity to post your résumé on their sites. Once posted, your résumé is available for employers to peruse, often using sophisticated search technology. Presumably, employers will contact you and invite you to apply for appropriate jobs. It seems an attractive proposition, but there are significant drawbacks. There have been many incidents of identity theft. Databases containing online résumés and job seekers' email addresses are sometimes sold or stolen. The consequences to you could be significant.

Important: If you choose to post your résumé on any Internet venue, you will probably receive unsolicited email and phone calls in response. Those contacting you might offer to conduct your job search for you, put you in touch with a number of companies or place you in a prime job within a short period of time. These offers may have a number of motives such as seeking payment of a fee for which you may obtain no benefit, or persuading you to make an investment in a new business such as a franchise or pyramid-selling scheme. Use due caution in responding to these offers.

Ads in Newspapers, Newsletters and Trade Journals

Traditional venues for job ads are still important. Until the Internet totally replaces print material, you must read the daily newspapers plus the industry journals and newsletters faithfully. You will find that many ads in the print media are also posted on Internet job boards and on organizations' web sites.

As you peruse newspapers and magazines, be sure to keep your eyes open for appointment notices and other news items that signal a change within an organization. It's good information for your networking efforts and can offer early signals of upcoming vacancies.

A sales executive from the hospitality industry read that a conglomerate had bought several world-class cruise ships. Recognizing that the acquisition could create the need for additional senior managers, he called the president of the acquiring company and explained his interest. The president was in Spain on holidays, but when he picked up his messages, he was so impressed that he returned the call personally, arranging a meeting for his first day back in the office.

The two main sources of job postings—print ads and the Internet—should be considered as one because they represent identical strategies on the part of the employer. They simply use different delivery channels. In each case, the employer has decided to advertise the available position to a broad market and collect as many résumés as possible. You will be one of hundreds or thousands responding to the posting. Your chance of being selected for the interview process is no better for jobs posted on the Internet than for traditional print ads.

Search Firms and Placement Agencies

Search firms and placement agencies play an important role in the active job search; however, don't make the mistake of thinking that you can register with a few well-chosen ones and then sit back and wait for results. These companies have no vested interest in finding you a job. They work for their client organizations and are focused on you only to the extent that you meet the criteria for one of their current assignments. If you are not a suitable candidate for any of the positions they are seeking to fill, they will keep your information in their database for an amount of time that varies from six months to a lifetime. Policies vary. Therefore, it's up to you to keep in touch and ensure that your qualifications stay top-of-mind with them.

Tip: Once your information is on file with a search firm or placement agency, you must continue checking their ads and Internet postings. When you see an ad that matches your interests, either call your contact or resubmit your application. Don't assume that you are in the process automatically.

Having said this, most search consultants are very interested in getting to know a large number of people and keeping track of their careers. It's their business to know who's who in the industries they serve, and they are conscious of the logical career moves that an individual needs to make in order to climb the ladder of success. Therefore, getting to know a few search consultants should be a part of your active job search plan. You will need a good networking introduction in order to meet them unless you are being considered for one of their assignments. An introduction from someone in one of their client organizations is often effective.

Tip: Researchers are the hidden treasures in many search firms. It's their job to compile the initial list of qualified candidates for an assignment. They are usually more accessible than the consultants and partners of the firm, and will often take the time to talk with you over the phone. They are an invaluable source of information once you have formed a relationship with them.

Search firms, also known as executive search firms or headhunters, differ from placement agencies in that they typically work exclusively at the senior management, professional and executive levels. Positions with starting salaries of less than $100,000 probably do not warrant their services. Search firms are usually paid on a retainer basis. Their fees are typically based on a percentage of the position's base or total cash compensation for the first year. With a retainer-based firm, fees are payable whether or not the search firm identifies a candidate who is successful in being hired by the organization. Once you have been identified as a candidate for one of their assignments, they will work very hard to help you.

Many search firms advertise the positions they are filling on their web sites, making it easy for the job seeker to evaluate the suitability of a particular firm. A few search firms also offer a confidential résumé-posting service where hiring organizations may peruse candidates' résumés. The occasional search firm will require you to fill out a lengthy online questionnaire as a way of registering with them. Many firms have linked their web sites to Internet job boards. Before posting your résumé on a search firm's or placement agency's site, read their privacy policy.

> *An operations manager from a major utility company who became a legend of the active job search game asked most of the people he met through his networking efforts to identify the search firms and placement agencies their organizations used. Doing this narrowed his list of firms for ongoing attention and contact, making this part of his job search as efficient as possible.*

Placement agencies often specialize in specific market niches. The jobs they fill cover the whole spectrum from full-time to temporary, seasonal or contract opportunities. They typically work on a contingency basis, being paid only when one of their candidates is hired. Although some agencies, particularly in the United States, charge an additional fee to the candidate, this is not a common practice in Canada. Placement agencies are interested in you only to the extent that your qualifications fit one of their current assignments.

Regardless, do your research and find the placement agencies that are active and respected in your industry. Keep in touch with a few carefully chosen ones either by checking their web sites regularly or by calling occasionally to see if there are any new possibilities.

GUIDELINES FOR USING SEARCH FIRMS AND PLACEMENT AGENCIES

- Do not expect these organizations to find a job for you. No more than 10% of your job search time and energy should be spent with them unless you are actively in consideration for one of their assignments.
- Use your network and do thorough research to determine which search firms and placement agencies typically have assignments that match your skills and interests. Check their web sites regularly and try to develop a relationship with someone in the firm.
- Some employers do not post their openings on their own web site but rather use a select group of search firms and placement agencies for all their hiring needs. Find out which firms are used by the organizations that are of interest to you, and stay in touch with them.
- If you approach a company directly for a position that has been contracted out to an agency, expect to be redirected to the agency. If the hiring organization proceeds independently, a dispute over the fee could ensue. You might be caught in the middle and ultimately lose your chance at landing the job.

- If you approach more than one placement agency, you might find yourself being presented for the same job by several firms. This is a problem. You must immediately decline the opportunity with the firm that was second in bringing it to you.
- Search consultants and placement agency representatives are expert interviewers. They will probe your background using a full range of interviewing techniques, particularly behavioural interviewing.
- In the initial interview with a search firm or placement agency, the name of the hiring organization will probably be withheld. This is done to maintain the confidentiality of the search so that neither an incumbent nor the competition will be prematurely alerted to changes.
- Once you are being considered for a position they represent, your consultant should be very helpful in providing inside information on the hiring organization. Talking with them should allow you to complete a large portion of your research.
- Your consultant should offer you feedback from each interview, with tips on what areas of your expertise should be highlighted in subsequent interviews.
- Always remember that the consultant is working primarily for the hiring organization. If there are several finalists for a position, the consultant will probably have input into the selection. It is therefore important that you continually manage your discussions with them as if you are being interviewed.
- Placement agencies and search firms will either help you with salary negotiations or negotiate for you. Stay involved with this aspect of the process.
- Hiring processes are often protracted, especially at more senior levels. If you are seen early in the process by the hiring organization, you may be a benchmark candidate, meaning that you appear to be ideally suited for the job and all subsequent candidates have the challenge of testing out above you. Although the wait can be disconcerting, you're in a good position unless you have other opportunities that need to be resolved.

Passive Search Techniques to Avoid

The ease with which you can distribute data through cyberspace has caused many job seekers to blast their résumés, unsolicited, to numerous prospective employers. Do not waste your time doing this, and do not pay a fee-based résumé distribution service to do it for you. It merely creates résumé spam, the scourge of corporate recruiters. It's the current equivalent of an old technique, the broadcast distribution of your résumé and generic cover letter by mail. This search method was, and still is, ineffective.

Beware of organizations that charge you a fee and promise to find you a job. Often, they represent you only by distributing your résumé, with minimal targeting and no follow-up, to vast numbers of hiring organizations. Your money is seldom well-spent on such services.

Chapter 17

Play to Win

An active search and marketing savvy will give you the advantage.

Winning athletes have effective strategies. They work hard to analyze the playing field and the competition. They know their advantages and vulnerabilities, and think about how to overcome obstacles. Their strategies include plans to sustain them through the long haul and tactics for generating a final burst of energy to cross the finish line first. They know what it takes to win. You need to know what it takes to win the employment opportunity you want.

Don't kid yourself. When you are looking for work, you're in a competition. Employers always have other alternatives to hiring you. They can leave a position vacant, choose someone else or restructure, precluding the need to hire. You must do everything possible to make working with you the most attractive option. Persevering with an active search to generate opportunities and knowing when and how to use bold marketing tactics are the keys to success.

Keep Your Search Active

An active employment search is just that—active! A passive search is reactive. It concentrates on the techniques that do not require a proactive approach to people and new ideas. This doesn't mean that a passive job search will be unsuccessful; it simply means that you are relying on circumstances and events outside your control to bring opportunities your way. Active job seekers go out and find new possibilities through creative thinking, probing research and an open-minded exploration of their targets. They talk with as many people as possible in carefully planned and appropriate ways.

Tip: When the going gets tough, just keep going. At all times be positive, patient, persistent and polite.

The following chart compares and contrasts the characteristics of the two approaches. Locate yourself on the chart and think about what you need to do to shift your attitude and activities to the "active" column.

Job Search Factors	Active	Passive
Attitude of the job seeker	• Feels in control and confident • Is willing to take up the challenge • Tries new approaches and techniques • Is open to feedback and suggestions • Is enthusiastic, highly motivated	• Feels victimized, blames others • Is unwilling • Is inflexible • Is defensive • Is despondent
Focus of the search	• Seeks external contact • Is involved and engaged • Focus is on the job search • Is interested in people • Has targets A, B & C in place	• Is turned inward • Is isolated • Has scattered energies • Is interested in inanimate resources • Is willing to take any job available
Scope of the search	• Looks at a variety of industries • Seeks out unfamiliar organizations • Thinks creatively about roles • Goes out to find new possibilities	• Stays with known industries • Has a limited list of organizations • Seeks to stay with known roles • Remains closed to new possibilities
Hours dedicated	• Works at the job search full-time • Spends 30 to 40 hours per week on dedicated job search activities • Makes a sustained effort	• Spends 10 to 20 hours or less each week on the job search • Counts all Internet surfing time and reading the comics in the 10 hours • Makes a sporadic effort
Methods employed	• Spends 80% of time actively networking • Follows up on all leads regardless of how unlikely they seem • Creates and follows a plan for using agencies or search firms • Answers ads and Internet postings • Posts résumé on Internet job boards • Plans time for self-care to keep energy and spirits high	• Answers ads and Internet postings • Posts résumé on Internet job boards • Contacts a few agencies or search firms without follow-up • Sends out broadcast letters with résumé attached • Sends out networking letters without personal follow-up • Networks with only a few close and well-known colleagues and friends
Resilience	• Manages to depersonalize rejection • Generates activity on many fronts • Recognizes and guards vulnerabilities • Is persistent	• Takes rejection personally • Puts all eggs in one basket • Remains unaware of vulnerabilities • Stops trying after setbacks
Measures of success	• Every plan implemented and every short-term goal attained is counted as a success and celebrated • Finds an ideal opportunity	• Uses only one measure: landing a job

The Employer's Point of View

Stand in the employer's shoes for a moment. When you have a vacancy to fill there are three objectives:
- Find the person with the right skills and the right fit for the position, the team and the culture of the organization.
- Fill the vacancy quickly.
- Minimize the cost of the search.

The major risk in hiring is the employer's limited access to information about a candidate's past performance and ability to deal with people. For this reason, hiring someone known to the interviewer or recommended by a trusted colleague or employee substantially minimizes the risk.

An experienced hiring manager will usually follow these steps in this order:
- Search for an internal candidate using personal observations and knowledge plus internal networking.
- Consider individuals outside the organization who are known first-hand.
- Follow formal internal job posting procedures.
- Use an external network of contacts to identify appropriate candidates.
- Check the organization's database of external résumés.
- Place the posting on an Internet job board or advertise using traditional print media.
- Use an executive search firm or placement agency.

Tip: Even when policy requires that all vacancies be posted internally, the informal networking and selection process is still active and powerful. If the best candidate is someone known or recommended, but who is outside the organization, executives will often find a way to hire them.

A CFO from an established communications organization was interested in making a move to a media company. He researched the industry and identified three companies that appealed to him. Using his network, he was able to meet with the CEO and founder of one company. He explained his professional skills and background, and was explicit about his interest in joining the founder's team. Although there was no immediate opening, the founder had been thinking about upgrading his management team in preparation for an acquisition within 24 months. That networking meeting was the catalyst for advancing the founder's plans. The CFO was hired, the acquisition successfully completed and the CFO launched a new phase of his career that was more closely attuned to his interests.

Your Point of View

As a job seeker, you want to have your potential candidacy identified as early in the selection process as possible. To achieve this you must be in touch with many people in numerous organizations so that your name will be raised for consideration during the initial steps of a search.

Ironically, most people prefer to focus their energies where the decision-makers least prefer to conduct their search. It's easy to surf the Internet, register on a few job boards, answer ads, talk with a search firm or two and believe that the best opportunities will eventually come your way. Excellent opportunities are often filled before they get to agencies, the Internet, newspapers or trade journals.

A senior retail executive got past his initial reluctance to network and quickly transformed his passive job search into a very active one. His weeks were filled with one meeting after another and all of his time outside meetings was devoted to preparation and follow-up. One day he got a phone call out of the blue from the CEO of a small manufacturing company. The CEO said, "I'm looking for a new VP of Operations, and the last five people I talked to mentioned your name! I don't know who you are, but I've got to meet you!" Although the job was not a good fit, their meeting generated a long list of new contacts and the CEO's ongoing support.

Barriers to the Active Job Search

Fear of Rejection

The primary barrier to conducting an active job search is the fear of rejection. Looking for employment can be one of the more daunting experiences that life has to offer. What you do for a living can be such a large part of your identity that it's difficult not to take everything connected with your search personally. Who would want to compound the stress of looking for a new opportunity with the small setbacks of phone calls not returned, meetings refused and polite brush-offs from those you approach for help? Of course, the answer is "No one!" It's easier to stay hidden behind your computer or busy with résumé revisions and broadcast emails than to brave the world of networking.

Those who master the techniques of the active job search don't entirely eliminate their feelings of fear and vulnerability; rather, they reduce them through good planning, research, well-crafted scripts, appropriate approaches to people and, most importantly, a strong support system. You need to acknowledge what will be most difficult for you and work hard to get yourself through it.

Introverts and Extroverts

Another often-cited barrier to conducting an active job search is the intrinsic difference between people with outgoing personalities and those who are more reserved and quiet. This distinction is important, and the issue is actually quite complex. Even naturally extroverted people might withdraw into a shell when they are experiencing the stress of a job search. Confidence is the critical factor. Regardless of your personality type, if you can muster the confidence, you can do what's needed to conduct an active job search.

Unquestionably, the job search methods that generate better success are easier for people who prefer an extroverted approach. Although there are distinct advantages throughout the career transition process to the introverted approach, the employment market consistently gives greater rewards to extroverted activities. Job seekers who are more introverted need to mimic extroverts, at their confident best, and those who are too outgoing can learn to rein in their effusiveness by observing their introverted colleagues.

Introverts tend to do an excellent job of thinking through their search plans and techniques before enacting them. This is advantageous in the early stages of career transition because it usually results in quality work in the more individual tasks of planning strategy, doing research and conducting a career assessment. In later stages, it can translate into good record-keeping, administration and follow-up, although many extroverts are also very well organized.

Extroverts are more inclined to talk about their job search before they plan it fully. These are the people who prefer to verbally form their strategy and do their research by asking questions of other people. Naturally drawn to action, extroverts risk interacting with their network too soon, confusing or tiring important contacts. However, they are usually more natural marketers who promote themselves and their experience with greater ease. Developing rapport with new contacts comes more easily and conversations flow with less effort.

In the networking process, virtually everyone has difficulty making telephone calls, particularly to people they don't know well. Making these calls can make you feel like you're asking someone to give up their valuable time to help you, a privilege that you think you don't deserve. As well, most people dislike appearing needy and when you are networking, you truly need information, advice and leads. For these reasons, making initial calls to ask for networking meetings is the crucial test of confidence for extroverts and introverts alike. The only way around this barrier is to trust in others' genuine willingness to be helpful, and plan an approach that is straightforward and credible. Remember that you will likely have something to offer them in return, if not now, at some point in the future. Tackle one call at a time, plan it carefully and give yourself full credit—even a reward—for making the call. Once a meeting is arranged, preparing for it and conducting it is a far easier task.

Introverted activities such as doing the research and developing targeted questions will help lower anxiety levels for both introverts and extroverts as they prepare for networking meetings. Showing reserve in meetings by listening attentively and not overstaying your welcome is also an introverted trait that is recommended for all. At the same time, introverts need to act more like extroverts and relate to networking contacts with their own expression of enthusiasm.

Tip: Don't let your natural preference for introversion or extroversion become a barrier to the active job search. Intentionally manage your behaviour to achieve a balanced approach, and remember that confidence is by far the more crucial factor.

Maintaining Motivation

An active search generates its own momentum and motivation. The law of inertia applies: objects, or in this instance, search activities, in motion tend to stay in motion. The notable reward for asking people for information, advice and leads is that you get what you request with encouragement as a bonus. Obviously, information, advice, leads and encouragement motivate you to initiate more meetings, which return additional information, advice, leads and encouragement, and so on.

Even with an active search under way, everyone has ups and downs as they go through the process. This is especially true for those with target markets that are quite specialized, very small or in a phase of consolidation or inactivity, resulting in a longer search. A protracted search is challenging for even the most optimistic individuals. Mood swings still need attention even though they are not as exaggerated as they were at the outset of the career transition process. Good coping techniques are crucial as the weeks go by.

Coping well entails recognizing your emotional needs and taking steps to manage them. Your method of dealing with your emotions is unique. You might need more time to yourself to recharge your batteries, or maybe you're the sort of person who seeks contact with others for a boost. Depending on your style, either working harder or backing off a bit might help you. Some people can talk themselves into a positive frame of mind, while others benefit from motivational books or inspiring speakers. Your support network and professionals such as your doctor, counsellor or career transition consultant can be excellent resources for the long haul.

Tip: Worry is a misuse of imagination!

The guidelines found in Chapter 3, for coping with the emotions accompanying loss and change, can also help sustain your motivation throughout your search for work. Regardless of the source of stress, the same techniques work. In addition to reviewing those strategies, use the guidelines that follow for more practical tips.

GUIDELINES FOR STAYING MOTIVATED THROUGHOUT THE JOB SEARCH
- Put a structure in place for your job search activities. Set business hours for yourself just as if you were expected to report to the office.
- Don't let hobbies, volunteer commitments, household chores, renovations or other activities unrelated to the job search take over your schedule.
- Have a plan with daily goals and objectives. Make them reasonable so that you can end each day by congratulating yourself on a job well done.
- Build stress-reducing activities into your daily schedule. Plan to go for a walk or a workout every day after you've completed your tough calls.
- Organize your day to accommodate your mood swings and energy levels. For example, if early afternoon is always a low time for you, don't make initial networking calls at that time.
- Use your high-energy moments as springboards for tackling the more daunting tasks. When you are feeling up, get tomorrow's calls out of the way early. Tackle the list of thank-you letters or get that cover letter finalized and dispatched.
- When you are feeling down, cut yourself some slack and seek out those things that you know will help restore your equilibrium.
- Keep weekends as time off for you and your loved ones.
- Do a weekly performance review. Since you are effectively paying yourself, evaluate whether or not you have earned your pay. What percentage of your time has been spent on the activities that are known to generate success?
- Counting the number of networking meetings you conduct each week is a good measure of the success of your search efforts. Between scheduling, doing the preliminary research, planning

your agenda, attending the meetings and following up with thank-you letters, six to eight networking meetings each week will keep you very active in the job search.
- Celebrate every success. Give yourself a reward for accomplishing your daily or weekly goals. Make the reward something that is healthy, fun or vitally interesting to you.
- Build some volunteer time into your weekly schedule. Helping someone whose needs are different from yours can be an excellent way to keep things in perspective.
- Remind yourself that your family and friends like you because you are *you*. It wasn't your identity as Vice President of Whatever at Previous Co. that held their affection and admiration.
- Keep the active job search going full speed ahead even when you are in the final stages of negotiating with an organization. It's devastating to have an opportunity that you really want fall through and have nothing else on the go.

A communications and public relations officer was feeling quite despondent at the outset of her job search. Although she was not usually in the habit of watching golf tournaments on TV, she tuned into the British Open. The announcer was talking about what factors differentiated the champions. He said that it had very little to do with physical build, natural athletic ability or a unique swing, but rather that it was the athlete's focus, determination and strength of character to sustain the long, arduous training that produced winners. She wrote down what the announcer said and began to think of each bit of research, and every phone call, letter and meeting as another practice swing. With this in mind, she knew she could do it, and she did. She landed a job that suited her to a T!

An active search, one with 80% of your time and energy allocated to networking, will result in two vitally important outcomes:

- An aware network to keep you informed
- Employment opportunities

An aware network will help you understand the marketplace, provide more contacts and alert you to opportunities. As you learn about market realities and the pragmatism of your targets, you expand your network and pursue new opportunities. One of them will be the right one for you.

Keep this proverb posted where you will see it often.

When nothing seems to help, I go and look at a stonecutter hammering away at his rock, perhaps a hundred times without so much as a crack showing in it. Yet at the hundred and first blow it will split in two, and I know it was not that blow that did it—but all that had gone before.

—Jacob Riis

Powerful Marketing Approaches That Work

The traditional components of an active and effective search can be mastered by just about anyone who has self-discipline and determination. With an accomplishment-focused résumé, effective research techniques, a planned and persistent networking effort, strong interviewing skills and a strategic focus based on targeting, many job seekers assume there's nothing else they can do to advance their search. They simply persist. This strategy works, but there *is* more that can be done. You can take an active and powerful marketing approach to compete for the work you want.

As your search progresses, there will be many circumstances in which you can demonstrate your capabilities by linking your value proposition to the situation at hand. Opportunities abound for more assertive marketing. The following list offers several examples. You will discover more if you look for them.

- You are networking with a key individual and want to bring one of your past experiences to life.
- An interviewer or networking contact mentions a specific problem or challenge and you have the experience or knowledge that would allow you to resolve the problem.
- There are multiple candidates for a role and you want to stand out from the crowd.
- You have a particular experience that is very relevant to the role you are seeking, but it is stated too briefly on the résumé to create sufficient impact.
- Your interviewer is a detailed, analytical type who likes to see data, not just hear stories.
- You want to emphasize your key points in a thank-you letter following an interview with a recruiter or hiring manager.
- The interview is over and there is one week or more to go while others are being met before decisions are made. You want to remain top-of-mind with the interviewers.
- There is no opportunity now at a company, but you love the company and want to show interest and stay in touch.

Don't let opportunities like these slip through your fingers. Take advantage of them with a bold approach. Once a contact has shared valuable information with you, making an extra effort to market yourself would not be inappropriate. It would reinforce your brand—both your image and value proposition—in the minds of the individuals who can deliver an on-target employment opportunity to you.

Marketing tactics that work start with an understanding of the target's needs. Narrow your focus so that you can concentrate on the challenges confronting the person or organization that you want to influence. Do thorough research (this includes having as many face-to-face conversations with your contacts as possible) to get a clear and complete picture of the issues. Based on your understanding of the situation, develop a case for what you could do. Explain what you would bring to the table to solve the problem. Link your value proposition directly to the market need, and use one of the following powerful strategies to deliver the message.

Case Studies

In Chapter 11 the process for creating case studies was explained and an example was provided. If you haven't already written some case studies, go back and work on one now. If you have already prepared a case study, you may wish to tweak it or write another one to exemplify your history of responding to a need that is similar to your target's. Ask for another meeting and walk your contact through the case. Be sure to include a full explanation of the situation, your actions and the results. Point out the link between your past contributions and the existing situation. If you cannot schedule a meeting, mail the case study with a well-crafted cover letter.

A Unique, Targeted Marketing Piece

Knowing what problem or need faces your target employer, create a one-page document that outlines five ways you could help. This marketing piece could be entitled *Five Ways to Increase Your Competitive Advantage* , or *Five Suggestions to Transform Your Operations*. Make it succinct and memorable. Here's an example:

Five Ways I Can Help Drive Your Business

1. The Benefit of Experience— as a former client, I understand what your service offers and how it is superior to the competition's.

3. A Developer of New Business— with extensive contacts, I am a proven relationship builder.

4. Fresh Energy— I am ready to meet the challenge and feel confident that we can successfully manage the obstacles.

5. Creative Thinking— I am an idea person who can deliver value to the customer through innovation.

6. Involvement in the Community— a willing community participant, I see community activities as a way to enhance the company's brand.

Tip: Communications experts suggest that people will not retain the information on a list containing more than five items.

Testimonials

If you have relevant letters of commendation, words of praise on a performance appraisal or quotes from a noteworthy source extolling your capability, incorporate these in a letter that expresses your interest in the job opportunity. If possible, ask an influential person to speak or write directly to the hiring manager on your behalf.

Relevant Data

When a contact talks about their issues and needs, you will have information, answers or solutions to help them if you are the right person for the role. Without giving away all of your suggestions, prepare a clear and concise exposition of the relevant data. Augment your existing knowledge with good research. Present the data in a format that will engage the reader. Deliver the document in person or mail it with a cover letter expressing enthusiasm for continuing involvement with your contact. Look at the following examples of formats you can use to present data.

Corporate Strategy Comparison Grid

Company	Strategy	Competitive Advantage	Image

Brand Positioning Map

Brand	Target Group	Key Benefit	Benefit Support	Image

Key Issue Summary

Issue	Implications	Potential Action to Resolve	Timing

An Alignment Chart

Search firms sometimes require candidates to fill out a form that matches the candidate's qualifications to the specifications of a job opportunity. Don't wait to be asked. When you are in competition for a specific position, create an alignment summary matching your qualifications and characteristics with the requirements of the role. Deliver it to the interviewers, including the search executive if one is involved. Use the headings on the following chart as an example and tailor your document to the specific opportunity.

Profile Alignment Summary

Requirements	Your Qualifications
Ideal Experience	
• Minimum 10 years' HR experience in a senior generalist capacity • Progressive, complex environments that have undergone cultural change and strategic re-direction • Shared services environment • International scope	
Education and Professional Designation	
• Post-secondary business degree required, graduate level an asset • CHRP	
Critical Competencies	
• Business acumen • Strategic thinker • Consultative leadership skills • Strong ability to influence at the executive level	
Personal Profile	
• Committed to ABC's values: "respect for the individual," "excellence in every endeavour" and "customer service" • Able to travel extensively • Willing to relocate internationally	

A Plan for the First 90 Days in the New Role

Developing and executing a thorough plan for the first few months on your new job will help you succeed. Chapter 19 deals with this more fully. While you are still in competition for a position, preparing a preliminary draft of a plan for the first 90 days allows decision-makers to see how you would approach your responsibilities. It shows that you have done the research and internalized the issues mentioned in interviews. The assessment activities that are listed on the plan and the points for aligning fundamental resources and processes to the organization's strategy make your intentions clear. Use the following example as an outline for such a plan, and deliver it yourself so that you can discuss it with decision-makers if the opportunity arises.

The First 90 Days for the CEO of a Charitable Foundation

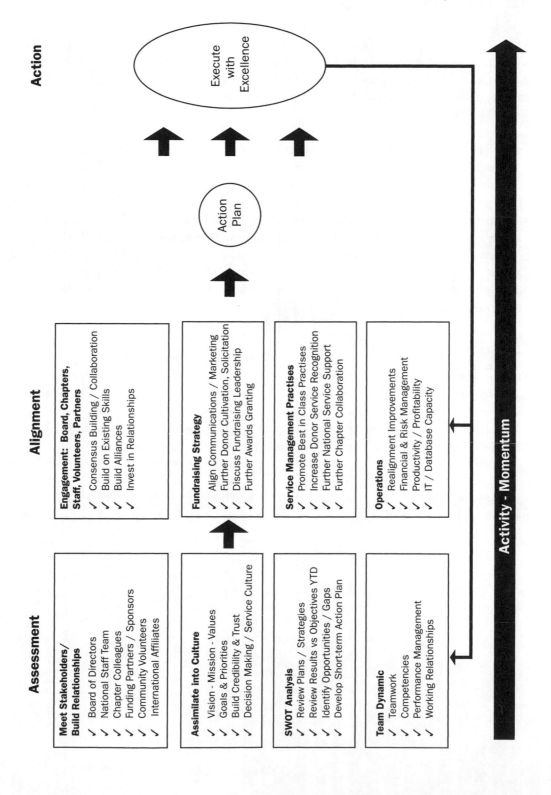

Taking an active and assertive approach to marketing yourself at opportune times will help you stand out from the crowd in a meaningful and memorable way. It demonstrates your genuine interest and enthusiasm for an opportunity and positions you as being strategically astute. It shows your ability to understand issues and respond with effective solutions. Powerful marketing gives you a competitive advantage and it can sway a decision-maker's opinion in your favour.

An experienced and successful consultant was intrigued by the prospect of joining an entrepreneurial professional services firm. Having worked on his own for five years, he wanted to rejoin a team. Although he had been told that the firm was not hiring, he met with the CEO who was the founder of the company. He listened carefully as the CEO expounded the industry's trends and issues. One challenge for the CEO was the scarcity of competitive intelligence. Following the meeting, the consultant did extensive research on the market, relying heavily on his many contacts' first-hand experience with the firm and its competitors. He created a positioning map illustrating the factors that distinguished one firm from another. His findings further convinced him that he would like to work for this organization. When he presented his map at a subsequent meeting, the CEO was so impressed that he immediately created a role for the consultant and hired him. The consultant had successfully linked his value proposition directly to the CEO's needs.

Stay with the Process and Success Will Follow

There is work out there for people with your skills and abilities! If you are not finding opportunities, have a look at the search techniques you are using. Are you truly engaged in an active search or are you allowing passive search methods to take up more than 20 percent of your time? Do you need to adjust your targets? Are you marketing your value proposition boldly every chance you get? If you feel stuck, call on your board of advisers and ask networking contacts for an infusion of fresh ideas. When you apply creative thinking and look at your situation from a different perspective, new paths often appear. Sometimes all that is needed is a change in your viewpoint.

Refer to Appendix A: Strategic View of Targeted Employment Search Process one last time. You have worked your way through the steps of a targeted search for employment. If you keep at it, the outcome will be positive.

Cross the Finish Line

Perseverance yields success.

Objectives

This final step takes you across the finish line and back to the starting point. It offers guidelines for getting off to the best possible start in a new role and recommends lifelong career management techniques. The chapters in Part Five cover:
- Managing your references well.
- Analyzing and aligning an employment offer with your key criteria for job satisfaction.
- Evaluating a remuneration package.
- The principles of win–win negotiations.
- Saying "No" to an offer without burning bridges.
- Planning what you need to achieve during the first 90 days on the job.
- Building good relationships at your new organization.
- Adapting to a new culture.
- Guidelines for ongoing career management.
- Goal-setting for the long term.

Rules to Follow

- Choose your references carefully. Prepare them through direct communication.
- Review your priorities and think about trade-offs as you evaluate your job offer.
- Think of negotiations as an opportunity to understand the interests of the other party.
- When starting a new job, eliminate as many extraneous responsibilities as possible so that the first 90 days will include ample time for planning and reflection.
- Remember to listen more than you talk.
- Adopt aspects of the new culture that will be noticed, such as the dress code, use of buzzwords and attendance at social events and opportunities for informal camaraderie.
- Get things done early in your tenure and be sure that your boss is aware of it.

- Keep noticing and recording your accomplishments.
- Keep your résumé up-to-date.
- Always have short-term and long-term learning goals.
- Value each job for being one step along your career path rather than thinking of it as one step up the ladder.

Moves That Can Set You Back

- Neglecting to deal openly with potential negative references.
- Negotiating too hard for concessions that your prospective employer is loath to make.
- Failing to understand exactly what you were hired to do.
- Arriving at your new job loaded down with old baggage.
- Thinking that this new job will be yours until you retire.
- Failing to start considering your next moves now.

Chapter 18

Close the Deal

You can't negotiate after you're hired.

Once you've nurtured a lead into a solid employment opportunity, finalize the offer with professionalism. Your references now play a leading role in helping you bring the transaction to a successful close. Manage their involvement carefully. At the same time, scrutinize the opportunity and the offer. You want to go in with your eyes wide open, or back away for valid reasons. When you discuss your questions and requests for amendments with your prospective employer, be conscious that your negotiating style will be on full display. You are setting the stage for the new relationship, and you want to establish trust, openness and goodwill.

References

From the beginning of the transition process you will have been in touch with the people who can now provide a reference for you. Some may have been part of your close support network, giving you counsel and support along the way. Others will be more distant, but presumably willing to step in and contribute to your success at this point. There may still be others who you feel would not be inclined to give you a positive reference. You must manage the involvement of every potential reference carefully and respectfully.

GUIDELINES FOR MANAGING REFERENCES

- Be thoughtful about the people you select as references. Their experience with you and your work should be relevant to the position.
- If you are currently employed, the hiring organization should not expect you to provide references from within your organization until an offer of employment has been extended and accepted. The offer can be conditional upon final reference checks.
- Call each person before offering their name to the prospective employer. Describe the position, explain why you are interested in it, how it complements your experience, skills and strengths and how you expect to add value. This will allow them to decide whether or not they feel comfortable providing the reference and it will help them in preparing for the conversation.
- Gain explicit permission from each person before giving their name to your prospective employer. Tell your references when to expect a call and who will be calling.

- Prepare a written list with your references' names, titles, contact information and one line of information about them that is relevant to the opportunity they are being called about.
- When you are offered the job, immediately call your reference providers with the good news.
- At the conclusion of the process, thank them in writing regardless of the outcome.

Tip: It is increasingly common for organizations to ask for references from a 360° perspective. This would include speaking with peers, subordinates, clients and other superiors as well as individuals who were your bosses. Give advance thought to this possibility, and be ready to contact a number of people who could provide meaningful and supportive references for you.

Managing No-Reference Policies and Negative References

There is growing reluctance on the part of organizations to provide references for former employees due to fear of legal liability. The confirmation of name, title and dates of employment is about as far as many will go. Some will also confirm salary. If your former employer has a no-reference policy, former co-workers and bosses who have since joined other companies are appropriate alternatives provided they have worked with you in the not-too-distant past. If you are stuck, you might approach trusted colleagues who are still employed with the organization; ask if they would consider offering a personal reference that does not represent the organization or speak to work-related issues.

Tip: A novel way of dealing with no-reference policies is to script your leaving story and provide it to those who will be contacted in the reference-checking process. Ask them to merely confirm its truthfulness when someone calls and relates the story as part of a reference check.

Potentially negative references must be handled with care, particularly if one of them is your most recent boss. It's best to deal with this honestly and openly. Contact the individual who concerns you and tell them where you are in the process of finding new employment. Describe the role you hope to land and how you believe you can make a contribution. Be honest about how you described the reason for your departure, your contribution, your strengths and areas in need of development. If there are particularly sensitive issues, consider putting your thoughts in writing before making the call. Have a trusted member of your support network vet the content of your message.

When you call, be brief and dispassionate. Seek to understand what is being said, and negotiate a way to acceptably express each point to your prospective new employer. If your potentially negative reference refuses to have the discussion or remains recalcitrant, pre-empt their remarks by explaining to your prospective employer what they are likely to hear from this person and why. Remain dispassionate. Respectfully provide your explanation of the situation before references are checked.

Evaluate the Offer

By the time you receive an offer of employment, there may be no question in your mind about accepting it. On the other hand, you might have some serious thinking to do.

The first step in conducting an in-depth evaluation of a written employment offer is to return to the reflective work you did at the outset of your career transition. Review the criteria you established for the ideal employment opportunity. Next, use the worksheets in this chapter for a thorough analysis of the position, the people and the organization. Finally, use intuitive questions to bring to the surface underlying issues that go beyond concrete facts.

Following these steps will be particularly helpful when you have more than one opportunity to consider. Even if you have only one written offer, surmise the terms of your possible alternatives and use the evaluation worksheet to score them. This can help you decide if it's worth taking the risk of losing one opportunity while waiting for another.

Tip: Don't think of this as an all-or-nothing exercise. Your objective is to develop a list of things to negotiate and rank them in priority order. Even if an offer seems acceptable, you might find ways to improve it.

WORKSHEET 18.1
Evaluate Employment Opportunities

Not all factors in an employment opportunity are of equal importance to you. First, establish the weighting for each, using a scale of 1 to 3, the higher number being the most important. Rank each element of the position, the organization and the offer with a score from 1 to 5. The final score for each factor combines the weighting and ranking.

Category	Factor	Weighting (A)	Ranking (B)	Score (A x B)
Job content	Degree to which your key skills will be engaged Elements of your style that will be useful Use of your knowledge Incorporation of your interests Match with your non-negotiable values and motivators Overall challenge Realistic performance expectations Alignment with your previous experience			
Job-related factors	Title Travel required (+ or -) Physical environment Resources available			
People	Fit with boss peers subordinates clients external contacts			
The organization	Reputation of the organization Positioning and direction of the industry Vision and values Ethics and principles Your compatibility with culture			

Future prospects	Direction of the industry Appropriate career direction Professional development opportunities Positioning for next steps (internally) Positioning for next steps (externally)					
Relocation issues	Suitability of housing Quality/accessibility of schooling Comparability of disposable income Opportunity to build equity or wealth Quality of business life Quality of family life and opportunities for your spouse Social relationships Balance between work and personal priorities Proximity to the "action" Ease of settling in Overall comfort Distance from home and extended family					
Remuneration	Base salary Variable pay* Equity Benefits Pension Vacation					
Perqs	Car Club memberships Parking Other					
Non-compete or Non-solicit	Restrictions on future activities if you resign					
Exit clause	Contracted amount of pay in lieu of notice					
Total Score						

* Variable pay includes bonuses, commission, profit sharing and long-term incentives. Be sure that you understand when your eligibility begins. There can be a waiting period of several months with no retroactive payment.

Intuitive Factors to Consider

- People are on their best behaviour during the interview process, and the organization will have been putting its best foot forward. If there is anything about them that does not sit well with you now, be forewarned that it's not likely to get any better.
- What is your gut feeling about this offer of employment? Are you genuinely pleased and looking forward to the job?
- What were your issues and questions at the beginning of the interview process? What early reservations did you mention to your spouse or partner and members of your support network or board of advisers? Has everything been addressed to your satisfaction?
- How will your colleagues and peers react to the news? Can you sincerely present this as being a good move for you?

An engineer was applying for a job in an aerospace firm. She arrived early and sat in the reception area observing her prospective colleagues as they came and went. They scurried past with heads down and eyes focused on their feet. No one spoke. She landed the job and accepted it, but quickly found the work environment oppressive. In hindsight, the clues had been there from the start, but because she wanted the job, she had not allowed herself to be honest about what she noticed.

Negotiate the Deal

The foregoing analysis should give you a clear picture of the positives and areas of concern regarding an employment opportunity. You need to be clear about how important the job is to you before opening negotiations. Don't feel that you must negotiate an offer of employment. If it's acceptable, take it as it is!

The salary and benefits have probably been negotiated to some extent prior to the organization making an offer. At this point, you are not likely to be able to achieve a significant increase in base salary, but there could be more room for improving the terms of variable pay. Think of remuneration and perqs as a composite, and don't get stuck on any specific point in isolation. If the organization cannot give you concessions in one area, they might have flexibility in another. Go for the best overall deal. If relocation is involved, comparable disposable income and the opportunity to establish equity in property must be considered as a part of the overall package.

Tip: If you come to a stalemate in negotiating remuneration, ask for an early review of both performance and remuneration. If agreed, ask that the offer letter be changed or sign it back noting the change. This precaution will give you some protection if the individual negotiating on behalf of the organization is no longer in the same position when the time for the review comes around.

Asking for a broader scope of responsibilities, a different job title or a different reporting structure may be met with a definitive "No." However, the more senior the role, the more competitive the market or the less bureaucratic the organization, the better your chance of success. Sometimes organizations will shape a role to fit an individual who brings a rare combination of skills and knowledge to the deal. Proceed with caution when negotiating factors that go beyond remuneration. Know your position well.

A senior executive from a large financial institution learned through a networking contact that a U.S.-based custodial services firm was considering expanding its business into the Canadian market. After a thorough round of interviews, the organization gave the executive a verbal offer. His job would be to establish and manage the Canadian arm of the business. Six months went by, during which time the executive and the organization negotiated not only his compensation, but also his authority, responsibility and autonomy. The prospective job description was much discussed, but the details weren't put in writing until the enterprising executive took the initiative of outlining the terms himself. Always confident that a formal agreement would be reached, and that the business venture would be a success, he moved ahead on locating office space and identifying capable support staff for the start-up, using his activities around building the infrastructure as leverage to bring the protracted negotiations to a successful close.

Use the worksheet that follows to list and prioritize your negotiating points, and then use the guidelines that follow the worksheet to plan and implement successful negotiations.

WORKSHEET 18.2 **Analyze Your Negotiating Points**			
Negotiating Points	**Terms of the Offer**	**Terms Desired**	**Priority**
Base Salary			
Variable pay: signing bonus individual performance bonus profit-sharing plan long-term incentive			
Equity: stock purchase stock options share ownership programs			
Benefits: life and disability insurance medical and dental coverage employee assistance program			
Pension plan or group RRSP			
Vacation time			
Car			
Parking			
Memberships: clubs professional associations			
Professional development opportunities			
Conference and convention attendance			
Executive coaching support			
Exit clause			
Non-compete clause			
Non-solicit clause			
Title and position with peers			
Work Arrangements: part-time schedule telecommuting flexible schedule job sharing			
Business development or sales targets			
Duration of initial mandate or time to first review			
Opportunities for sabbaticals			
Equipment: laptop, cell phone, pager home system connection Internet connection			
Product or service discounts			
Leave policies: sick days personal days parental leave compassionate leave			
Start date			

Tip: Have an employment lawyer review the offer, especially if it contains complex variable pay arrangements, equity, options, a non-compete clause or an exit clause. Don't finalize the deal on the back of an envelope or rely on a verbal agreement. Sign back the offer just as you would with an offer to buy a house.

GUIDELINES FOR NEGOTIATIONS

- The best time to negotiate is when you have a written offer of employment in hand. The organization clearly wants you to sign up, and it will be interested in a speedy resolution of the process. This puts you in one of the best negotiating positions you will ever have.
- Don't let this advantage go to your head. Every organization has a maximum tolerance level, and you don't want to push it too close to that line. These negotiations will have an effect on your ongoing relationship with your new employer.
- Know your position:
  - Before negotiations begin, use worksheet 18.2, "Analyze Your Negotiating Points," and make a complete list of the points you would like to improve or add to the offer.
  - Establish your minimum acceptable level for each of the negotiating points listed and know your priorities. If the existing terms of the offer are not close to your minimum levels of acceptability, it's going to be an uphill push, and you need to be thinking about alternatives.
  - What might you be willing to trade off (e.g., variable pay for base salary)? Think about equivalent values. If you are in a period of life when your cash-flow needs are great, higher base salary might be much more important than it is for someone closer to retirement.
  - What is non-negotiable for you?
- Know your alternatives:
  - What other opportunities realistically await you if you cannot come to a satisfactory agreement on this offer? You don't want to drive too hard a bargain if there is no fallback position. Even if you win your points, you risk tainting the relationship.
  - Keep all of your other job search initiatives going.
  - If you are waiting for offers from other organizations, evaluate those opportunities and see how they would score in comparison to the offer in hand. This will give you clarity regarding the wisdom of stalling to see if something better comes through.
- Learn as much as you can about the organization's position. Use your network, ask the search or placement consultant, check with your career transition consultant or ask the individuals conducting the final interviews.
  - What does an average remuneration package contain for your peers in this organization?
  - What are the standard compensation levels and where does your position fit?
  - How are incentives and equity ownership terms usually structured?
  - What is the range for performance bonuses at your level?
  - How much authority and flexibility does the person negotiating the deal have?
  - If flexibility is limited in some areas, is it less limited in others?

- Get comparable industry data. Know what others are paying for people like you in similar positions.
- Enter the negotiations with the intention of finding a resolution that leaves both you and the organization feeling like winners.
- Negotiate in person if at all possible. Negotiating over the phone or through a third party is not as effective.
- Begin by affirming your interest and enthusiasm for the opportunity. Confirm items that you agree on, and enumerate the items to be discussed in order of priority.
- For each item, explain your interest or point of view and the rationale behind it.
- Listen carefully and ask probing questions.
- Focus on the rationale for the organization's responses to your requests, not just the answers. Find out what policies or practices make it difficult for them to meet your needs.
- Remember that you are always communicating with your body language and voice, as well as your words. Reaffirm your enthusiasm for the position where appropriate throughout the process.
- If you relent on one point, make sure that you get something else in return.
- Your goal is to build an amicable working relationship with the people in the organization. Do not give in too soon and do not create a problem for yourself by insisting on having a better deal than they can afford.

Stalling Techniques

Although it may seem a nice problem to have, it's not easy to delay accepting one offer while waiting for another that you would prefer. Anticipation and early prevention, as discussed in Chapter 12, are the best remedies to this situation but may not always be possible. If you find yourself struggling for ideas, use these guidelines.

GUIDELINES FOR DELAYING AN OFFER WHILE WAITING FOR ANOTHER

- If you haven't been given an offer in writing, ask for it before you start negotiations.
- Find credible reasons to meet with specific individuals before indicating your willingness to enter negotiations. Perhaps a key person was on holidays during the round of interviews, and you would like a chance to meet them. Ask for another discussion with someone that you have already met to ensure that your understanding of the mandate is clear. Indicate that you want to present your ideas about how to handle the mandate to see if they are acceptable to the organization.
- Negotiate slowly.
- Return phone calls on the same day, but do it late in the working day to delay the process. Keep your cell phone turned off as if you are busy in meetings.
- Have your lawyer review the contract.
- Ask for one more weekend to review the offer with your spouse or partner.
- Ask for an extension.

Tip: Be very careful with these delay tactics. You do not want to send a message of waning enthusiasm in case you do finally take the job. Also, the community is very small, and you might be found out.

When you are in this situation, do everything you can to speed up the process with the other organization. If there is a search firm or placement agency involved they might be able to help as long as you trust them to do so tactfully. Be honest with the organization you would rather join. Don't deliver ultimatums, but let them know about your dilemma.

Saying "No"

When you decide to turn down an offer, do so with great care. Be honest about your reasons and state them in a way that depersonalizes the message. If you are joining a competitor of the organization you are turning down, or think that you might do so in the near future, focus your reason for refusing the offer on a characteristic or issue that is a known point of differentiation between the two organizations. Try to steer clear of sensitive issues.

> *A business developer was offered a job by an entrepreneurial firm that had a small but healthy niche in a localized market. Although the offer was tempting, he decided that it would take a mandate with larger scope to interest him. After three months, he joined a competitor to the entrepreneurial firm and assumed responsibility for nationwide business development. He was promised an international mandate following a successful orientation period. His reputation with his competitors remained intact because his reason for turning down their offer was consistent with his reason for accepting the other.*

When you go through a round of interviews that results in an offer of employment, a significant relationship is established between you, the organization and the people you have met. Regardless of the outcome, it is important to preserve those relationships. You might have opportunities to work with these people in the future, either as a fellow employee or through joint ventures or partnerships. Write letters of regret and sincere thanks to each one of your interviewers.

Saying "Yes"

Once the ink is dry on the offer, contact each person you met in the interview process and let them know that you are pleased to be joining the team. Call the individuals who provided references and let them know the good news. Follow up with a formal letter of thanks. Begin to draft your "I've Landed" letters, and have them ready to send the first week on the job.

After your thank-yous are made, prepare yourself for the first 90 days on the new job.

Chapter 19

Prepare for the First 90 Days in Your New Job

*First impressions
are lasting impressions.*

Success in your new position will depend on your ability to get things done, your skills at building relationships and your flexibility in adapting to the new culture. It sounds simple, but the challenge is real. Once you have successfully negotiated your deal and know your starting date, focus your thinking on how you will handle the crucial first 90 days on the new job. Create a plan to immediately deliver results and shift your status from "new kid on the block" to "familiar face."

Know Exactly What's Expected of You

The mandate presented to you during the interview process will inevitably require further explanation and clarification at the outset of your employment. Job descriptions are seldom fully comprehensive and objectives are rarely documented in advance of your joining. In the first few days, meet with your boss and anyone else who will evaluate your work. Now is the time to find out exactly what's expected of you. You cannot wait until the end of the first 90 days to be clear about your goals and the activities that will lead to attaining them.

Gather information from multiple sources. Make an effort to meet with every stakeholder associated with your mandate. Include colleagues, team members, direct reports, support staff, internal resource providers, front-line salespeople, external suppliers and, most importantly, clients. Target your questions to get to the heart of the issues. Take notes! Find out if the people whose cooperation you need share the priorities given to you. If your mandate does not match the key stakeholders' needs, you have a problem. Raise your concerns with your superiors early and propose a solution.

A market research specialist joined a small entrepreneurial firm with a reputation for providing excellent customized service to its major corporate clients. The methodologies used by her new employer were creative, costly and radically different from traditional research methods. Selling them required extensive explanation with top-quality demonstrations to convince prospective clients of their value. The owner of the firm told the new employee that achieving her established sales targets would be dependent on scheduling and conducting numerous face-to-face meetings with clients. He identified four performance markers: develop a list of at least 25 qualified prospects; schedule and conduct one introductory meeting each week; use the established follow-up guidelines to take the client through the sales cycle; and submit PowerPoint files from product demonstrations to the internal quality review team. With such clear performance markers in place, there was no mistaking the firm's expectations.

Tip: Go for some quick wins. If you can solve a problem, contribute to a project, suggest a novel approach or make a sale during the first 90 days on the job, it will be noticed and appreciated.

Identify the Support and Resources You Need

The support and resources available to you were, no doubt, discussed to some extent during the interviews. Once you are on the job, you need to check out who and what is available, determine their suitability for the task and develop an inventory of what's needed. Make sure that your list is reasonable and affordable. Present it tactfully and only after you have built a relationship with your boss. Have a fallback plan in place in case your requests are denied or delayed.

Your co-workers and subordinates are probably your most important resources. If you are the manager, evaluate your staff quickly. Look for factual evidence of their abilities and delegate as much responsibility as you can without sacrificing quality. If performance problems are present, deal with them immediately. When you put the right people in the right jobs and give them the training and supervision they need for the task, *your* chances of success increase dramatically.

If you do not have managerial responsibilities, be sure to learn how your co-workers' responsibilities relate to yours. Take the initiative to understand the materials, systems and processes that are already in place and use them to the full. When you need resources, ask. Chances are good that they are there for the asking.

Tip: New employees who busy themselves reinventing the wheel waste valuable time and irritate co-workers. If the resources you need are available, use them as they are. Opportunities to suggest improvements will arise in good time.

Look at your own skills and capabilities. Honestly evaluate your strengths and weaknesses as they relate to the tasks at hand. Reflect on the most difficult and daunting aspects of the job, and make a commitment to yourself that you will get the help you need. Whether it's technical support, strategic thinking, planning, communication, implementation or detailed follow-up, there is most likely something that is best shared with someone better suited for the particular task than you. Do not shirk responsibility, but don't leave your Achilles' heel exposed.

Finally, arrange your other responsibilities so that you can concentrate fully on your mandate. During your orientation to the organization, your new colleagues might solicit your help with their projects in a well-meant attempt to bring you on board. Handle this with diplomacy, being careful that fulfilling your mandate is not jeopardized, and that you are not overstepping the boundaries of your role. Distractions also come from outside the organization. Previous responsibilities, family issues, volunteer commitments and even poor health can sabotage the first 90 days. Plan ahead, be cautious and keep your personal calendar clear to make the best possible start.

The scope of what needs to be accomplished will come into focus as you do the above analysis. With this information, create a 90-day plan to keep yourself on track. Establish specific, measurable, realistic, time-limited goals. Document the steps to be taken toward your goals and create an inventory of the resources needed. Give yourself realistic deadlines. Use the worksheet on the next page to aid this process.

Tip: During your first 90 days, create a six-month and one-year plan for the attainment of the goals that the organization has outlined for you and your own development goals. Outline the steps to implementation and make a diary note of checkpoints.

WORKSHEET 19.1
Set Targets for Your First 90 Days in the New Job

Goals	Steps to Implementation	Resources Needed	Deadlines

A very capable executive was hired as CEO of a major financial services company. His plan for the first 90 days of his tenure was to develop a five-year strategy to improve shareholder value. He conducted exhaustive interviews with his executive team and many of their direct reports for an in-depth understanding of internal operations. He met with external advisers, business partners and major clients to gain a view of their forecasts and expectations. By the end of the 90-day evaluation period, he had written a 200-page document containing summaries of the information he had collected, his analysis and his goals for the next five years. Priorities and implementation steps were laid out. The board was duly impressed. At the end of the five-year period the company was sold at a substantial premium. The CEO's copy of the plan, now dog-eared and tattered, stood as a record of the value of using the first 90 days to set things up.

Build Good Relationships

You are joining an established group of people and your presence will change the dynamic. Enter with caution and a willingness to understand each individual. Take the time to learn how the group interacts before you barge into the process. Regardless of your role, they have a set way of doing things and it's best to ask, "How can I help?" rather than saying, "I suggest that we do it this way!"

Ask questions. When you are first engaged in discussions or problem solving, wait until you understand each person's assessment of the situation before forming your own. Find out what's been suggested and tried in the past. When asked for your opinion, offer suggestions rather than delivering edicts. Use phrases such as, "Here's an idea," or "Has the possibility of doing such-and-such been considered?" If you are the one in charge, your opportunity to take the lead will present itself. Spend your early days listening to the collective wisdom of your team and colleagues.

Get to know your most important customer—*your boss*. Become an astute observer of how they prefer to communicate and make decisions. Note who they trust, and seek to understand why. Analyze the challenges and issues that are putting pressure on them, and learn what performance markers lead to their success. Find ways to make a direct contribution to this success.

Build a network inside the organization. Take the initiative to meet your boss's peers. This is especially important in an environment of constant turnover. If your boss changes jobs before your capabilities are widely known, you will need another advocate quickly. At your peer level, seek out and introduce yourself to people across the organization, especially those associated with your mandate or department. Clarify their roles, and learn how their areas operate and interact with yours.

Tip: If you are shy and reserved, make a conscious effort to initiate contact and conversation. Shyness is often mistaken for unfriendliness or arrogance. Remember to smile.

Find a mentor within the organization. This should be someone who can point out the potholes and land mines before you run into them. A mentor is usually someone who has been around for a while and can give you tips on communicating. They can steer you through the decision-making channels and tell you who's who. It's probably best if your mentor is not in the immediate chain of command above you. They need to be willing and able to act as your confidant, free of any conflict that would arise from having influence over your future.

Understand the decision-making process in the organization, and learn to communicate effectively through the appropriate channels. Listen to stories about initiatives that have been proposed and were accepted or rejected. Observe others going through the process of getting something approved. Float your hypotheses in confidence with a few trusted co-workers and ask what it would take to get a green light. Think about everyone whose work would be affected by your proposals and share your preliminary ideas with them. Ask what they see as the benefits and drawbacks. Listen carefully to their responses, and do not immediately try to defend your position or influence theirs.

Adapt to the Culture

In Chapter 4, you did an analysis of the cultures you have experienced in the past. Use that reflective exercise to guide your observations of this new environment. Notice how things get done, how people interact and what is valued. As mentioned earlier, be aware that the stated norms are not always practised. In the first 90 days on the job, make it one of your goals to understand both the main tenets and subtle nuances of the culture.

Leave all signs and habits of your previous organization behind. Purge your briefcase, golf bag and T-shirt drawer of any evidence that you have worked elsewhere. Do not decorate your new office with anything bearing your previous organization's name or logo. Guard against discussing how things were done at your previous place of employment. Your new colleagues do not want to hear, "Over at Old Co., we did this."

Leave all of your baggage behind. This includes frustration with your previous employer's policies and bureaucracy, suspicion of motives, disrespectful treatment of subordinates, an entitlement mentality or anything else that was destructive, yet prevalent, in your previous organization. You have a clean slate—don't write old lines on it!

To succeed, you need to become comfortable in the new culture quickly. This does not mean completely suppressing your unique personality and approach. Remember that the interviewers were pleased with your personal qualities. However, you need to adapt your style and modify your behaviour somewhat to the new environment.

Use these guidelines to remind yourself of the basic rules for adapting to a new workplace:

GUIDELINES FOR ASSIMILATION INTO THE NEW CULTURE
- Observe how information is communicated.
- Notice how meetings are conducted.
- Learn how decisions are made.
- Listen for commonly used jargon and buzzwords, and begin to integrate them into your vocabulary.
- What interpersonal qualities are respected and admired?
- Watch how people interact. How do they dress? How do they use humour?
- How do your peers conduct themselves in day-to-day operations and in meetings, and under stressful circumstances?

- Go to meetings well-prepared to contribute and participate, but sit back and watch the group dynamics first.
- What are some of the corporate legends and anecdotes? What do they indicate about behaviours, values and ethics?
- Why have long-term employees stayed with the company? Why have others left?
- How does the corporate mission statement apply, or not apply, to day-to-day operations?
- On what basis have people been promoted? Why have others been dismissed?
- Who are the rising stars of the organization and what identifies them as such?
- How formal or informal is the workplace?
- What clues do you pick up from the way the offices are furnished and laid out?
- What are the guidelines for dealing with clients or customer complaints?
- How are special events handled? Promotions? Celebrations? Sales goals? Casual days?
- Pay attention to the small things. Learn how to use the electronic filing system, and know who makes the coffee and orders the stationery.
- What discrepancies do you see between what is said and what is done?
- Remember that many of the organization's important rules and regulations will be the informal, unspoken ones. They won't be written down in the handbook. You have to discern them through observation.

A training and development specialist left an organization where the terms "programs," "seminars" and "participants" were used. In her new role she had to consciously adopt the terminology used by her new organization and refer instead to "workshops," "hands-on learning" and "clients." She knew that as long as she used the old references, she would be labeled as one still learning the ropes, rather than being accepted as part of the team.

Tip: If the culture is a poor fit for you, or your values do not match those of the organization, it will be obvious within the first 90 days. Don't fool yourself hoping that everything will work out for the best, or expect that either you or the organization will make significant compromises. Start planning your exit now, even if you need to wait some time before finding the right opportunity.

Build reflection time into each day. If you charge ahead too quickly, you are likely to miss the important clues that are right in front of you. Notice the minor, seemingly unimportant comments and unexpected events. Think about what you should be learning from them. The small things are almost always signposts for more crucial issues. To pick up these subtleties and understand the dynamics, you need to carve out time for reflective analysis. Continue to call on your support network or board of advisers throughout this crucial period to help you understand your new environment.

WORKSHEET 19.2
Do a Daily Review During the First 90 Days

- What introductions did you initiate today?

- What did you learn about the people you met? Make note of their role, challenges, communication style, level of influence and demeanour, and of any personal factors you have observed or been told.

- Who do you want to meet tomorrow?

- What new information do you have about your boss?

- Are you on track with getting things done?

- What steps did you complete toward the implementation of your goals?

- What needs to be done tomorrow to stay on track?

- What new feature of the culture did you observe today?

- What did you do today in an attempt to fit into the culture?

Restart the 90-Day Clock

The energy and enthusiasm that typically accompany a new job make it easier to do all that is necessary during the first 90 days in a new organization. Once you are acclimatized it's more difficult to recognize that each significant change in the organization signals a new beginning. Every time you have a new boss, mandate, structure or goal, you need to implement some of the same 90-day techniques in order to ensure a smooth transition. Major changes in your job should signal a new 90-day period to build relationships with the boss and co-workers, adapt to the new communication and decision-making styles, understand the values and get done what's important given the recent change.

Of equal importance to understanding that the first 90-day trial period happens again and again is realizing that you need to be consciously renewing your career management efforts throughout your entire working life. In this new world of work, it's always time to think about future options and next potential moves.

Chapter 20

Start Planning Your Next Moves Now

If you don't know where you're going,
you'll end up somewhere else.

—*Yogi Berra*

Once you've successfully been through the career transition process, you can be confident in the knowledge that your skills are employable in another work setting. Career change will likely never again present the same degree of emotional challenge for you, and the skills you've acquired in relation to planning, research, writing a résumé, networking and interviewing will be there to serve you for years to come.

But you're not finished with this process yet. As soon as you've settled into your new role, it's time to put a revised plan in place. It should build on the one you've been following and focus on moving you even closer to your ideal employment opportunity. It might entail further development in this new role, attaining another role within your new organization or choosing to move externally. Don't allow yourself to become fed up with your job, and don't wait for something beyond your control to create a career crisis for you. Start managing your own career *now*.

Notice What You Like Doing

Focus on your accomplishments! At this point, instead of looking back over your career to bring up memories of past experiences, *pay attention to your achievements in the present*. They do not need to be grandiose, out of the ordinary or recognized and rewarded by your employer. They might not be part of your specific responsibilities or mandate, but they will flow from your strategic advantage. The key criteria are that they give you a sense of pride and make work worthwhile for you.

Noteworthy accomplishments arise from situations where your creativity finds expression. Everyone has creative potential, not just inventors, musicians and painters. For a teacher, there is creativity in finding a technique that unlocks a door to learning for a struggling student. For a manager, it could be enlivening a workplace with humour and encouraging words. For a consultant, it could be finding the unexpected solution to a client's problem. Satisfying work offers regular opportunities for you to make enjoyable contributions.

Record your accomplishments. Start a journal and jot down the pertinent facts, describing the situation, your actions and the quantifiable results. Doing this will make revising your résumé a much simpler process. If you cannot name on-the-job accomplishments on a regular basis, you need to put career change plans in effect as soon as possible.

Revise Your View of Career Progression

It's old-fashioned to think that each new job should be one rung higher on the bureaucratic ladder than the previous job. It makes more sense to strive for a spiral career in which you might change occupations and/or employers several times, learn new skills and stay vitally interested in your work. This kind of career progression entails finding a role that more closely fits your strategic advantage and offers a work arrangement that better suits your lifestyle.

Professions and occupations evolve as trends come and go, and market conditions change. People often move forward by directing their search for new opportunities toward the leading edges of their profession. In the dynamic employment market, one path leads to another.

A woman who originally trained as a librarian left the school system behind and worked for an industry association that operated a busy reference library. The exposure to numerous business people afforded her the opportunity to transfer her research skills into the consulting field, working on projects where extensive research on the client's competitors was crucial. Through this she was at the forefront of business trends and was well positioned to use the first electronic databases developed by the major newspapers. She shifted her focus to concentrate on electronic information collection and retrieval and did product development work, looking for early applications of the databases for market research. Following her interests, she launched an entrepreneurial endeavour, providing a leading-edge market research technique to a number of blue-chip corporations.

Lateral moves, project-oriented assignments and working as an independent consultant, contractor or sole proprietor are all options for you. With far too many managers vying for the few openings in the executive suite, not everyone with executive capacity will get there. Be content with satisfying work, a great group of colleagues and reasonable remuneration. These things typify the enlightened view of career progression for everyone.

Keep Your Network Healthy

Perhaps the only concept mentioned in this book as frequently as accomplishments is *networking*. The importance of staying in touch with people who helped during your career transition has already been emphasized, and a variety of ideas for doing this have been described. Don't wait until you're looking for another employment opportunity to give these people a call.

Expand your existing network by intentionally seeking out people who are involved in activities, occupations, industries or organizations that interest you. Broaden your perspective beyond the boundaries of your current organization and industry. The more people you know, the easier it is to keep up-to-date on trends. Initiate conversations and be eager to learn what others find interesting, amusing, problematic and exciting.

Don't burn bridges! Try to make every client, supplier, peer, subordinate and superior your ally. You don't have to like everyone, but it's important to develop a reputation for being open-minded and reasonable. Try to find a way to get along with everyone, even with those who are the least magnanimous. Everyone you meet might someday be in a position to either advance your career or set it back.

Find a mentor outside your current organization. In the same way that an internal mentor helps you through the decision-making maze and communication avenues within your organization, an external mentor can guide you through the power channels of your industry. Your mentor should be at a more senior level than you and ideally have more years of experience. Go to your mentor for advice on professional development and career direction as well as challenges and opportunities that arise on the job.

A young woman who was starting her career in commercial real estate was unhappy with her current employer and looking for a new job. She had gotten to know a senior executive in a large real estate development company because they were active members of the same volunteer service organization. When she was offered an opportunity to join an individual in an entrepreneurial real estate venture, she checked her prospective employer's reputation with her friend, the senior executive. Immediately stepping into the role of mentor, the executive warned his young colleague that she ought to steer clear of the opportunity. He knew the entrepreneur well and was certain that if his colleague took the job, she would quickly find that her values and the entrepreneur's were mismatched.

Tip: Your mentor should be someone with whom you feel comfortable sharing your values. It's important to have someone who can remind you of what's truly important to you when you are in danger of deviating from your values.

Be Committed to Lifelong Learning

Keeping your professional and functional skills current is rudimentary. It's your responsibility to see that you get the training you need. If everyone is using a new project management process, take a refresher course. If business process outsourcing is revolutionizing your functional area of expertise, attend conferences and seminars where industry leaders are speaking about it. When your profession moves toward requiring additional credentials or designations, don't let yourself fall behind. Do what's required for accreditation, even if you could teach the qualifying courses yourself.

Explore learning opportunities outside your area of expertise. Do this especially as it relates to your longer-term plans. In addition to learning from traditional resources and networking, arrange an experiential learning opportunity. People often have mistaken ideas of what other occupations would be like, and the easiest way to dispel these notions is to give an occupation a temporary try. If you are currently employed as an accountant and you think you'd like to own and run a little bookstore as a step toward retirement, get a part-time job in a bookstore now.

Major career shifts often involve retraining. This is possible only if you have the patience for going back to the classroom, sufficient financial means and very supportive loved ones. However, for some people in mid-career, the realization that they have become what they are because it was expected of them can inspire a courageous decision. If you will be studying to embark on a radically different second career, do extensive research on the options available for your education, and network diligently to ensure that you will be pleased with the educational institution you choose. In mid-career, you don't want to waste your time taking courses that are poorly taught, too elementary or unnecessary.

Tip: When exploring institutions of higher education, find out what philosophies, theories, social mores, theologies or political convictions they espouse. They may claim neutrality, but there will be a bias, and if it doesn't match yours, you're likely to be unhappy.

A woman who was a stay-at-home mom until age 38 entered the world of paid work as an administrative assistant at an international development agency. In that role she was in frequent contact with a group of clergy who encouraged her to further her education and ultimately became her role models. She enrolled in school part-time and took 10 years to complete her bachelor's degree, following which she studied full-time for her Master of Social Work degree. She entered private practice at age 50. Two years later she decided that her ideal would not be fulfilled until her work directly involved her spirituality and deep religious convictions. She prepared for parish ministry and was ordained at age 56. Fourteen years later she retired from full-time ministry and began a part-time practice as a spiritual director. She never let her age deter her quest for lifelong learning or her commitment to making a contribution through her profession.

In addition to keeping up-to-date in your field, learn about something that truly interests you with no economic or professional goal in mind. Interesting people usually have some hobby or pastime that fully engages their curiosity. Become an expert in Renaissance cartography, or grow prize peonies. Study Mayan archeology or become knowledgeable about every wine-producing region in France. Understand the nuances of the toughest green at every golf course on the professional tour. These are the sorts of things that offer personal enrichment and enliven your time away from work. If there's nothing like this in your life, it's time to change that.

Tip: Capitalize on the exploding opportunities for learning over the Internet. Everything from graduate degrees to advice on hang-gliding is readily available.

GUIDELINES FOR GOOD CAREER MANAGEMENT

- Set realistic, measurable, time-specific goals for personal development, lifelong learning and career progression. Map out the steps to implementation and the resources needed.
- Build time into your daily and weekly schedule to chart your progress toward these goals. It's best to record your progression in writing as if you were doing a performance review. As a minimum, think through your progress as you commute or exercise.

- Carve out time at least once every five years to redo the long-term reflective exercises in Part Two of this book. At the same time, review your previous reflections and take notice of what has changed and what has remained the same. The constants probably hold important clues to your ideal work in the longer term. Revise your vision statement of the ideal employment opportunity for you.
- Look at every job, assignment or new piece of business as a temporary stop along the way. This is your journey toward your goal. Be content to move forward in stages.
- Come to grips with non-stop change. It's important to recognize and understand your unique reaction to change, and to develop effective coping techniques. Resilience and flexibility are required in today's workplace.
- Keep your résumé up-to-date. This provides impetus for recording your accomplishments and equips you to respond to any employment opportunity that arises.
- Keep your five sound bites ready to go. Have a 30-second, 2-minute and full 10-minute version prepared so that you can give quick updates to networking contacts or present your background and capabilities to a new boss or prospective employer.
- Don't look to anyone else to take responsibility for your professional development and career progression. Keep your long-term direction under your own control, using those who traditionally manage careers—your boss, the organization or the industry associations—as input providers.
- Identify opportunities to advance your career and put yourself forward to take assignments that point toward your desired future. It's surprising how few people step up and tell their boss that they want a specific opportunity.
- Train your replacement! Make yourself available for the next move by preparing one of your subordinates or co-workers to step into your shoes. This will also earn you an excellent reputation for developing people.
- Maintain balance in your life. Don't sacrifice your personal relationships for the sake of the job. It's much easier to adjust to an unwanted career change when work isn't everything to you.
- Don't focus on your age; rather, look at how many productive years you have to go. As mentioned earlier, trend-predictors suggest that you will retire in stages, moving into full retirement at a much later age than previous generations.
- Get the important people in your life on board with your long-term plans. Share your dreams with them and involve them in the planning.
- Help your spouse or partner with their career planning. If your ultimate ideal employment opportunity requires a radical change of any kind, your life partner will probably need to make adjustments as well.

Tip: When your phone rings and someone asks for 15 minutes of your time for a networking meeting, schedule it without hesitation.

Extend Your Timeline

This is not a formula for longevity; it's the completion of the reflective exercise in Part Two where you created your historic timeline. Pick up at today's date, and record your vision for the chapters of your life that are yet to come. Set goals for your career progression, work arrangements, continual learning, personal enrichment and finances. Predict how your personal priorities are likely to change.

Given the speed of change in this environment, set 18 months as the time frame for the first chapter, and then project three years ahead, five years and on to retirement. Don't worry if retirement is six or 36 years away for you. It's always helpful to have a picture of what you want to be doing at the end of your working days.

Tip: Pipe dreams are useful as long as you keep exploring what would be required to make them a reality.

Use the final worksheet to extend your timeline and create a picture of a future that's worth the effort it will take to get there.

WORKSHEET 20.1
Extend Your Personal Timeline

	Today	18 months	3 years	5 years	Retirement
Personal priorities					
Career goals					
Work arrangements					
Learning goals					
Personal enrichment plans					
Financial goals					

Keep a Balanced View

Having a comprehensive vision of the future that includes a realistic picture of your ideal employment opportunity in the longer term is a good strategic move. Whether your current circumstances allow you to pursue these goals right away or require you to postpone them in favour of a purely pragmatic approach to the job search, having this vision gives you a sense of direction and purpose.

There are also cautions regarding visions of future employment. If they are completely unattainable, they can set you up to feel discouraged and inadequate. They can also rob you of the ability to enjoy and make the most of present opportunities. Your long-term plan needs to be tempered with realism if it's going to be helpful. It should be a plan that you are continually taking steps to implement, even if it will take many years to fully achieve. Ensure that your vision of the future offers some present-day activity that keeps you motivated and gives you a feeling of accomplishment.

Another factor that needs to be kept in balance is the search for individual meaning and purpose through work. Many people use a time of transition to think about how their work can serve a purpose that transcends self-interest. Some speak of contributing to the ultimate good of society, while others say they want to leave a legacy, make a difference, fulfill their destiny or serve a divine purpose. These are enormously complex issues, going far beyond what any job or work environment alone can provide.

Take a practical view that seeks to encompass four very important facets of life. They are:

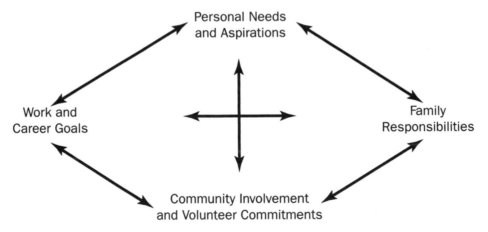

It's not healthy to let any one of these areas become the only focus of your time and energy for extended periods of time. Ideally, they should co-exist in harmony, and there should be no need for you to pretend to be a different person when you move from one role to another. The key is to keep striving for balance.

If your working life is to deliver its fair share of that balance, you need to find work that utilizes as many aspects of your strategic advantage as possible. When you achieve this, even for a short time, your work will make an appropriate contribution to your sense of meaning and purpose, and you will have a degree of contentment, knowing that you don't need to grasp for more.

You know the new rules and all the right moves. Now it's up to you to put yourself in the game and be a winner on your own terms.

Recommended Resources

The following resources are recommended. They offer additional information on the topic noted, and have been helpful to many people who are in the process of career transition.

The Transition Process and Its Emotional Dynamics
Bridges, William. *Managing Transitions: Making the Most of Change.* Cambridge, Mass.: Perseus Publishing, 2003.

Career Direction
Pathfinder, a web-based career assessment instrument available through Cash Lehman & Associates, Toronto, ON. For information go to www.cashlehman.com.
Tieger, Paul D. and Barbara Barron-Tieger. *Do What You Are.* New York: Little, Brown, 2001.

Alternative Employment Options
Block, Peter. *Flawless Consulting: A Guide to Getting Your Expertise Used.* San Francisco: Jossey-Bass Pfeiffer, 1981.
Business Planning Tools, a web-based guide for writing business plans and more, www.bplans.com.

Using Internet Technology to Dispatch Your Résumé
Whitcomb, Susan Britton and Pat Kendall. *eResumes: Everything You Need to Know about Using Electronic Résumés to Tap into Today's Job Market.* New York: McGraw-Hill, 2002.

Negotiating
Fisher, Roger and William L. Ury. *Getting to Yes.* Boston: Houghton, Mifflin, 1981.

Preparing to Start a New Role
Deep, Sam and Lyle Sussman. *Smart Moves for People in Charge.* Reading, Mass.: Perseus Books, 1995.
Watkins, Michael. *The First 90 Days.* Boston: Harvard Business School Press, 2003.

Appendix A

Strategic View of
Targeted Employment Search Process

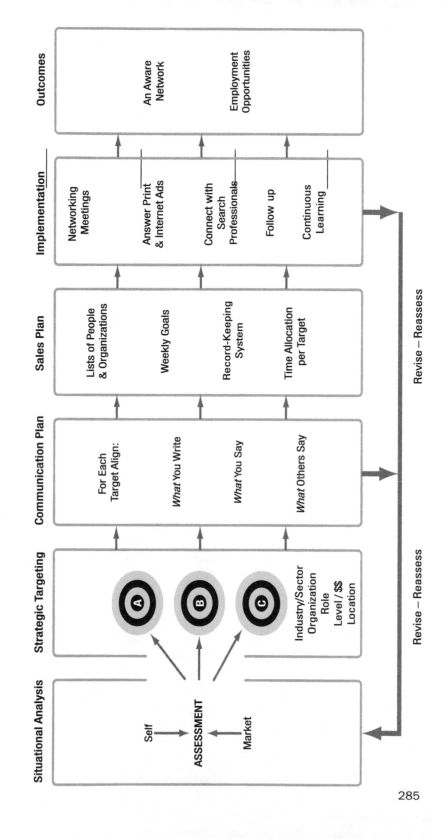

Appendix A – Strategic View of Targeted Employment Search Process

Appendix B

Sample Search Activities Project Plan

Task — Week of	Feb 02	Feb 09	Feb 16	Feb 23	Mar 01	Mar 08	Mar 15	Mar 22	Mar 29	Apr 05	Apr 12
Get Your Head in the Game											
Financial plan, legal advice, sign off	▓	▓									
Inform family, friends, close contacts		▓	▓								
Build support network, consider references			▓								
Develop Your Strategy											
Self-assessment				▓							
Market assessment				▓	▓						
Set strategic targets and get input from advisers					▓						
Gather Your Resources											
Résumé and other written materials				▓	▓						
Verbal pitch — five sound bites					▓						
Correspondence preparation					▓						
Move into Action											
Sales plan, record-keeping system					▓						
Search firms, ads, the Internet for all targets							▓	▓	▓	▓	▓
Target A—time allocation							80%	80%	80%	60%	60%
Research, align resources, input from advisers								▓			
Active networking											
Assess target, revise if necessary										▓	
Target B—time allocation							20%	20%	10%	20%	30%
Research, align resources, input from advisers								▓			
Active networking											
Assess target, revise if necessary											▓
Target C—time allocation									10%	20%	10%
Research, align resources, input from advisers										▓	
Active networking											
Assess target, revise if necessary											
New Targets—time allocation											
Research, align resources, input from advisers											
Active networking											
Assess target, revise if necessary											
CROSS THE FINISH LINE											

Note (handwritten): *Family Ski Trip* (Mar 08)

Note (handwritten, bottom with arrow): Preferred Date for Re-employment

Note (handwritten, top right with arrow): Aug 30

Acknowledgements

By far, the greatest contribution to *It's Your Move* has come from my colleagues at KWA Partners, Toronto. For more than a decade, we have worked together, designing and delivering career transition programs to thousands of individuals. Constantly striving to find more effective ways to help our clients, this team has shown dedication to professional excellence and innovation and has brought fresh ideas to each edition of the book.

In this third edition, the marketing-oriented approach to the search process is the creative work of one person in particular, Kevin O'Leary. I am grateful to Kevin for his vision, to the consultants who took his ideas and incorporated them into our practice, and to the clients who successfully used them in the employment market. Together we have developed a truly unique method for winning the competitive game of employment search.

My thanks goes to all of my colleagues, including those who contributed to the earlier editions and those who have helped with this edition, for enthusiastically supporting me as I recorded our collected wisdom. Their encouragement has been uplifting and most appreciated.

I am indebted as well to the nationwide KWA Partners organization, Canada's quality leader in career management services. Not only has their input and generous support made this third edition possible, it has also facilitated the publication of the French version of *It's Your Move*, *À Vous de jouer*, in 2005. KWA Partners has made these two Canadian resources available to our clients from coast to coast.

None of these accomplishments, especially the writing of this book, would have been achieved without John Knebel's extraordinary efforts. I am deeply thankful for his partnership in both business and life. It is a joy to know that our collaborative work has helped so many people.

Index

Notes

Notes

Notes

Notes

recent graduate
COVID.
volunteer w/
banana Republic